Bowen Family Systems Theory in Christian Ministry

Grappling with Theory and its Application Through a Biblical Lens

EDITED BY

JENNY BROWN
LAUREN ERRINGTON

Copyright © Jenny Brown & Lauren Errington

First published 2019

Published by The Family Systems Practice & Institute
30 Grosvenor St Neutral Bay, NSW
Australia 2089
E-mail – contact@thefsp.com.au
Web – www.thefsp.com.au

All rights reserved. No part of this publication may be reproduced, stored in a retrieval system, or transmitted in any form or by any means—electronic, mechanical, photocopy, recording, or any other—except for brief quotations for printed reviews, without prior permission of the publisher.

ISBN 978-0-6485785-0-5

All Scripture quotations, unless otherwise indicated, are taken from the Holy Bible, New International Version®, NIV®. Copyright ©1973, 1978, 1984, 2011 by Biblica, Inc.™ Used by permission of Zondervan. All rights reserved worldwide. www.zondervan.com The "NIV" and "New International Version" are trademarks registered in the United States Patent and Trademark Office by Biblica, Inc.™

Any profit from the sale of this book will provide financial assistance for people in ministry to study Bowen theory at the Family Systems Institute and/or the Family Systems Practice.

Cover design: Boheem Design

"Grappling" is an apt description for this important book. Throughout its sixteen chapters, the authors grapple with Bowen's ongoing influence on Christians in the helping professions. Their irenic approach provides as much of a model of how to engage a prominent theorist as the practice implications they suggest. By taking Bowen seriously, they help the reader avoid the false choice of remaining true to Christian convictions or benefiting from the common wisdom of someone like Bowen who has much to offer the Christian helping profession practitioner. I deeply appreciate their own expressed security in Christ which enables a teachability that includes learning from those with whom the Christian shares humanity but not redemption.

I am very grateful to the editors and authors for this rich contribution to the literature. Throughout many years of working with pastors and other Christian helping professionals, I have observed an alarming lack of informed wisdom when it comes to understanding systems in general and family dynamics in particular. This timely resource deepens the understanding and enriches the practice of Christians toward fruitful ministry.'

Donald C. Guthrie, EdD, Executive Director of the Centre for Transformational Churches, Director of the PhD (Educational Studies), Professor of Educational Ministries, Chair of Educational Leadership, Trinity Evangelical Divinity School, Deerfield, IL. USA.

'Bowen family systems theory is a very useful tool for understanding and managing relationships. I have been fascinated with its application to the task of Christian leadership and ministry over the last decade and have benefited enormously from its insights. This varied collection of essays provides a much-needed contribution to the field, in reflecting on the theory from a distinctively Christian biblical perspective. The book's great value is its melding of the practical, theoretical, theological, and personal aspects of the theory. It will be helpful to those in Christian ministry, both beginning practitioners of the theory and seasoned system thinkers alike.'

The Rt Revd Dr **Richard Condie**, Bishop of Tasmania, Australia.

'This is a book I've been waiting for. I've clocked up some years in ministry and have "dabbled" in family systems theory for the last ten years. Here at last is a book that looks at Bowen theory through the biblical lens I share; and it applies both lenses to the kind of relationship challenges I know only too well. I will be dipping into this book for years to come. I see this as a resource to equip me to be a calmer and more thoughtful servant of God and others, through growing a better understanding of what is going on in, and around me.'

Caroline Spencer, Program Manager, Trainer, Evangelist, City Bible Forum Australia.

'As I have presented Bowen family systems theory to pastors and seminary students for two decades, I have often received questions that begin, "Yes, but how does this relate to…" followed by some aspect of Christian theology or some biblical passage or concept. Jenny Brown, Lauren Errington and their colleagues in Australia have done an admirable job of bringing Bowen theory into conversation with a faithful evangelical biblicism. They critically connect their commitment to Scripture as authority for faith and practice with their experience of learning and living with a natural systems perspective on congregational and personal life, allowing the former to critique or enhance the latter at times. I recommend their good work to any who are thinking through their Christian faith in relation to Bowen's understanding of human behaviour.'

R. Robert Creech, PhD
Hubert H. and Gladys S. Raborn Professor of Pastoral Leadership Director of Pastoral Ministries Baylor University's George W. Truett Theological Seminary Waco, TX. USA, Co-author of *The Leader's Journey: Accepting the Call to Personal and Congregational Transformation* (2003, 2016, 2nd Ed. Forthcoming 2020). Co-author of *Ethics for Christian Ministry: Moral Formation for Twenty-First-Century Leaders* (2017). Author of *Family Systems and Congregational Life: A Map for Ministry* (2019).

'This book makes a valuable contribution to those who want to apply Bowen theory to the practice of ministry and of life. People from many theological perspectives and ministry settings can benefit from seeing how ministers seek to put this theory to work in a way consistent with their principles and beliefs. Reading the essays in this book can deepen your understanding of the theory and broaden your view of how to apply it.'

Margaret Marcuson, Author of *Leaders Who Last: Sustaining Yourself and Your Ministry, and Money and Your Ministry* & ministry coach, USA.

'It is a common and dangerous activity to unreflectively migrate a model developed outside of the Christian community into the Christian life. This is often the case with psychological and counselling models. A better method is for the secular insights to run thoughtfully alongside ministry, much as a supporter does an athlete: sometimes assisting and sometimes distracting them. Bowen family systems theory is like the supporter. It explains relationships well and offers a beneficial way for a person to develop. It is compatible with much of the life of faith, but at times parts company with us. This volume has a variety of contributors who are well respected Christian thinkers from a wide variety of situations, who understand the theory, and have employed it in practice. They have reflected at a deep theological level to show the theory's strengths and its shortcomings and how it might be helpfully applied Christianly. Here you find a great conversation, from many different angles, from Christians who have used and engaged with Bowen family systems theory. I will certainly be recommending this collection of essays.'

Archie Poulos, Head, Ministry Department, Moore Theological College, Newtown, Australia.

Relationships and our understanding of human functioning is such a driving force behind Bowen family systems theory. This book overlaps Bowen's theory with biblical principles and will be a resource for those in ministry and for Christian people, wherever they are in their faith journey. It may be helpful for people from other faiths who are considering how to critique a psychological theory through the lens of their beliefs. The chapters in this book reveal the complexity and layers of what it means to be relational and Christian. We are faced with challenges in so many of our everyday relationship encounters, and in life and ministry work, such complexity provides fodder for a deeper and fuller understanding of God.

This book provides insight from several perspectives that will illuminate this complexity. I will use it as a resource for growing my understanding of human functioning, relationships, how to face life challenges, and for growing in my Christian faith.

Veronica Peters BSc (Psych) MAPS, MAAFT, Psychologist and Family Therapist, Faculty at The Family Systems Institute, Sydney, Australia.

Bowen Family Systems Theory in Christian Ministry: Grappling with theory and its application through a biblical lens brings together the voices of Christian leaders and workers who have engaged Bowen theory in their ministry contexts—churches, schools, workplaces, and pastoral care situations.

Christian ministry inevitably involves working with, and for, a wide range of people. And where there are people, there is a plethora of relationships. Many of these relationships bring joy, while others are fraught and frustrated. This raises questions about when and how to turn to psychological relationship theories for assistance. When we hold a high view of the Bible's wisdom, we want to take care to ensure that secular ideas do not contradict or replace biblical guidance.

This book provides a strong intellectual consideration of where Bowen theory may be compatible with a biblical view and where it may be in tension. Additionally, it discusses the usefulness of Dr Murray Bowen's theory to the practical aspects of working with different relationships in Christian ministries. We trust it provides rich fodder for grappling with family systems, or indeed any secular theory, as it relates to Christian ministry and biblical truth.

Jenny Brown and Lauren Errington — Editors

Contents

Preface	x
Acknowledgments	xii
Contributors	xiv
Introduction JENNY BROWN & LAUREN ERRINGTON	1
SECTION 1 **The Interplay Between a Biblical Lens and Bowen Theory**	19
1. Critiquing Bowen Family Systems Theory as an Approach for Pastoral Care RUTH SCHROETER	21

2. Can a Focus on Self be Unselfish?
      Evaluating Bowen's Concept of Differentiation of Self
      ANNA MOSS
	36

3. Bowen's Multi-Generational Research and the Family Diagram / Genogram JENNY BROWN	52
4. Anxiety and Differentiation in the Ephesian Church PETER FRITH	68

5. "A New Teaching—and with Authority!"
      A Theological Reflection on Bowen Theory
      ANDREW ERRINGTON
	86

SECTION 2 **Applying Bowen Theory in Different Ministry Contexts**	101

6. Church Unity and Anxious Togetherness Forces
      Discerning the Difference
      JENNY BROWN
	103

7. Applying Bowen Theory to Pastoral Care
      From Rescuing Pastor to Coaching Pastor
      TARA STENHOUSE
	120

8. Quarrelsome or Caught in a Quandary? — 134
Triangles and the Complex Position of the Ministry Spouse
LAUREN ERRINGTON

9. Can Bowen Theory Help us Avoid Burnout? — 150
Bowen Theory and the Practice of Sustainable Pastoral Ministry
ANNA MOSS

SECTION 3 — 169
Working In Christian Ministries During Anxious Times

10. Conflict Resolution in the Workplace — 171
A Case Study on Using Bowen Theory in Collaboration with the Bible
CRAIG FOSTER

11. Denominational Leadership Interventions in Local Congregation Conflict — 189
The Benefits of a Bowen Theory Perspective
VIVIAN GRICE

12. Bowen in Leadership Coaching — 208
Walking with Leaders Through Challenging Times
KEN MORGAN

13. Church Planting and Systems Anxiety — 226
DUNCAN ANDREWS

SECTION 4 — 245
Personal Accounts of Applying Bowen Theory as a Christian

14. "Angels and Devils" in the Family — 247
An Exploration of Reciprocal Functioning in the Moral Domain
MARGARET WESLEY

15. Three Psychologists and a Funeral? — 262
A Personal Reflection on a Bowen Theory Approach to a Family Crisis
MICHAEL CRICHTON

16. Grappling with Bowen Theory in Ministry — 280
An Interview with Simon Flinders and Paul Grimmond
LAUREN ERRINGTON

Index — 297

Preface

Since establishing a Bowen training institute in Sydney, Australia in 2004 (The Family Systems Institute), several clergy people have shown an interest in family systems training programs that have predominately attracted mental health clinicians. A few ministry people have committed to the effort of in-depth study in the Institute's 3-year Certificate program. Others have come to short training events and formed peer reading groups to take their understanding of theory further. Some specific systems in ministry workshops have been offered by the Institute since 2008. There have also been people in ministry in Australia who came across Edwin Friedman's version of Bowen theory during their time in seminary.

In 2014 the Family Systems Institute hosted its first symposium applying Bowen theory to faith communities. This attracted attendees from a spectrum of Christian organisations and churches. It provided an opportunity for students of Bowen theory, who work in ministry, to present their thinking to others and begin more rigorous grappling with the applications of systems thinking in a Christian context. A second ministry symposium was held in 2016 on the topic of the minster's family of origin. Many of the papers in this book were first presented at these ministry symposiums.

The contents of this publication represent variations in people's knowledge of Bowen theory. Some authors have been studying the theory for well over a decade and some for a few years. As editors we have corrected some areas of confusion about theory but allowed each paper to remain an expression of where each author's exploration of theory is at. We are confident that this collection of papers has a unique contribution to make to the effort of critiquing a psychological theory through the lens of Christian belief. It invites readers into the journeys of a range of Christian workers as they live under the guidance of Jesus, as both Saviour and Lord, and seek to draw on Bowen theory in managing themselves more usefully in the complexities of relationships.

Acknowledgements

It has been a privilege to work together on this publication as editors and to collaborate with a fine group of authors. Many people have contributed to this book becoming a reality, the roots of which have developed over many years in conversation with different folk about the challenges of ministry and how systems thinking might be useful. A significant contribution has been made by the many people in local ministry who have engaged in testing Bowen's ideas for their usefulness in church and in their personal lives over many years. It has been especially helpful to have a small number of people express caution and criticism of ways the theory may be out of line with biblical wisdom. Such challenge has appropriately sharpened our own work in applying a biblical lens to ways we utilise Bowen's theory. A sincere thank you to all our contributors-busy people serving in various contexts who have been generous in sharing their ideas, personal applications and concern to uphold biblical understanding. Jenny is deeply grateful for the generous backing on many levels provided by her husband David. Lauren would especially like to thank Andrew, for helping keep the enthusiasm and vision for this project amidst the personal changes in their last few years. A special acknowledgment is due to Bronwyn Windsor for her dedicated proofreading and astute suggestions. Dr Murray Bowen's theory must be acknowledged as an extraordinary offering to seeing the many complex ways that we humans are inextricably linked to our relationships. And above all, a deep gratitude to our God who has given us His truths and charged us to use our minds to reverence Him, grow in godly understanding and wisely serve others.

'Blessed are those who find wisdom, those who gain understanding' (Proverbs 3:13)

Jenny Brown & Lauren Errington

Contributors

Jenny Brown
BSoc Stud, MSc, PhD.
jbrown@thefsi.com.au

Jenny has been a scholar of Bowen's theory since discovering it in a postgraduate couple and family therapy program in New York in 1992. In 2004 she founded a training institute in Bowen family systems theory in Sydney, Australia. Jenny has been providing training for many people interested in exploring systems thinking in both mental health and in ministry for many years. Her current professional interest extends from her doctoral research in involving parents in systems interventions in the treatment of their children's mental health issues. She is author of *Growing Yourself Up: How to bring your best to all of life's relationships* (2012, 2017). Jenny is married to David and has adult children and grandchildren. She is actively involved in her church congregation and para-church programs.

Lauren Errington
BA, BSocial Work, MCouple and Family Therapy.
ljberrington@gmail.com

Lauren is an Accredited Mental Health Social Worker and Family Therapist who lives in Canberra with her husband Andrew and their three children. Over the past ten years Lauren has worked in child and adolescent mental health services and private practice in Australia and Scotland, and is currently working at headspace Canberra. She has published articles with the Australian and New Zealand Journal of Family Therapy and teaches a Relationships and Family subject with Charles Sturt University's Pastoral Counselling course. Lauren is a graduate of the FSI's Graduate Certificate Program in Bowen Family Systems Theory and Practice. Since first encountering Bowen theory through her family therapy work, Lauren has found it a compelling description of the challenges we all face in life's relationships, with the ideas resonating across therapeutic, workplace, and ministry contexts.

Duncan Andrews
BEd, BDiv.
duncandrews@gmail.com

Duncan is the senior pastor of Trinity Church Victor Harbor, a church plant within the Trinity Network of Churches, Adelaide. Duncan was a primary school teacher in Sydney, before training for ministry at Moore Theological College, Sydney. His interest in Systems Theory began while completing a ministry apprenticeship with the Sydney University Evangelical Union and has provided valuable insights for his ministry. Duncan is married to Miriam, with three young children, and loves living in one of the most beautiful places in Australia.

Michael Crichton
BEc, B Th.
pigeon.pastor@gmail.com

Michael has been an Anglican minister in a variety of parishes in Sydney over the past 30 years, including St John's Park, Parramatta, Kensington, and Lindfield. He has always had a keen interest in people, and what makes them tick. This led him to complete the Advanced Certificate in Family Systems Theory and Practice at the FSI in Neutral Bay. In his role as a Senior Minister, Michael longs to see people find their identity in Christ and to grow in spiritual and emotional maturity. Michael is married to Karen and they have three adult children.

Andrew Errington
BA, MA, BDiv, PhD.
andrewerrington@gmail.com

Andrew Errington teaches theology at St Mark's National Theological Centre, in Canberra. An Anglican minister, he previously worked in parishes in the inner city of Sydney. He is the author of *The God who Speaks Life* (Sydney: Mountain Street Media, 2017), and *Every good path: Wisdom and practical reason in Christian ethics and the book of Proverbs* (T&T Clark: Edinburgh, 2019).

Craig Foster
BEc, BDiv, Dip Min, Dip Ed, MEd.
craig@norwestanglican.org.au

Craig Foster is an Anglican Minister at Norwest Anglican Church in the North West of Sydney. He works part-time with The Family

Systems Practice at Neutral Bay offering coaching services for people and teams in Christian ministry. He has spent the past 16 years working in church and Christian school settings. He is a graduate of the FSI's Advanced Certificate and has found Bowen theory to be such a helpful tool for those in Christian ministry. Craig is married to Terese and they have four children, the majority of whom are now teenagers.

Peter Frith
BTh, MA, DMin.
peterfrith@gmail.com

Peter started his working life as a jewellery designer before entering full-time ministry. He has pastored four churches including two suburban church plants plus two in rural and inner city settings. Currently he specialises as a chaplain in mental health care. Peter's parish experiences caused him to reflect deeply upon human functioning and prompted him to learn more about systems theory. He completed his masters degree majoring on the congregation as a family system and has recently earned a doctorate studying the experiences of Anglican clergy encountering the emotional system in their first parish. In his spare time he plays tennis, is learning grandparenting skills and mentors young church leaders using Bowen theory. He intends to write a book on systemic leadership.

Vivian Grice
BA, BTh, MTh, DMin.
vgrice@nswactbaptists.org.au

Originally a secondary school teacher, Vivian Grice has been an ordained and accredited minister with the Baptist Association of NSW since 1984. He has served in solo, associate, and team leader roles in three local Baptist churches (1982 – 2006). Since 2006 he has worked as a denominational leader with the Baptist Association of NSW/ACT. His role focuses on building resources and policies to assist pastoral leaders to be healthy: spiritually, personally, and professionally. He is married to Rhonda, and they have three adult children and five grandchildren.

Ken Morgan
Dip Min, MBus.
kmorgan@melbourneanglican.org.au

Since 1998 Ken Morgan has worked as a consultant, trainer, and coach to church planters, church ministers, and denominational leaders in a wide variety of traditions across Australia and beyond. He is currently the Head of Parish Mission Resourcing for the Anglican Diocese of Melbourne. A graduate of Tabor College and Victoria University, he makes his home in Melbourne.

Anna Moss
BSW LLB, Grad Dip CS, Grad Dip Div.
amoss@thefsp.com.au

Anna is an accredited Mental Health Social Worker and studied theology at Sydney Missionary and Bible College. She has completed the Advanced Certificate program at the FSI. She currently works at the Family Systems Practice as a clinician, seeing mostly Christian clients, many of whom are serving in vocational ministry roles. She also works for the Presbyterian Church of NSW, supporting and equipping women who are employed in ministry roles and helps facilitate a reflective ministry course at Moore

Theological College. Previous to this she worked for ten years as a women's pastor and has also worked with adolescents and families as a school counsellor. Anna is married to Clayton and they have three children.

Ruth Schroeter
BTh.
ruth.schruth@googlemail.com

Originally from the UK, Ruth moved to Sydney to study at Moore Theological College and is now an associate minister at St Andrew's Cathedral, Sydney, where her work revolves around teaching, training and discipleship. Having developed an interest in Bowen theory while at Moore College, Ruth went on to pursue further training at the Family Systems Institute and is particularly interested in the application of Bowen Family Systems Theory within pastoral ministry.

Tara Stenhouse
BSc Hons (Psych), BTh, Dip Min, MA (Th).
tara.stenhouse@moore.edu.au

Tara Stenhouse has been working at Moore Theological College since 2009, as a lecturer in the Ministry Department and as the Dean of Women. Prior to this she was the women's pastor and trainer at Unichurch@UNSW for nine years, after studying a theology degree at Moore College. She lives in Newtown, Sydney with her husband, Ian, who is a Presbyterian minister. She's found Bowen's theory invaluable over the years personally through her own counselling, as well as in her pastoral care roles with women through professional supervision.

Margaret Wesley
BSc, MDiv, ThD.
margaret@wesley.nu

Margaret is a graduate of the FSI's Advanced Certificate program and is particularly interested in applications of Bowen theory to Christian character and leadership. Her book, *Son of Mary,* examines the family relationships of Jesus in the Gospel of John. She was ordained in 2017 and is part of the ministry team in the Anglican parish of East Redlands, Queensland, where she works with six congregations that seek to express God's love into very diverse communities. As a spiritual director, theological teacher, minister, and mother, Margaret loves to see people mature towards their unique embodiment of the likeness of Jesus.

INTRODUCTION

Jenny Brown & Lauren Errington

This collection of papers seeks to apply a biblical worldview to Bowen family systems theory and its application in church ministry contexts. Dr Murray Bowen's family systems theory has garnered interest from clergy for some decades, especially since the publication of Rabbi Edwin Friedman's *Generation to Generation: Family Process in Church and Synagogue* (Friedman, 1985). Numerous organisations have emerged in the USA who consult to church workers, drawing from Bowen theory. Many books have been published that apply systems thinking to the functioning of congregations and to pastoral leadership.[1] One can assume that the premise of these publications is that Bowen theory is relevant across divergent theological and denominational positions, as it refers to relationship process rather than the content of belief. While applications of Bowen theory to the church do refer to the Bible in passing, the literature is sparse in considering Bowen theory through the lens of biblical truth—starting with the view that "All Scripture is God-breathed

---

1 For example: Friedman (1999, 2006), Richardson (1996, 2005), Galindo (2004, 2009), Steinke (2006), Gilbert (2006, 2009), Marcuson (2009), Herrington et al. (2003, 2016).

and is useful for teaching, rebuking, correcting and training in righteousness, so that the servant of God may be thoroughly equipped for every good work" (2 Tim 3:16-17). The authors in this book all subscribe to this authoritative view of Scripture as well as being scholars and appliers of Bowen theory to church contexts. The papers presented do not attempt to provide a thoroughly rigorous critique of Bowen theory through a biblical lens, however they do represent thinking and application of Bowen theory that engages critically with the Bible's view of the human condition. The aim is to raise many questions about the usefulness of Bowen theory to the Christian church, as opposed to providing definitive conclusions. It is hoped that these papers will provide rich fodder for continued grappling with Bowen theory as it relates to Christian ministry and biblical truth.

Bowen theory and its central concepts[2]

Before outlining what to expect from this publication it is appropriate to give an overview of Murray Bowen's family systems theory. It might be tempting to skip over a description of the theory; however the effort to make sense of the basis of Bowen's framework will enhance the reading of the applications and critiques contained in this book. Bowen was a US army physician during World War II who became interested in psychiatry after seeing the varying effects of trauma on soldiers. Observing variation in human functioning in the face of life challenge was part of what fuelled his research orientation. He originally trained in Freud's psychoanalysis but departed from this theory as he observed that human difficulties went beyond unresolved issues in the individual's psyche and was, rather, embedded in each person's

---

[2] Sections of this outline of theory are taken from the book *Growing Yourself Up* (Brown, 2012, 2017, pp. 47-48). For a more rigorous understanding of this theory, a reading of core texts is recommended (Bowen, 1978; Kerr & Bowen, 1988; Papero, 1990; Kerr, 2019).

family system. In researching whole families at the US National Institute of Mental Health in the 1950s, Bowen noticed patterns of managing anxiety in families that were similar to the instinctive ways other species dealt with threats in (or to) their herds and packs. In this way it is a natural systems theory that has developed out of field research of the human in families and groups in the same way that a natural scientist observes the activity of a troop of chimpanzees or the cellular behaviour in a particular organ. Bowen was strongly influenced by the writing of Charles Darwin in seeing the way species and groups make adaptations to their environments that have ramifications for survival.

Anxiety, the engine room of reactive patterns in relationships

Bowen's theory is constructed around eight concepts and some important notions about types of anxiety and emotional (instinctually embedded) process. All of the relationship patterns described by Bowen are mechanisms for us as humans to manage the anxieties of life and relationships. Hence the understanding of systems anxiety is pivotal in Bowen's theory. Bowen theory is built around the notion of *two counter-balancing relationship forces*: the *togetherness force* that seeks attachment and the *separateness force* that seeks autonomy. Both are viewed as essential for human survival as a social mammal. A balance of being connected to others while also being sufficiently separate to function as an individual is core to a person's development. The challenge to balance these forces is what fuels tension in relationships. For example, the perception of another's efforts towards more autonomous functioning can easily trigger separation anxiety. Conversely the sustained push for more connection can trigger a sense of suffocation in another. This flow of anxiety renders any two-person relationship as somewhat unstable. From such instability humans have developed mechanisms that deflect or absorb their experience of tension in relationships. The concepts that Bowen describes in his theory are all connected to our human management of this relational insecurity.

Bowen described two different types of anxiety experienced by humans, and these reside in our family and other significant systems. The first is *acute anxiety*: that is the response to a real adverse event. Humans can usually find sufficient resources over time to recover from such challenges, as long as the adversities are not unrelenting. The second is *chronic anxiety*: this presents complex and longer-term challenges for us in relationships. Chronic anxiety is an exaggerated sense of potential threat that generates a continued sensitivity to and scanning for the presence of the feared outcome. Bowen proposed that this "what if" chronic anxiety is the engine room of anxious patterns in relationships: conflict, distance, over and underfunctioning, triangling, and projecting onto a vulnerable family member (e.g., a child). Chronic anxiety is seen as being largely generated by perceived threats to important relationships. Such perceived threats are understood in the context of the two life forces of being close and having emotional space. The degree of chronic anxiety flowing back and forth is a key contributor to symptom development in a relationship or in a member of the anxious system. Higher chronic anxiety equates to lower differentiation of self/maturity. Chronic anxiety, which is present to varying degrees in all families, is also the driver of over-dependent relationships which in turn can lead to distancing in an effort to manage the relational intensity.

An important observation behind Bowen theory is that the family functions as a single emotional unit. While anxiety and tension is part of each individual's physiological response it also belongs to the family as a single emotional unit. The family is viewed as a collection of interdependent members who each affect the functioning of others.

The following is a brief overview of Bowen theory's eight concepts. Bowen's concept of the *triangle* describes the way a three-person system can contain tension by spreading it around three relationships. The triangle enables two people to divert their insecurities to a focus on a third. This triangle focus can be a rescuing, blaming, or mediating focus. Other people are easily drawn into responding to the triangle through side-taking or blaming. Hence interlocking triangles are easily formed in any group.

Bowen's cornerstone concept of *differentiation of self* describes the human challenge to balance the need for connection with the need for autonomy. All humans are on a continuum of differentiation (or maturity) in that they vary in capacity to self-regulate and maintain connection with important others in the face of tension. Alternatives to well-differentiated relationships are *fusion,* which sacrifices autonomous functioning for the sake of harmony, and *cutoff,* which sacrifices connection for the sake of independence. Emotional cutoff is when the sensitivities between one generation and the next are managed through breaking away. Distance is used to manage tension between parents and adult children, which in turn intensifies the fusion in replacement relationships.

Nuclear family emotional process describes the patterns for managing stress and immaturity (undifferentiation) in a one-generational family. The patterns of over- and underfunctioning, conflict, and distance in a marriage, and over-investment in a child are all predictable ways that family members contain the stressful overload of life relationships. These patterns can become stuck in place and in time lead to the emergence of symptoms in a marriage, a spouse, and/or a child.

The *family projection process* is one of the patterns of adaptation mentioned above where parents' insecurities are detoured through a focus on the next generation (focusing on one or more children). Bowen saw the importance of this process in understanding how different degrees of maturity are transmitted from one generation to the next. The *multigenerational transmission process* is the way in which each child moves into adult life with varied degrees of relationship sensitivity. This is linked to how much relationship intensity they were a part of with their parents.

Bowen drew upon Walter Toman's research (Toman, 1992) on family sibling position to see how this impacts the patterns of relationship involved in establishing a marriage and family. This concept is much more complex than simple profiles of eldest, middle, and youngest. It looks at the interplay of marriage partners' sibling profiles with the way they attach and parent their children. Bowen's final concept, *societal emotional process*, identified ways that family patterns play out in society with each influencing the other.

Bowen theory doesn't focus on mental illness but on the challenges of being human in the relationships which affect us all. The therapy that comes from the theory aims to reduce chronic anxiety in a system and to assist people to lift out of fusion and reactivity in order to grow more into maturity (differentiation of self). A system lens means that a change in one member will necessitate adjustments in others. Hence the efforts of one can improve the functioning of the entire system. It is a complex theory to grasp, as it focuses on the big-picture patterns of a system rather than the narrower view of what causes difficulties for one individual.

Bowen theory and the process of change

Bowen posited that the change process is about working to be a bit more differentiated in relationships. This process requires observing one's *self* in relationships and identifying patterns driven by fusion with others. Exploring one's family of origin can assist with greater awareness of what we have inherited in terms of patterns of managing anxiety as well as gaining a more objective view of family members. It is critical to point out that awareness alone does not result in improved functioning in relationships. Change occurs in very small steps of practising being more autonomous while in meaningful connection with others. It is an active and long-term research project in a person's life. An underlying principle is that all family members (or members of a relationship system such as a ministry team) play a part in all that goes on in the group. It is not useful to try to change another, however it is possible to change the part that one's self plays. A change in one person necessitates compensatory changes in others which may promote improved functioning for the whole group. Bowen writes:

> The modification of self requires that the person be sure of self on all life principles that involve him [her] self and his [her] family, to have the courage to act on his [her] convictions, and to devote primary attention to becoming the most responsible person. (Bowen, 1978, p. 449)

It is interesting to note the centrality of a person becoming surer of their personal beliefs in the process of differentiation. Bowen does not discuss what these beliefs might be but emphasises the importance of a person developing core beliefs gradually from within rather than quickly adopting them from others in the group.

The therapy approach in Bowen theory is called *coaching*, given that it is based on collaborative investigation of a person's relationship patterns rather than providing a healing corrective relationship. The coach works to stay out of side-taking triangles with the person they are assisting. They place the focus on descriptions of interactions in real life and not on what is happening in the "therapeutic relationship".

Bowen theory applied to non-family systems

Bowen theory has been applied beyond families since its earliest disseminations. In particular the theory has been extended to work systems with Bowen writing about his observations of his research staff team's reactivities in 1965 and his own anxious patterns as a lead administrator in 1972 (Bowen, 1978, pp.131-133, 461-465). While patterns of managing anxiety are more generationally entrenched in family groups, the same patterns will be evident (perhaps less intensely[3]) in any group of people that regularly interact. It is worth noting in relation to work groups and congregations that while an individual may bring their family reactivity to the group, the manner in which members of the group respond to the individual will affect the extent of turbulence to the group as a whole. This systems thinking means that no individual can be viewed as "toxic" to the group, given the vital contributing factor of another's capacity to be in less anxious contact with, and define self to, the sensitive individual.

Bowen theory, secular psychology, and the Bible

Broadly speaking, Bowen theory has a natural application to the church with its big picture view of a system or body of interconnections—where every member affects others' functioning. The church as a body is a central idea in the apostle Paul's letters and this lends itself well to thinking of the church as an interdependent system: "Just as a body, though one, has many parts, but all its many parts form one body, so it is with Christ" (1 Cor 12:12). The key to systems thinking is to consider how every person impacts others in a constantly moving reciprocal

---

[3] Bowen (1978) writes: "Basic relationship patterns developed for adapting to the parental family in childhood are used in all other relationships throughout life. The basic patterns in social and work relationships are identical to relationship patterns in the family, except in intensity... However there are exceptions to this in which the intensity of relationships in work systems approximates the intensity in the original family." (p. 462)

dynamic. It is a paradigm shift from individual, cause-and-effect thinking. The core implication is that change occurs through a person's effort on themselves and the problematic impacts they have on the overall health of the group—whether that be through distancing, reactive conflict, side-taking, or taking on too much or too little responsibility. This is expressed clearly by Richardson:

> Rather than asking the question, 'How can I change the church?' Bowen family systems theory suggests that the minister should ask, 'What do I need to work on to improve my functioning within the emotional system of the church so that I can better represent the Gospel? (Richardson, 2005, p. 401)

The quest to appraise a secular psychological theory through a biblical worldview is complicated with a diversity of approaches appearing in the field. These include: the integrations view, levels of explanation view, Christian psychology view, transformational psychology view, and a biblical counselling view (Johnson, ed., 2000, 2010). This collection of papers does not endeavour to work uniformly within any of these views. Readers will most likely find themselves considering the efficacy of each chapter's approach to a biblical perspective of Bowen theory. An example of a well-developed framework for examining a theory through a biblical lens is found in the writing of David Powlison from the current stage of the biblical counselling movement. Powlison writes:

> First, read the Bible for the humanity portrayed, as well as for the divinity revealed, and above all for the interaction between the two. Though myriads of significant details about individuals and social groups are not contained within the Bible, learning to think the way Jesus thinks will rightly align all that you learn from other sources. (Powlison, 2010, p. 254)

In engaging Powlison's approach I (Jenny) have found the following series of questions that he utilises to be valuable for thinking Christianly about any extra-biblical knowledge (Powlison, 2003)[4]:

- At what level does the theory capture the human condition?
- What valuable extra-biblical information does the theory provide?
- How does the theory interpret the information it deems important?
- What does the theory "blinker out"? How would a biblical worldview fill in what's missing?
- What interventions for change emanate from the theory's interpretations?
- What does the Bible have to say about change?

And an added question of Jenny's own:

- What is the partnership between the Holy Spirit and human obedience/effort in the work of change?

This sequence of questions has been useful in this author's writing in Chapter 3 on Bowen's family of origin approach. Other authors in the book ask key questions about the absence of notions of sin in Bowen theory and a process of change that leaves out the sanctifying work of the Holy Spirit. One notable area of Bowen theory which warrants further theological critique in the future is its deep reliance on evolutionary theory to shape its understanding of natural systems theory. As a theory that views the human as part of millions of years of evolutionary processes, Bowen theory does not give credence to the hand of an intelligent designer who has

---

[4] This framework is taught in the course by D Powlison:"Theology and Secular Psychology", at Christian Counselling and Education Foundation, CCEF, Philadelphia, USA.

crowned the human as the pinnacle of creation—the concept of *imago Dei*:

> Then God said, "Let us make [human]kind in our image, in our likeness, so that they may rule over the fish in the sea and the birds in the sky, over the livestock and all the wild animals, and over all the creatures that move along the ground". (Gen 1:26)

Our view is that Bowen theory's understanding of evolutionary processes of adaptation, plus the theory's attention to what humans share with lower life forms, is an important contribution to understanding human relationship systems. Nevertheless, from a biblical perspective, a purely Darwinian lens diminishes the uniqueness of the human in creation. Bowen's natural systems view of the human species, unsurprisingly, leaves out human responsibility and accountability to his/her creator. While the papers in this book do not take on this critique in any depth, it is necessary to flag that engaging with natural systems theory is an important area for Christians to grapple with in appraising this, and other, scientific and psychological theories.

Change: The work of the Holy Spirit and human responsibility

Any theory that leaves out the activity of a sovereign God will present the process of change as the domain of human effort. From a biblical perspective, a very different view is presented of how people change: it is with God's "activity imperative" *by His Spirit*. The question of what is in God's domain and what remains the responsibility of each human creature in change efforts is a complex theological issue. Jerry Bridges' concept of "dependent responsibility", where each human is simultaneously completely dependent on God while also responsible for their own application of Scripture's call to godly living, is an example of such biblical examination (Bridges, 1983, 1996). Bridges writes, "Though the power for godly character comes from Christ, the responsibility for developing and displaying that character is ours" (Bridges, 1996, p. 61). Salvation is gifted by grace alone while the Christian walk is mobilised by a thankful response to this gift.

As a Christian working in the secular psychology and social science fields, I (Jenny) have endeavoured to keep my biblical thinking and application authoritatively ahead of the thinking and application that is generated by secular theory, and in particular Bowen theory (given this is the theory I have been studying for over 25 years). In the recent edition of my secular publication on Bowen theory I write the following in my acknowledgments:

> I don't view Bowen theory as my primary lens of understanding myself and others and my life's purpose. I seek to utilise my biblical Christian faith as the overriding compass in my life journey. I endeavour to filter all ideas through the lens of being dependent on my creator God and staying conscious of my tendency to arrogantly live as if I am capable of independently controlling my life. (Brown, 2017, p. 277)

It has been a useful exercise in preparing for this collection of papers to collate a statement of my beliefs without drawing on anyone else's writing, and consider the question, How clear am I about the beliefs of my Christian faith and their implications for how I live in relationships?

Outline of this book

The chapters that follow provide examples of biblical critique and application of Bowen theory to church contexts. They represent many "works in progress", both in learning Bowen theory and in applying a critical biblical lens to the theory. Our hope in bringing such a collection of papers together is that they provide a platform for clarification of aspects of Bowen's broad theory about human interactions, and facilitate further investigation of how these sit within a biblical worldview. It is a lens that understands humans as God's image bearers, who live the present and generational consequences of rejecting God, and a lens that sees humans and the creation as part of a big picture story of God's rescue and redemption culminating in the life, death, resurrection, and future return of his Son Jesus Christ.

The book has two sections. The first section includes papers which are more theoretical in nature, considering the complex interplay between theology and Bowen theory, with authors critiquing several of the theory's concepts. **Ruth Schroeter** begins this section with Chapter 1, observing that Bowen theory has a unique contribution to make in understanding and enhancing human relationships, and critiquing emotional immaturity and relational processes through a biblical lens of a broken world in which only God can restore the core problem of the relationship between humanity and God. **Anna Moss** further critiques Bowen theory's concept of differentiation of self in Chapter 2 by asking the pertinent question of whether a focus on self can be unselfish, grappling with what a Christian view of self-awareness might entail through an examination of the biblical doctrines of humanity, sin, and forgiveness. In Chapter 3, **Jenny Brown** recognises the value of understanding one's multigenerational family history, but cautions the use of such knowledge as merely an explanatory framework for human problems, and instead considers how such knowledge might be a catalyst to turn to God with a deeper understanding of our human weaknesses and immaturities. The church in Ephesus is conceptualised by **Peter Frith** as an anxious system in Chapter

4, in a detailed description of how Paul encourages Timothy to be more differentiated in his leadership of the church in 1 and 2 Timothy. And in Chapter 5, the final paper in this section, **Andrew Errington** addresses head-on the question of whether as Christians we ought to be skeptical about what a secular psychological theory has to offer, using ideas from the Bible's wisdom literature about how one might approach this issue.

The second section in the book contains a range of papers by authors who have been grappling with applying Bowen theory in various ministry contexts and have worked to articulate their own thinking and practical knowledge to contribute to the dialogue about the opportunities and challenges this raises. This section begins with four chapters that highlight the usefulness of Bowen theory in pastoral ministries. **Jenny Brown** introduces the theme of thinking about churches as anxious systems with Chapter 6, considering the difference between unity and togetherness and how working on relating to others, rather than reacting to others, is a key to healthy church communities. **Tara Stenhouse** then provides a thoughtful reflection on her journey from being a "rescuing" pastor to a "coaching" pastor in Chapter 7, and how relational principles from Bowen theory have guided her to be relationally connected with people without being overly responsible for them. The concept of triangles is illustrated by **Lauren Errington** in Chapter 8 who uses the example of the minister's spouse to describe the way anxiety is passed around relationships in the church relational system. And **Anna Moss** considers in Chapter 9 whether Bowen theory can help ministry leaders work in such demanding roles in a way that is more personally sustainable, thus potentially preventing burnout.

Working to manage one's own reactivity and engage well in relationships in families, workplaces, and communities that are anxious is a challenge for everyone. The next few chapters in this section include reflections from those working in or with those in Christian ministries where anxieties are high, triangles multiply rapidly, and conflict escalates quickly. The biblical reflections **Craig Foster** offers in Chapter 10 alongside relational principles from Bowen theory in dealing with workplace conflict provide stimulating thinking about what a godly response to difficult relationships involves. In Chapter 11 **Vivian Grice** reflects on his unique role in providing "interventions" when required to Baptist churches in need of external support and how Bowen theory provides a way to observe and manage one's own emotional reactivity in a situation and to work towards being a useful resource for the church. The case studies **Ken Morgan** offers in Chapter 12 are an example of the way a leadership coach grounded in Bowen theory can help ministry leaders work effectively in anxious communities, namely by working on one's self and noticing the ripple effect a leader who is clear and consistent in their own values and principles can have on a system. As **Duncan Andrews** discusses in Chapter 13, such systemic thinking can particularly assist leaders of new church plants, where the stressors of church planting contribute to creating conditions that breed systemic anxiety amongst a new congregation.

Much of Bowen theory depends on individuals increasing their self-awareness through understanding how they participate and function in their own families and relationships, and working to manage one's self differently. The last three chapters in this book are personal accounts of how this process has taken shape for the various contributors. In Chapter 14 **Margaret Wesley** describes how understanding her family of origin has contributed to understanding her own functioning, and raises the difficult question of how reacting to others shapes one's own moral functioning. **Michael Crichton** then gives a personal account in Chapter 15, of the influence of Bowen theory on how he responded to a family crisis when his daughter became unwell. And the final chapter, Chapter 16, highlights how understanding Bowen theory and grappling with it through a biblical lens is an ongoing conversation. **Lauren Errington's** interview with **Paul Grimmond** and **Simon Flinders** features their thinking about conviction versus coercion, compassion, biblical and relational principles, and the challenges that arise when trying to do things differently.

We would like to take this opportunity to thank each of these contributors—for working to turn their thinking and experience into papers that allow readers to engage with the opportunities and challenges that arise when applying Bowen theory to Christian ministry and thinking about the theory through a biblical lens. We hope our readers find this book as stimulating and challenging as we have in thinking about what it means to love and serve people, and we hope that it might contribute to more thinking about how we can best contribute to the building up of healthy and mature churches that bring honour to our Saviour, Jesus Christ.

References

Bowen, M. (1978). *Family therapy in clinical practice*. Jason Aronson.

Bridges, J. (1983, 1996). *The practice of godliness*. Nav Press.

Brown, J. (2012, 2017). *Growing yourself up: How to bring your best to all of life's relationships*. Exisle Publishing.

Friedman, E. (1999, 2006). *A failure of nerve: Leadership in the age of the quick fix*. Church Publishing Inc.

Friedman, E. (1985, 2011). *Generation to Generation: Family process in church and synagogue*. Guilford Press.

Galindo, I. (2004). *The hidden lives of congregations: Discerning church dynamics.* Rowman & Littlefield.

Galindo, I. (2009). *Perspectives on congregational leadership.* I Galindo Press.

Gilbert, R. (2006). *Extraordinary leadership.* Leading Systems Press.

Gilbert, R. M. (2009). *The cornerstone concept: In leadership, in life.* Leading Systems Press

Herrington, J. Creech, R. Taylor T. (2003, 2016). *The leader's journey: Accepting the call to personal and congregational transformation.* H B Printing.

Johnson, E. ed. (2000, 2010). *Psychology and Christianity: Five views.* IVP Academic.

Kerr, M. E., & Bowen, M. (1988). *Family evaluation.* WW Norton & Company.

Kerr, M. E. (2019). *Bowen Theory's Secrets: Revealing the Hidden Life of Families.* WW Norton & Company.

Marcuson, M. (2009). *Leaders who last: Sustaining yourself and your ministry.* Abingdon Press.

Papero, D. (1990). *Bowen family systems theory.* Allyn & Bacon.

Powlison, D. (2003). *Seeing with new eyes.* P&R, Phillipsburg, NJ

Powlison, D. (2010). A biblical counselling view, Ch. 6 in *Psychology and Christianity: Five views.* Ed. Johnson E. J. InterVarsity Press.

Richardson, R. W., (1996). *Creating a healthier church.* Fortress Press, Minneapolis.

Richardson, R. W. (2005). *Becoming a healthier pastor: Family systems theory and the pastor's own family.* Fortress Press.

Richardson, R. W. (2005). Bowen family systems theory and congregational life, *Review & Expositor,* 102(3), 379-402.

Steinke, P. (2006). *Congregational leadership in anxious times: Being calm and courageous no matter what.* Rowman & Littlefield Publishers.

Toman, W. (1992) *Family constellation: Its effect on personality and social behavior.* Springer Publishing Company.

Section 1

THE INTERPLAY BETWEEN A BIBLICAL LENS AND BOWEN THEORY

Chapter 1

CRITIQUING BOWEN FAMILY SYSTEMS THEORY AS AN APPROACH FOR PASTORAL CARE

Ruth Schroeter

"No man is an island, entire of itself; every man is a piece of the continent, a part of the main. If a clod be washed away by the sea, Europe is the less."

— John Donne, Meditation XVII

Introduction

When Rabbi Edwin Friedman made the claim that the church functions more like a family than does any other organisation (1985, p. 364), he provided insight into the surprising relationship between Bowen family systems theory and Christian ministry. Surprising because Murray Bowen was a secular humanist who described man as "an assemblage of cells who has arrived at his present state from hundreds of millions of years of evolutionary adaptation and maladaptation" (1993, p. 158), and it was in part Bowen's reaction against the prevailing view that humans were the crowning glory of God's creation that influenced the development of the family systems theory. This theory assumes that all natural systems, from the least complicated organism to *Homo sapiens*, are guided by the same processes that govern all life forms. This raises the question, Why does Bowen theory appeal to those who hold to the belief that mankind is indeed the pinnacle of creation, made in the image of God, with the noble task of exercising dominion over all other life forms as described in Genesis 2?

Despite their different starting points, several observations that Murray Bowen made about the interconnectedness of all life resonate with the biblical view of humanity. This paper proposes that two of Bowen's concepts seem to particularly correspond to Christian doctrine: the *multigenerational transmission process* and *differentiation of self*. Considering these two points of intersection may help to explore the potential for concepts of Bowen theory to be applied in Christian ministry.

Multigenerational transmission process

As society becomes more individualistic, it is reasonable to anticipate that each generation will become less interested in who came before them and less concerned about who will come after. Both Bowen theory and the biblical worldview have a different perspective and believe that no person can be understood in a vacuum, or as John Donne described, no man is an island.

There is, in both Bowen theory and the biblical view, a strong sense of context and of legacy. How we live and interact with those around us now is the result of an inherited prescription handed down through generations. In moving away from the cause-and-effect approach of Freud and others, Bowen moved closer towards a biblical anthropology and its understanding of the interconnectedness of humans. Bowen calls this the "multigenerational transmission process", whereby a person can only be understood when considered in their position in a network of relationships, spanning the generations.

Bowen theory

The starting point in Bowen family systems counselling sessions is the creation of a family diagram (also known as a *genogram*). This is a family tree where names and dates and facts form the basic framework, but where the primary focus is on charting relationship patterns by exploring the emotional connections between family members. The individual is invited to begin exploring their own history in order to better understand themselves within their unique framework. As they dig deeper into their family of origin, patterns may begin to emerge, and these patterns can be picked up and passed on like batons in a relay race. Michael Kerr states:

> The intensity and characteristics of the emotional patterns in one generation are significantly influenced by the intensity and characteristics of the emotional patterns in the previous generation. These patterns reflect orderly and predictable relationship process that connects the functioning of family members across generations. (Kerr & Bowen, 1988, p. 224)

Bowen describes how in times of heightened stress, families react in various ways to reduce the experience of tension: sometimes by pulling together tightly to bind up the anxiety (the *fusion* force), sometimes by pulling apart to cut the connecting wires through which anxiety flows (the *distancing* force). He identified patterns of *triangling*, when the intensity in a dyadic relationship becomes unbearable and a pressure valve is introduced in the form of a third person or object of focus. These emotional patterns, among others, illustrate the capacity of a family to manage the anxiety or tension in the relationship system, and, as work in the family of origin continues, it can be observed that these responses form part of the inherited patterns of relating passed from one generation to the next.

The biblical perspective

This sense of legacy resonates strongly with Scripture. God promises Abraham that he will be "a father of many nations" (Gen 17:5), and that "all peoples on earth will be blessed through you" (Gen 12:3). Genealogies abound in the Old Testament as an individual's identity is marked by their place within the nation of Israel, God's chosen people (e.g., Gen 11:10-32; Ex 6:14-25; 1 Chron 1:1-9:1). The connection between the generations are conduits both for blessings: "Because you have done well in accomplishing what is right [...] your descendants will sit on the throne of Israel to the fourth generation" (2 Kgs 10:30), and for curses: "I [...] am a jealous God, punishing the children for the sin of the parents to the third and fourth generation [...]" (Ex 20:5).

Bowen theory and the biblical worldview both emphasise that what happens in one generation, even with one individual, can impact and change what happens in future generations. But whereas Bowen theory necessarily works within the earthly boundaries of biology, the overarching message of the Bible is that there is an inheritance which transcends genetic lineage, reaching back to creation, stretching forwards to the gathering up of the elect upon Christ's return (Mt 24:31) and broadening out to include all nations, tribes, people, and languages (Rev 5:9). And it is here that biblical ontology goes beyond the limits of Bowen theory and speaks to the heart of what it means to be human. The Bible describes an immutable prescription received by every human being of *imago Dei*, the image of God, by which every human receives the indelible mark of their Creator: "So

God created mankind in his own image, in the image of God he created them; male and female he created them" (Gen 1:27).

But sadly, that is not the only permanent mark received by the human. After the events of the fall in Genesis 3 humans earn another prescription: "Therefore, just as sin entered the world through one man, and death through sin, and in this way death came to all people, because all sinned" (Rom 5:12). Through the events in the Garden of Eden, as humans pushed at the boundaries placed safely around them by their Creator, no longer can humans revel in *imago Dei*.

Theologian John Calvin offers a sobering description of the state of mankind, observing that "even though we grant that God's image was not totally annihilated and destroyed in him, yet it was so corrupted that whatever remains is frightful deformity" (1960, p. 189).

Purely through his mercy, the image of God is not completely lost, and Calvin goes on to explain how it is that the deformed will be reformed:

> Consequently, the beginning of our recovery of salvation is in that restoration which we obtain through Christ, who also is called the Second Adam for the reason that he restores us to true and complete integrity. (1960, p. 189)

This recovery of something that is almost, but not quite, ruined is powerfully portrayed by the prophet Jeremiah in his image of the potter and the clay:

> So I went down to the potter's house, and I saw him working at the wheel. But the pot he was shaping from the clay was marred in his hands; so the potter formed it into another pot, shaping it as seemed best to him. (Jer 18:3-4)

God, the potter, does not throw away the deformed pot and start again, but remoulds it, his loving hands coaxing it into the shape it was destined for, his divine fingerprints pressed into it and his plan for it unaltered. For the Christian, the multigenerational transmission process is historical and eschatological. The inherited prescription is written out in creation, marred but not destroyed by the fall, stewarded by the patriarchs, and restored by the Creator.

Sin, blame, and forgiveness

One of the implications of viewing the family as a multigenerational emotional system is that it potentially removes the opportunity for blaming self or others for problems which occur in self or others. Blame is a natural response when something goes wrong. There is a human urge to deposit anger somewhere, to identify the place where the debt belongs, to state who owes you, and to receive appropriate payback. Michael Kerr asks, "If humans are linked together emotionally across the generations by a process that is fuelled by automatic reactions and reinforced by subjectivity, who does one blame?" (1988, p. 255). Bowen theory disables blame because there is no place to put it.

Blamelessness is also the status of those who have been declared righteous through the atoning death of Christ. But, whereas in Bowen theory there is no blame because no one person can be held accountable, in the biblical worldview, *all* are accountable: "All have sinned and fall short of the glory of God" (Rom 3:23). But through his mercy God has removed the debt from humanity by pointing the finger of accusation not at those who deserve it, but back upon himself, so that those who are to blame are instead "justified freely by his grace through the redemption that came by Christ Jesus" (Rom 3:24). The gospel disables blame by removing it from those who are guilty and transferring it to the one who is not.

This is not to say that either Bowen theory or the biblical view do away with human responsibility. Bowen theory naturally takes a systems view and, rather than pinpointing a problem, would say all members of a system are part of the problem; as Kerr suggests, "Getting beyond blame does not exonerate people from the part they play in the creation of a problem" (1988, p. 255). However, according to the principles of Bowen theory even the part they play may be predetermined by factors beyond their control and so the buck endlessly circulates and stops nowhere.

The biblical doctrine of sin includes moral culpability, in that sin is systemic but it is also absolutely personal:

> What comes out of a person is what defiles them. For it is from within, out of a person's heart, that evil thoughts come—sexual immorality, theft, murder, adultery, greed, malice, deceit, lewdness, envy, slander, arrogance and folly. All these evils come from inside and defile a person. (Mark 7:20-23)

Until a person realises that the devil didn't make them do it, they cannot know their greatest need, and they will be strangers to God and to the forgiveness he offers through Christ.

Where there is no sin, there is no blame, and where there is no blame there can be no forgiveness. Forgiveness is the free choice made by the one who has been wronged, not to seek revenge or to demand payback for a wrong committed against them. Bowen theory aims to disarm the destructive power of blame within relationships and to develop a non-judgmental neutrality, but in doing so it misses out on the richness of grace which can only be experienced by those who know they are forgiven sinners.

Differentiation of self

The development of maturity is a focus of Bowen theory and for Christians. Both are heavily invested in restoration of relationships, and consider individual maturity to play a key role.

Bowen theory defines maturity as differentiation of self. This concept is described as "the ability to be in emotional contact with others yet still autonomous in one's own emotional functioning" (1988, p. 45). Christian maturity is Christlikeness. In his letter to the Ephesians the apostle Paul speaks of the purpose of church "[...] so that the body of Christ may be built up until we all reach unity in the faith and in the knowledge of the Son of God *and become mature, attaining to the whole measure of the fullness of Christ*" (Eph 4:12-13 [emphasis mine]).

Both views consider maturity to be a process, a gradual inward change with outward consequences. As a humanist, Bowen locates the potential for change in human effort, whereas the Christian view is that "Christlikeness" is first and foremost the sanctifying work of the Holy Spirit enabling human cooperation rather than depending upon it.

Bowen theory

Murray Bowen developed the idea of a continuum called "the scale of differentiation" (1988, p. 97) which measures, theoretically, the degree to which a person can distinguish between the feeling process and the thinking process. This was intended as a hypothetical scale for descriptive purposes, not for accurately diagnosing people's levels of maturity, but it identifies the capacity for responding thoughtfully and consciously rather than automatically and emotionally.

Those at the lower end of the scale tend to experience tightly bound, or enmeshed, relationships. Bowen described the inflexible pattern of relating as *fusion*, where emotional processes override intellectual processes. There are two extremes of fusion: intense togetherness where members borrow and lend "self" in an anxious dance to maintain equilibrium at all costs, abandoning individuality and relinquishing personal boundaries. At the other extreme is emotional *cutoff* where anxiety is controlled by completely disengaging from the system. Creating such distance is an enforced shutdown of the relationship and is often an extreme response to too much togetherness. At the higher end of the scale are those who are consciously able to function independently of the emotional system, thoughtfully maintaining their own principles and values while maintaining a warm and open connection to others. They demonstrate the capacity to preserve a calm sense of self when under pressure to respond in predictable ways to stress within the system.

While Bowen considered perfect differentiation to be out of reach, humanly speaking, he believed that a person's basic level of differentiation could be improved upon. Dan Papero writes, "While the basic level of differentiation of self is established early in life it can be expanded in later life through disciplined effort" (1990, p. 48).

Bowen theory presents the idea that differentiation of self can be "expanded" by first exploring one's place in the family of origin and by understanding the way anxiety travels throughout the system. Having recognised patterns and themes of emotional reactivity, and through repeated efforts to engage with the relationship system, it is possible for an individual to act as a circuit breaker and to change the embedded patterns of reactivity. For Bowen theory to be applied successfully the individual must first realise that they themselves hold the potential for change, and to actively attend to the relational connections between multiple members of the system, rather than identifying an individual problem that needs to be fixed. In Bowen theory, therefore, the potential for updating the inherited prescription lies within the will and discipline of the individual.

Christian maturity

The Bible presents a contrasting perspective. It claims that perfect maturity is God's ordained end goal for humanity. It is guaranteed because change does not depend upon the disciplined effort of the individual but upon the work of God himself. He lovingly recovers *imago Dei* in his people, and restores humanity's broken relationship with him. The Bible grounds this restoration in past activity: "those God foreknew he also predestined to be conformed to the image of his Son" (Rom 8:29). Christlikeness has been the plan and purpose of God for his people from all eternity. It is also a present and ongoing work of the Spirit in the lives of believers: "And we all, who with unveiled faces reflect the Lord's glory, are being transformed into his image with ever-increasing glory, which comes from the Lord, who is the Spirit" (2 Cor 3:18).

And there is a future perfection: "Dear friends, now we are children of God, and what we will be has not yet been made known. But we know that when Christ appears, we shall be like him, for we shall see him as he is" (1 John 3:2).

The Christian realises that they can do nothing to mend the relationship between themselves and their Creator, but that Christ has done it all. Only then does the Holy Spirit take up residence and begin to chip away at the old self and replace with the new (Eph 4:22-24) in the ongoing process known as sanctification.

However, this does not mean that disciplined effort is not part of the Christian's life; on the contrary, they strive to reflect the inner sanctification in their words and deeds. Herman Bavinck describes the relationship between God's work and human effort as the "all encompassing activity of God in grace and the self agency of people maintained alongside of it" (2008, p. 254).

In his letter to the Ephesian church Paul describes what maturity in the Christian life looks like:

> Then we will no longer be infants, tossed back and forth by the waves, and blown here and there by every wind of teaching [...] Instead, speaking the truth in love, we will grow to become in every respect the mature body of him who is the head, that is, Christ. From him the whole body, joined and held together by every supporting ligament, grows and builds itself up in love, as each part does its work. (Eph 4:14-16)

With these words, Paul perfectly expresses the individual, relational, and corporate nature of maturity. In using the example of infants, Paul speaks of a progression away from childish uncertainty towards the maturity which defines the Christian life. Those who are not mature are at the mercy of the elements, lacking the anchor of a strong sense of self, impressionable and easily drawn.

For Paul, this maturity includes speaking the truth in love. This is surely an expression of differentiation of self, speaking of the balance between autonomy and connectedness. Speaking is only effective if there is connection with a hearer. Speaking the truth requires the speaker to be personally convicted of that truth, and to be prepared to be persuasive. Speaking the truth in love suggests a close relationship with the hearer. In fused relationships "speaking the truth" may be an obstacle to those who may forfeit their truth for the sake of harmony, and equally "in love" is not something that can be expressed where there is emotional distance.

The image is of a body, made up of individual parts each with their own peculiar structure but all containing the same DNA, different but dependant, all working in coordination towards the same end, namely, becoming the mature body of Christ. There is individual responsibility as each part does its work, in the context of loving relationships, for the unity of the body, under the headship of Christ.

This is the Bible's description of church, and when Rabbi Edwin Friedman made the connection between church and family (1985, p. 364) he hinted at the potential for the principles of Bowen theory to be helpful for those who work within the emotional system of a congregation.

Bowen theory applied in Christian ministry

Whilst society at large is organised into any number of systems, it is the concept of the emotional system which connects the idea of family with the idea of a church community as a type of family. Bowen made the distinction between a relationship system, which describes the system, and the emotional system, which explains the processes which can be observed wherever people gather and interact with one another.

The early church as described in the book of Acts was a mutually supporting community. They were "together and had everything in common. They sold property and possessions to give to anyone who had need [...] they broke bread in their homes and ate together" (Acts 2:44-47). There is an interdependence, a personal investment, and a shared purpose which binds this community in ways that are deeper and more profound than experienced by other systems, displaying characteristics akin to a family system and therefore functioning similarly. The apostle Paul uses the metaphor of the body to describe the emotional system of the church:

> Just as a body, though one, has many parts, but all its many parts form one body, so it is with Christ [...] If one part suffers, every part suffers with it; if one part is honoured, every part rejoices with it. Now you are the body of Christ, and each one of you is a part of it. (1 Cor 12:12, 26-27)

This beautiful corporal image celebrates both individuality and togetherness, the two forces which Bowen realised were fundamental to being human. Jesus himself used familial language when talking about his relationship to the community of believers: "Someone told him, 'Your mother and brothers are standing outside, wanting to see you.' He replied, 'My mother and brothers are those who hear God's word and put it into practice'" (Luke 8:20-21).

It is unsurprising then that a church congregation might be described as a church family. Therefore, the normal dynamics of family relationships can be seen to be operating within a congregation, for better and for worse, on a larger, and possibly more complex scale. Not only is the church itself a family system, but it is made up of individual families, and every person carries the script of their nuclear family's emotional system with them. Ronald Richardson writes:

> Being aware of the emotional process in the community, and relating to it as a more emotionally mature person is one of the best things we can do for individual members of the church in our pastoral care for them. (2017, p. 31)

The interrelatedness of life means that those involved in the pastoral care of congregations will always be dealing with emotional processes that connect individuals in a relationship system. The ability to recognise anxiety as it manifests itself in various ways and to respond non-anxiously, to spot the myriad of triangles that endlessly multiply and to calmly resist being drawn in, and to understand that every person carries with them the weight of their own inherited prescription, can only contribute positively to the building up of the body under the headship of Christ. The skill to remain authentic and connected, rooted and flexible, takes effort and discipline but above all a prayerful dependence on the Spirit of God: "being confident of this, that he who began a good work in you will carry it on to completion until the day of Christ Jesus" (Phil 1:6).

Conclusion

This paper has sought to identify and explore potentially useful intersections between Bowen theory and the biblical view of humanity. It has considered the value of seeing humans as part of systems patterns for pastoral ministry.

The observations that Bowen made about why individuals react, respond, and relate the way they do have the potential to assist in the restoration of relationships. Bowen theory encourages the development of maturity in the individual, enabling a less anxious, more compassionate mode of connecting with others without compromising one's sense of self.

But it cannot restore the relationship between mankind and God.

The Bible grounds these observations in the activity of God in his people and in his world. The assurance of the gospel is that among the broken relationships, the patterns of sin, the inevitable sufferings which are part of being human, there is a crucified Messiah who has restored the one relationship that we were powerless to fix: "and the God of all grace, who called you to his eternal glory in Christ, after you have suffered a little while, will himself restore you and make you strong, firm and steadfast" (1 Pet 5:10).

References

Bavinck, H. (2008). *Reformed dogmatics: Holy Spirit, church, and new creation.* (J. Bolt, Ed., J. Vriend, Trans.). Grand Rapids, Mich: Baker Academic.

Bowen, M. (1993). *Family therapy in clinical practice.* Jason Aronson.

Calvin, J. (1960). *Calvin: institutes of the Christian religion.* (J.T. McNeill, Ed., F. L. Battles, Trans.). Philadelphia; London: Westminster John Knox Press.

Friedman, E. H. (1985). *Generation to generation:* Family process in church and synagogue (1st edition). New York: The Guilford Press.

Kerr, M. E., & Bowen, M. (1988). *Family evaluation* (1st edition). New York: W.W. Norton & Company.

Papero, D.V. (1990). *Bowen family systems theory.* Boston: Pearson.

Richardson, R. W. (2017). *Pastoral care of congregations: Selected workshops: Volume 1.* CreateSpace Independent Publishing Platform.

Chapter 2

CAN A FOCUS ON SELF BE UNSELFISH?
Evaluating Bowen's Concept of Differentiation of Self

Anna Moss

Introduction

The idea of selfless service is a valued attribute within Christian ministry. Putting others first and having a ministry marked with compassion, generosity, and love is something many ministers aspire to. Despite these values being generally accepted as positive attributes of ministry work, the actual practice of these values within the nitty gritty of relationships can be less clear. Bowen family systems theory (hereafter Bowen theory) has been used in various ways to equip pastoral workers in their practice of healthy and sustainable ministry in the local church.

A central idea of Bowen theory is that of learning to manage oneself more maturely in the face of complex and challenging relational systems. The idea of focusing on oneself may at first glance sound like selfish navel gazing and its practice may seem the antithesis of appropriate ministry which is other-person centred and self-sacrificing. However, the theory may provide a helpful framework of "managing self" in a way that is neither sel*fish* nor self*less*.

While Bowen theory might be useful, its application may be challenging due to some limitations with the available resources. Most pastoral resources which discuss Bowen theory are based upon a North American church context and for the most part do not articulate a robust theology of the church, nor provide a theological critique of Bowen theory (e.g., Friedman, 1985; Galindo, 2009; Richardson (1996, 2005); Steinke (1996, 2006a, 2006b)).

In order to thoughtfully assess Bowen theory's potential contribution to the church and to pastoral ministry, it is important to critique it biblically and theologically, neither dismissing it outright as a secular humanist theory, nor "baptising" it naively and applying it to the church context as though the church were merely another type of relational system.

This paper will offer a biblical and theological critique of Bowen theory. It will argue that understanding and applying Bowen theory through a biblical lens has potential to enhance and deepen the ways in which the theory is employed.

The first section of this paper will outline Bowen theory's concept of differentiation of self and explore Bowen's conceptualisation of humanity within a natural systems framework. The second section of the paper will critique Bowen theory with particular reference to the concept of forgiveness and the biblical doctrines of humanity, sin, and the Trinity.

A biblical and theological critique of Bowen family systems theory

Introduction to Bowen family systems theory

Bowen theory was developed by the psychiatrist Murray Bowen in a process that began in the late 1940s. It is a theory of relationships, which postulates that there are predictable relationship patterns in all human emotional systems. The family is seen as an emotional unit, in which relationships and behaviours are shaped by reciprocity, symbiosis, and interdependence.

A central concept of Bowen theory is *differentiation of self* and it is this concept which forms the basis of this discussion. Differentiation is described as the capacity of the individual to function autonomously by making self-directed choices, while remaining emotionally connected to the intensity of a significant relationship system (Kerr & Bowen, 1988). It is the management of "two counterbalancing life forces—individuality and togetherness" (Kerr & Bowen, 1988, p. 59). It involves the ability to remain emotionally present, engaged, and non-reactive in emotionally charged situations, while expressing one's own goals, values, and principles (Wright, 2009). Titelman describes it as "the ability to act for oneself without being selfish and the ability to act for others without being self-less. Differentiation involves the ability to be an individual while simultaneously functioning as part of a team" (2003, p. 20).

Integral to the process of differentiation is the establishment of a self, yet to equate this process with self-enhancement, self-assertion, or egotism is to misunderstand the foundations of the theory. Differentiation of self is viewed in Bowen theory as existing on a theoretical scale, ranging from low to high differentiation and forms a significant goal of therapeutic work. Growth in differentiation of self involves an individual learning to more clearly define oneself and make efforts to live this out in one's close relationships: to carefully think through and articulate one's own principles, beliefs, responsibilities, and decisions at both the internal (intrapersonal) and external (interpersonal) levels.

Bowen theory encourages individuals to do their own objective, mature thinking rather than borrowing from others' thoughts and ideas. This idea echoes the exhortations in Scripture for Christians to not be taken "captive through hollow and deceptive philosophy, which depends on human tradition… rather than on Christ" (Col 2:8), and to "no longer be infants, tossed back and forth by the waves, and blown here and there by every wind of teaching" (Eph 4:14). As followers of Christ we are encouraged to be mature in our thinking and to have our character, thoughts, and actions shaped by the Bible, rather than being swept up in worldly ideas and values. Both Bowen theory and Scripture exhort us to see ourselves with humility as learners, and so it is with these frameworks in mind that the following observations are offered.

Bowen's conceptualisation of humanity within a natural systems theory

Bowen sought a scientific basis for his theory, which places humans and human behaviour in the context of natural systems. The theory "is based on the assumptions that the human is a product of evolution and that human behavior is significantly regulated by the same natural processes that regulate the behaviour of all other living things" (Kerr & Bowen, 1988). Bowen sought to devise terms that were consistent with a conceptualisation of humans as biological beings.[1] Bowen's theoretical foundation in Darwinism has significant implications for how humanity and human behaviour are conceived.

In outlining the natural systems basis for the theory, Kerr states:

> We have for the most part taught ourselves to view the human race as a unique form of life on the planet… we have also been inclined to regard the human as the most important form of life on Earth, the crowning achievement of God's creation. (1988, p. 3)

Bowen theory sees the conceptualisation of humanity as a unique life form to be an exaggeration of our own importance, one that hampers our understanding of ourselves and our relationship to all of life. A cornerstone of Bowen theory is the assumption that the behaviour of all forms of life is driven and regulated by the same fundamental *life forces* (Kerr & Bowen, 1988, p. 28). Bowen theory likens the *togetherness force* in an emotional system with the "herding" instinct seen in social animals that react emotionally as a group when under threat and heightened anxiety.

In Bowen theory, humanity is set apart from other animal species by the "capacity to know, to understand, and to communicate complex ideas… it is that part of man that makes him a unique part of life" (Kerr & Bowen, 1988, p. 48). This view closely resembles Descartes' 17th century "I think therefore I am" philosophy of humanity (Descartes, 1999). This is arguably a reductionistic

---

[1] The term "differentiation of self" is taken from the activity of cell differentiation; the process by which cells specialise and form separate entities within the biological system.

view, one that diminishes the relational, spiritual, and physical aspects of humanity and potentially undermines the dignity and humanity of those who are intellectually impaired.

Dysfunctional behaviour and altruism

By placing human behaviour within evolutionary biology, the theory proposes that "much of man's virtuous behaviour, as well as his dysfunctional behaviour is rooted in his evolutionary heritage" (Kerr & Bowen, 1988, p. 22). Thus, in the same way that a troop of chimpanzees shifts from a calm and orderly state to an anxious and disorderly one, humans may act destructively toward one another given certain conditions of heightened systemic stress. Bowen theory contends that seemingly negative behaviours may be regarded as purposeful in evolutionary biology. Kerr suggests that "aggressiveness, discord and selfishness are not 'bad' characteristics. Evolutionary theory assumes that natural selection has preserved these properties in certain species and that they therefore have a function" (Kerr & Bowen, 1988, p. 91).

One of Bowen theory's strengths as a science is its emphasis on observing behaviours in a family system with a non-judgmental posture, in the role of a "researcher" seeking to better understand self and others. Therapy that draws on Bowen theory seeks to assist individuals in gaining more objective awareness about oneself and significant others. Adopting a research posture enables individuals to become curious about relevant facts within their own family of origin and their relationship interactions. This approach can encourage non-judgmental curiosity of other people, rather than reactive judgment, and can open up a broader awareness and understanding of significant others. Working to suspend judgment enables one to consider what others may have been up against; what challenges and hardships they may have faced. This openness can potentially lead to increased empathy for others, rather than an approach which remains stuck in assumption and conjecture. Systems thinking seeks to ask questions about the relational processes that have taken place and applies a broad lens through which to assess these interactions and patterns of relating. The curious researcher is potentially better able to approach others with humility and with an understanding that one can never ascertain the exact motives (the "why") behind another's actions.

In *Family Evaluation*, Kerr (1988) posits:

> Despite the limits of our objective understanding of human behaviour, we have not been especially constrained in terms of our willingness to passionately adhere to certain viewpoints about the nature of human problems... The vast majority of the admonitions and directives that swirl around us are hopelessly entangled in subjectivity. (p. 18)

Kerr is making the point that the complexity of human behaviour and the combination of factors that contribute to the way humans behave make objective judgment very difficult. It is correct to say that humans are often caught up in and limited by our subjective experience and thinking, yet to allow human limitations to cast doubt on the existence of objective truth is to venture into dangerous territory that may give humanity more power than is warranted. One could argue that objective truth can exist outside of a human's ability to perceive it correctly.

Within this awareness of the complexity of human behaviour, Bowen theory does not clearly articulate a concept of human wrongdoing. As a humanistic theory, the concept of human sinfulness and depravity is absent from the theory. Behaviour is instead seen as being maladaptive and affecting differentiation of self. Bowen's articulation of the family as an emotional unit emphasises the relational process rather than individual pathology. This broader view of human behaviour has significant strengths, which will be further explored, yet this view leaves minimal space for individual accountability. The concept of forgiveness is hence given very little attention in the theory. The absence of the idea of sin and the need for forgiveness are distinct features of Bowen theory that differ from a Christian worldview.

Bowen theory does acknowledge the challenge and mystery that human altruism poses to the theory of natural selection. Kerr proposes that "man's ability to remember the past and to plan for the future allows him to engage in acts of 'reciprocal altruism'… Altruistic acts can be traded at different times and spaced over long periods, even generations" (Kerr & Bowen, 1988, p. 91). Bowen theory's reliance on Darwinism results in a reductionistic view of the human capacity for both evil and good.

Although the biblical doctrine of humanity conceives what is arguably a deeper and fuller picture of humanity, one must not dismiss Bowen theory's concept of humanity outright. It takes a certain humility to perceive our own weakness and brokenness, mirrored in the creation in which we live. Bowen theory proposes that we see ourselves as "far more like other life forms than different from them" (Kerr & Bowen, 1988, p. 3). In doing so, we may helpfully perceive our creatureliness, perhaps being less likely to overestimate our innate wisdom and ability to rise above our instinctual natures without help. However, a biblical lens can provide much depth to Bowen theory's concept of humanity. The next section will outline ways in which the biblical doctrine of humanity can enhance and deepen Bowen's conceptualisation of humanity and human relationships.

Applying a biblical lens: How a theological framework can enhance Bowen theory

This section will explore the ways in which a theological framework can enhance Bowen theory and deepen the ways it is employed within the church ministry context. The doctrine of humanity, the doctrine of sin, the concept of forgiveness, and the doctrine of the Trinity will be applied to the theory as part of this exploration.

The doctrine of humanity

Biblical anthropology is grounded in the notion that humanity is created in the image of God (Gen 1:27). This concept can provide a rich understanding of anthropology, arguably one more complex and nuanced than Bowen's articulation. The biblical lens offers humanity a distinctiveness from lower animal species that is grounded in more than intellectual capacity. Our spirituality and relational capacity are tied in with our nature as image bearers.

The doctrine of humanity enhances Bowen's insightful observation of the togetherness force and individuality force which he posits propels individuals to act in certain ways to either be connected to the group, or to distinguish themselves as a separate entity. Bowen rightly recognises that humans are hardwired for relationship; we seek belonging and connectedness with one another. Bowen theory also helpfully observes our need to be separate selves, with distinct identities, not being fused with others, but able to relate freely and authentically with them as individuals.

As image bearers we possess the unique ability to know God, to know ourselves, and to know others. These capacities are interrelated and contingent. Bowen theory emphasises the benefits of making self-directed choices and expressing one's own values and principles. However the process of establishing substantive, worthy values is less clear. Adopting an objective posture is central to Bowen's thinking about managing oneself less reactively in relationship processes. Working on defining and communicating one's principles is indeed a key process in managing one's own reactivity as an individual working to operate out of a more authentic self. However, the theory's emphasis on objectivity may limit its willingness to assess whether particular values or principles are commendable and constructive. Instead, a biblical lens can assist us in the determination of God-centred values and accurate self-expression which is based on humans being under the authority of God. Calvin articulates the central truth that the knowledge of God and the knowledge of ourselves are mutually connected (McNeil, (ed) 1997). In other words, without knowledge of ourselves there is no knowledge of God and without knowledge of God there is no knowledge of ourselves. From a biblical perspective, an expression of self, anchored in values and principles which are rooted in God's own character and self-revelation is one that is authentic, life-giving, and truly purposeful. Theologically constructed, the capacity for differentiation of self is the capacity to be truly the person that God intends us to be, to know fullness of self while knowing fullness of relationship with others and especially fullness of relationship with God himself, through his Son, Jesus.

The doctrine of sin

The biblical doctrine of sin provides meaningful insights into the human experience of togetherness and individuality. Bowen helpfully outlines maladaptive patterns in the emotional process, such as emotional cutoff, withdrawal, fusion, and loss of self. The doctrine of sin can be seen as undergirding these dysfunctions. The Bible's story is that God lovingly and joyfully created humans as distinct individuals (Ps 139:14-16), whose personhood would be expressed fully in relationship with their creator and with one another. Sin has led to the distortion and corruption of these processes. We no longer define self and identity through our relationship with God, we fear moving toward others in loving relationship and meaningful connectedness, and either anxiously fuse with them or anxiously distance and hide ourselves.

Romans 3:10-18 describes the way in which our turning away from God has led to profound dysfunction in our relationships with one another. The doctrine of total depravity holds that every aspect of our being has been distorted by sin and that our very basic instincts are compromised. Through the lens of evolutionary biology Bowen saw that human emotional functioning is better understood through "instinct" and "forces" (Kerr & Bowen, 1988, p. 28) rather than through socialisation. Bowen states, "Focused as we are on psychological reasons; it is easy to forget that humans... are motivated to do many things on the basis of processes that have roots deeper (older in an evolutionary sense) than thinking and feeling" (Kerr & Bowen, 1988, p. 31).

The doctrine of sin helpfully nuances the role of instincts and biological forces in understanding human behaviour. Bowen theory does not explicitly discuss human wrongdoing and has no actual concept of sin, but perhaps Bowen's proposal of "deeper" and "older" forces could be considered as aspects of creation and original sin. Genesis 3 and Romans 8 highlight the fact that all of creation has been affected by sin and thus the instinctual drives of humans and animals alike have been distorted from their originally intended purposes. This systemic nature of sin is a helpful lens through which to understand human emotional functioning as well as the functioning of the natural world. However, a biblical framework will require a balance of systemic sin and individual sin. Bowen's ability to perceive pathology within the emotional process of the broader system (rather than residing solely in the individual) is valuable, yet one must be wary of an approach which undermines individual responsibility: Romans 14:12 states that each individual will give an account of themselves to God. A biblical perspective will encourage an approach which encapsulates both systemic and individual factors.

Forgiveness

Considering Bowen's lack of emphasis on human wrongdoing, it is perhaps not surprising that the concept of forgiveness features sparsely in the theory. In his application of Bowen theory to the local church context, Ronald Richardson (2005) states:

> Remember that this work is not primarily about giving or getting 'forgiveness' in the family. Forgiveness is a very tricky issue, and we can disguise a lot of emotional process behind it. Forgiveness can sometimes imply a one-up or one-down relationship that simply doesn't fit with a system analysis of the situation and that will only continue the emotional process in place. (p. 145)

Forgiveness is indeed a complex and challenging relational issue. Bowen theory leads us to calmly observe the broader systemic process rather than prematurely blaming an individual, as well as considering our own role in the problem and managing our own reactiveness. These are helpful processes to adopt. However, accountability and truth-telling must be also applied. Forgiveness is a powerful, biblical concept and its value in the relationship process should be considered as integral to the way God's people manage relationships in a fallen world under Christ.

In his discussion of forgiveness and relationship restoration, Miroslav Volf (1996) argues that in order to embrace the other and to experience full restoration in relationship, the truth must be said, wrongdoing must be acknowledged, and justice must be done (reconciliation). Volf asserts that "the will to give ourselves to others and 'welcome' them, to readjust our identities to make space for them, is prior to any judgment about others, except that of identifying with them in their humanity" (1996, p. 29). The "willingness to readjust our identities" may initially appear to contradict differentiation of self as a concept. However, Bowen theory emphasises one's ability to be appropriately open and flexible while maintaining self, rather than taking defensive, closed, and rigid relationship postures.

The doctrine of the Trinity

The doctrine of the Trinity, which presents the relationships in the Godhead as interrelated but not compromised by each other, offers a profound example to think about in light of Bowen's concept of differentiation of self. The doctrine of the Trinity proposes that God is within himself as he is toward us; namely that God's inner person is completely consistent with the actions of his outer person. Put another way, God's intrapsychic self is thoroughly coherent with his interpersonal self and therefore demonstrates complete differentiation of self.

The concept of *perichoreses*[2] was further developed by John of Damascus in his statement that the persons of the Trinity are "with one another in one Being in such a way that they have their Being in each other and reciprocally contain one other without any coalescing or co-mingling with one another and yet without any separation from one another."[3] *Perichoreses* demonstrates the way in which the distinct persons of the Godhead interrelate without fusion and loss of self or conversely without distancing or self-protective withdrawal.

---

2 This term, which literally means "proceeding around" was developed by the Cappadocian Fathers. It encapsulates the idea of an intimate relationship dance.

3 John of Damascus, *De fide orthodoxa*, 1.8. As cited in T. F. Torrance, *Christian Doctrine of God, One Being, Three Persons* (London: T &T Clark Ltd, 1996), p. 170.

In discussing the aseity of God, which embodies the notion that God is self-sufficient and independent, Volf (1996) notes that the free, personal activity of the divine life "does not occur in self-isolation, but rather through constitutive relationships with the Son and Spirit" (p. 77). God in his very being is persons-in-communion. God's self-expression and identity are bound up in his inter-personal, inter-related nature. Volf further argues that, "if behind the action of the divine persons there is no 'I' of these persons, then the three persons are superfluous in the economy of salvation... God's external works are not to be attributed to one undifferentiated divine essence, but rather proceed from the divine persons" (p. 205). The ontology of God provides a powerful example of differentiation of self: each person of the Trinity being distinct in individual personhood and purpose, yet existing in intimate connection with the other, without loss of self. It is the very distinctiveness and individual fullness of the three persons of the Trinity that enables them to relate to one another, and to humanity, in completeness of purpose and connection.

Conclusion

In order to consider the ways in which Bowen theory's concept of differentiation of self may be useful to those in Christian pastoral ministry, it is first necessary to apply a biblical and theological lens to the theory so we understand the foundation in doing so. This paper has explored and critiqued the concept of differentiation of self using biblical anthropology, the doctrine of the Trinity, the doctrine of sin, and the concept of forgiveness. It is argued here that the application of a biblical and theological framework can enhance the useful contribution of Bowen theory to the church, not dismissing its potential value nor naively applying it without thoughtful and appropriate scrutiny.

A common dilemma for many pastoral workers is how to manage oneself maturely and wisely in the face of complex, difficult relational situations. Many of us in ministry may recognise that neglecting ourselves and failing to attend to our basic needs is unsustainable, and yet questions about how to most helpfully interact with others can be personally confusing, exhausting, and painful, especially when the relationship system is upset and in turmoil. Bowen theory can help us focus on ourselves in a way that is not selfish and self-absorbed, but rather in a way that promotes responsibility for self, greater self-awareness, and an improved understanding of others. Rather than bowing to relational pressures that can render us invisible, voiceless, and resentful, the concept of differentiation of self can encourage compassionate, sacrificial acts that originate from a place of solid self—a thoughtful, robust, intentional, and more sustainable choosing to love others and serve them rather than engaging in behaviours that are driven by one's own insecurities and others' expectations.

References

Descartes, R. (1999). *Discourse on Method and Related Writings.* London: Penguin Books

Friedman, E. (1985). *Generation to generation: Family process in church and synagogue.* New York: Guildford Press.

Galindo, I. (2009). *Perspectives on congregational leadership: Applying systems thinking for effective leadership.* New York: Educational Consultants.

Kerr, M. & Bowen, M. (1988). *Family evaluation.* Ontario: Penguin Books.

McNeil, J. (ed.) (1997). *Calvin: Institutes of the Christian religion.*

Philadelphia: The Westminster Press.

Richardson, R. (1996). *Creating a healthier church.* Minneapolis: Fortress Press.

Richardson, R. (2005). *Becoming a healthier pastor: Family systems theory and the pastor's own family.* Minneapolis: Fortress Press.

Steinke, P. (1996). *Healthy congregations: A systems approach.* Herndon: The Alban Institute.

Steinke, P. (2006a). *Congregational leadership in anxious times.* Maryland: Rowman and Littlefield.

Steinke, P. (2006b). *How your church family works.* Herndon: The Alban Institute. Titleman, P. (2003). "Emotional Cutoff", in P. Titleman, ed. *Emotional Cutoff: Bowen Family Systems Perspectives.* New York: Haworth.

Torrance, T.F. (1996). *Christian Doctrine of God, One Being, Three Persons.* London: T&T Clark Ltd.

Volf, M. (1997). *After our likeness: The church as the image of the Trinity.* Grand Rapids: Eerdmans.

Volf, M. (1996). *Exclusion and embrace: A theological exploration of identity, otherness and reconciliation.* Nashville: Abingdon Press.

Wright, J. (2009). A recursive intrapsychic and relational process: The contribution of the Bowen theory to the process of self-soothing, *Australian and New Zealand Journal of Family Therapy, 30*(1), pp. 29-41.

Chapter 3

BOWEN'S MULTI-GENERATIONAL RESEARCH AND THE FAMILY DIAGRAM / GENOGRAM

Jenny Brown

The family diagram (or genogram) has become a popular tool in counselling for visually presenting information about the generations of people's families. In particular it is used as an assessment and treatment tool in the family therapy field. This chapter will explore the aspects of investigating family history that are compatible and can add value within a biblical worldview. Murray Bowen's use of this tool will be presented as well as that of other prominent therapists who espouse the value of family of origin research as part of a clinical approach. In particular it will consider the various ways a diagrammatic tool may express different interpretations of the human condition and about the process of change. A key question asked is, To what extent is the family diagram utilised as a fact-finding and information gathering tool rather than as an explanatory framework for understanding human problems? While there are clearly helpful aspects to the data provided in a family diagram, this paper will analyse potential areas of blinkering and distortions in the use of this tool and its family systems perspective.

Bowen is recognised as one of the first theoreticians in the psychiatry field to propose multigenerational research (Guerin, 1976) and the use of the family diagram in clinical work (Bowen's term for this is *coaching*). In a definite move away from Freudian thinking, Bowen did not look at past generations as the cause of an individual's problems but as a resource to better understand the complexity of human relationships in which their problem was situated. Bowen's family diagram has been popularised as the genogram; however his original label will be the primary term used in this chapter.

Bowen theory and family history

Dr Murray Bowen's use of gathering and diagramming family history stemmed from his research effort as a psychiatrist in the 1950s and 60s where he facilitated National Institute of Mental Health funded research with entire families admitted to a hospital unit with their symptomatic young adult child. He aimed at gaining more factual data about humans in contrast to what he viewed as subjective explanations of human life problems emanating from Freudian theory. Hence his effort went to collecting details of the past generations of the family, including dates and places of births, deaths, migrations, people's education, jobs, sibling order, adverse life events, and symptoms. He endeavoured to avoid what he saw as the humans' preoccupation with "why" and with cause-and-effect thinking that ascribes blame to others (usually one's parents) for one's own failures (Bowen, 1978, p. 491). In reflecting on the outcome of his early analytic training, Bowen stated that:

> During my psychoanalysis there was enough emotional pressure to engage my parents in an angry confrontation about childhood grievances that had come to light in the snug harbour of transference. At the time I considered these confrontations to be emotional emancipation...

> The net result was my conviction that my parents had their problems and I had mine, that they would never change, and nothing more could be done. (1978, p. 484)

Bowen was not satisfied with this outcome as he began to see from his research that each family member participated in a reciprocal (circular) process of making compensations for others. He observed that every response in the family affects other family members in a back-and-forth manner. Bowen and those who utilised his family systems theory diverged from the basic viewpoint in psychotherapy that "My family is the cause of the problems in my life." He espoused an alternative to this viewpoint: "that every family member, including one's parents, is embedded in a multigenerational emotional [relational] process and everyone, including oneself, has a responsibility to grow up as much as possible within that process" (Kerr & Bowen, 1988, p. 306).

The effort to investigate one's family back for at least three to four generations was primarily introduced as a way to research transmission of family characteristics and symptoms from one generation to another. Bowen was careful to acknowledge that the historical information could at best provide indirect impressions rather than definite interpretations, owing to the human difficulty "to get beyond myths, pretense, and emotionally biased reports" (Bowen, 1978, p. 491). Bowen alleged that the information about family history is meaningless unless it conveys principles of relational processes that assist in understanding regressions and improvements in different family members' life-functioning. This could be gleaned through considering indications of life challenges and patterns of relationship breakdown in some lines of the family compared to other generational lines. The information deemed to be important in this approach was factual details of past generations and impressions about family relationship patterns such as distance between generations (indicated by people falling out of contact, not attending family weddings, etc.) or dependencies between the generations (indicated by family members not leaving the parental home or living in close proximity to each other).

The family diagram as a tool

The tool of the family diagram was employed primarily as a way of managing voluminous material. It provided a kind of shorthand for gathering generational information and enabled a visual sense of a person's small place within the broad patterns of the distant past. A method of using symbols and graphics that record and diagram family members' positions, key facts, and relationship patterns is part of this tool. Bowen's clinical purpose of this information was to steer an individual away from immaturely seeking their personal need fulfilment and to replace this with a broader sense of being part of a multigenerational process. The gathering of facts of family life over the generations provides information about both symptoms and strengths and how these relate to a family's response to challenges and prosperity.[1]

With careful research of family history and patterns, the individual can begin to relate more from their relational awareness and less in reaction to others. From a more objective position within the multigenerational family, the individual may improve their capacity to develop a person-to-person relationship with each member of his/her family where differences can be expressed without attacking, defending, or withdrawing. A feature of this gathering of fairly factual family history is that it moves away from the self-referencing that can be the focus of individualised secular psychological theories. It places each person in a broad network

---

[1] Described clearly by Victoria Harrison (2018) in Chapter 1, The Family Diagram as a Tool.

of relationships across the generations that paints a picture of how small each of us is in the ebb and flow of life and death. It can also raise a person's self-awareness of patterns and symptoms that they may be more prone to repeating, such as cutting off from people in the face of tension, or intense expectations in a marriage (evidenced by marital conflict or divorce), or patterns of disparate functioning in marriages (evidenced by a vulnerable spouse with a seemingly resilient spouse) or patterns of overfocusing on children (evidenced by certain children struggling to grow into adult responsibility).

This lens avoids concepts of "sick patients" and diagnosis. Instead the focus is on relationship patterns that either enhance or impair each person's ability to cope in their life. Symptoms are viewed as belonging to the interconnections and interactions within the family as a system. For example, symptoms such as alcoholism, that might be prevalent in the histories of some families, are seen to emerge "in the context of an imbalance in functioning in the total family system" (Bowen, 1978, p. 262). Immaturity can be unevenly distributed within the family through anxiously focusing on another, sidelining a family member, or excessively managing another within the family dynamic. Bowen's approach avoids the more reductionist labelling of a medical model and avoids the need for a corrective therapeutic experience to redress perceived inadequate parenting.

When the family diagram is used as a change intervention

The tool of the family diagram has been championed by a number of others since Murray Bowen. Most proponents of the clinical value of the family diagram have tended to elevate its use beyond Bowen's formulation of cautious impressions about each person. Social worker and family therapist, Monica McGoldrick, has written some texts on the use of the genogram (her terminology for the family diagram). While she shares Bowen's view that people and their problems do not exist in a vacuum but are inextricably interwoven into broader family interactional systems, she presents the genogram information as somewhat more authoritative for understanding *self*. McGoldrick writes that the genogram enables people and families to "understand their current dilemmas and provide solutions for their future" (McGoldrick et. al., 2008, p. 4). This potentially elevates the family diagram beyond a data organising tool to an explanation for why families behave as they do. If generational patterns are used to explain a person's present behaviours it risks bypassing the biblical understanding of human sinfulness and need for repentance in order to change.

Edwin Friedman (family therapist and Jewish rabbi) is another who has espoused the value of the family diagram and family of origin research, particularly for clergy and others in faith communities. He saw great potential for the information in a family diagram to help people to change. He proposed that seeing repeating patterns of behaviour across the generations "helps people to get distance from their immediate problems and as a result become freer to make changes" (Friedman, 1985, p. 32). In Friedman's writing about relationships in faith communities he doesn't mention sin as a problem for church leaders; rather the focus is primarily seen in relationship anxieties. Like McGoldrick, Friedman seems to have a more optimistic view than Bowen of what can be achieved through the research of one's multigenerational family. He writes that "genogram information can make the difference in the life and death of a marriage, for, like many malignant processes, many marital problems would never have had such influence had they been recognised and treated at an earlier stage of their development" (Friedman, 1985, p. 93).

Bowen and other long-term scholars of his theory have cautioned of the dangers of simplification and distortion of the use of the family diagram (Titelman, 1987). One such danger is, if its use is reduced to clinical technique it can present the mistaken view that a person will solve their life difficulties by gathering family history. Bowen made it clear that any improvements in a human's maturity would be a slow and lifelong effort and that an understanding of family generational data was just one component of improving self-awareness. In a recent publication on the family diagram, long-term scholar of Bowen theory, Victoria Harrison, warns about misconceptions about the change benefits of this tool: "There is nothing magical about developing and drawing your family diagram" (Harrison, 2018, p. 25). She clarifies that this tool needs to be in partnership with a longer-term project of being a less reactive person in all family relationships.

Family of origin research and the Bible

Seeing the human as part of a multigenerational context conforms to a biblical view that regards genealogies as evidence of God's sovereign purposes over time: "For the Lord is good and his love endures forever; his faithfulness continues through all generations" (Ps 100:5). When biblical truth is critically applied to human ideas and discoveries it is always interpreting and then reinterpreting these through its worldview. This can be seen to be the case with Bowen's theory and use of the family diagram. There are lessons to be learnt and reinterpreted from Bowen's research discoveries in that "extra-biblical knowledge—of ourselves and our world—is always the grist with which biblical truth works continually to extend the range and depth of understanding" (Powlison, 2007, p. 15).

A common grace element of Bowen theory and generational histories

There is a case to be made for a common grace component of knowledge of human relationships within Bowen's intergenerational theory. Bowen's descriptions of patterns in families that affect people's maturity may be part of God's providential activity in allowing a secular researcher to make advances in knowledge of how families operate in this anxious, fallen world. It can add extra-biblical information about influences of family history that complements biblical truths. For example, the Bible reveals the centrality of relationships in God's good design and the God-ordained unit of the family for raising each generation. It also gives wisdom on particular ways that relationship patterns become distorted in the anxiety of the fallen world outside of Eden. Bowen's careful observational research of families has enabled him to describe common patterns of interaction in dealing with the strains of relationships (this includes the pattern of *triangling* or detouring to a third party through side-taking, or as an alternative focus that avoids truthfulness in another relationship).

The church as a body, where each member affects the whole, bears similarities to Bowen's observations of the family as more than a collection of individuals. It can be reasoned that Bowen's observations of the human, while God-bypassing, are closer to a biblical lens than many other secular theorists. Bowen is amongst the secular theorists who aimed to be more of a research scientist than a psychotherapist. He has contributed much observational-descriptive detail that helps to get to more facts of human functioning in relationships. Bowen could recognise the human as a narcissistic creature with limited capacity to be objective and make progress in maturing self through his/her own efforts. Bowen writes:

> The human is a narcissistic creature who lives in the present and who is more interested in his own square inch of real estate, and more devoted to fighting for his rights, than in the multigenerational meaning of life itself. (Kerr & Bowen, 1988, p. 385)

Bowen theory and blinkers about humanity

While Bowen observes much that fits a biblical lens, it is impossible for a secular theorist to not have blind spots in their effort to understand the human phenomenon. Hence it is necessary to reinterpret Bowen's theory and use of the family diagram with the eyes of a biblical worldview. While Bowen's theory is less "self-referential" than much secular psychology, it is certainly not "God-referential". The clear blinkers in Bowen's interpretations of family history data is the absence of the notion of human sin as central to the aetiology of family relationship dysfunctions. The Bible's view of human sin is that it is more than willful acts of selfishness and harm to others. Rather the Bible speaks to the inner struggles and relationship struggles of us all "that stem from the deep inner hold of sin" (Powlison, 2003, p. 194). In the Gospels, Jesus' teaching speaks to this inner problem of humans:

> For it is from within, out of a person's heart, that evil thoughts come—sexual immorality, theft, murder, adultery, greed, malice, deceit, lewdness, envy, slander, arrogance and folly. (Mark 7:21-22)

Without a perspective on the consequence of human defiance against God and the selfish heart that drives this, Bowen is left to explain human life problems merely as the consequence of anxious patterns of family survival. Family patterns are described as facts of nature as if they exist apart from God. With this God-suppressing blockage, Bowen draws from Charles Darwin's theory about all species' patterns of survival or extinction as the main basis of his interpretive framework for family dynamics.

It is helpful that Bowen gets beyond the common psychological view of human difficulties as inner wounds caused by inadequate caregivers. The broad scope of intergenerational history reduces the propensity to blame parents and can promote a more gracious posture towards one's family of origin. Nonetheless Bowen's use of family history is also blinkered by missing the extent of the morality problems of sinful humans who act in evil ways towards other humans. This dampening down of the problem of human sin against God and others is reflected in Bowen's writing about how generational family research risks removing personal accountability and need for repentance:

> Gaining more knowledge of one's distant families of origin can help one become aware that there are no angels and devils in a family: they were human beings, each with their own strengths and weaknesses, each reacting predictably to the emotional issue of the moment, and each doing the best they could with their own life course. (Bowen, 1978, p. 492)

On one hand this quote conveys a more grace-filled, compassionate view of family members in our past but it also reveals a blinkering out of God's moral order of right and wrong. When family patterns are deemed most useful for understanding challenges for people, "human responsibility is muted" (Powlison, 2003, p. 196). The deceitfulness of the human heart is rationalised away and replaced with social-environmental explanations as sufficient in accounting for our problems.

McGoldrick and Friedman present a similar blinkering to Bowen about the human as essentially good:

> An important assumption behind all family questioning is that human beings are always doing the best they can, given the limitations of their particular perspectives. (McGoldrick, 1997, p. 48)

This is clearly a secular humanist interpretation of the human condition in viewing the human as inherently good and the external environment as the context for life problems. Humanism as a worldview asserts the answer to life problems "can be found unequivocally by humanity looking to itself" (Thompson, 2007, p. 105). In contrast the Bible reveals that no amount of human effort can achieve a right relationship with God, which is viewed as our deepest relationship problem. The gospel speaks to our inability in addressing our waywardness. Our reconciliation with our creator is provided for through the sacrifice of Jesus Christ, transferring his perfect goodness to those who turn to him in faith and repentance. This doesn't mean that we are without sin but that we have forgiveness that enables us to relate intimately to God. Change comes in response to this undeserved gift:

> For it is by grace you have been saved, through faith—and this is not from yourselves, it is the gift of God—not by works, so that no one can boast. (Eph 2:8-9)

Unlike most psychological theories, Bowen observes that the human is incapable of substantial internal change. Unbeknown to Bowen, this observation actually points to the need for God's intervention. Bowen however does not see the need for supernatural intervention. He is left with a somewhat pessimistic view that small human improvements rely on an awareness of a person's part in family patterns to work at improved responsibility (maturity) in relationships. This in effect denies the sanctifying power of God's word and Holy Spirit to heal and change

(Powlison, 2003). It leaves aside the Holy Spirit's sanctifying work that occurs when people abide in Jesus Christ and his word and so are continuously being "transformed by the renewing of [their] mind" (Rom 12:2).

As an exploratory and descriptive tool, the effort to document intergenerational family history can contribute to the human understanding themselves within God's revelation of the fall and of his redemptive purposes. The identification of patterns of relationships and symptoms may be helpful to assist people to understand the particular challenges of their families in dealing with the effect of sin and fallenness. If, however, this data becomes authoritative as the explanation as well as the solution for human life challenges, it runs the risk of promoting distortions and suppressing God's revelation of his purposes. Without including the vertical relationship of humans and their creator God, the multigenerational patterns can so easily be misinterpreted and potentially over-emphasised. Humans who have all turned their backs on God live with the effects of sin by nature, nurture, and choice:

> For all have sinned and fall short of the glory of God, and all are justified by his grace through the redemption that came by Christ Jesus. (Rom 3:23-24)

A biblical reinterpretation—change under Jesus' redeeming transformation

The Bible speaks of the family as part of God's good creation but, importantly, it reveals that God the Father adopts children into a new family through the death and resurrection of his Son Jesus. In this way the language of family is one of the ways by which God explains himself and his church. This extends well beyond the secular family theorists' notion of the family and its influences on each human. Family can only rightly be understood in relation to God as Father. His new family of the church, the bride of Christ, to be presented faultless in the age to come, replaces the intergenerational heritage of our biological families: "He predestined us for adoption to sonship through Jesus Christ, in accordance with his pleasure and will" (Eph 1:5). The family diagram, when used as a predictor of our life functioning, does not make room for the marvellous eternal inheritance of the family of Christ.

The counselling approach emanating from Bowen's emphasis and interpretations is "directed at helping the family to modify its patterns of functioning" (Bowen, 1978, p. 262). The most resourceful family member is encouraged to use the awareness of their part in anxious relationship patterns to modify the way they are reacting. In turn, one person's shift facilitates others to adjust to less anxious relating. While this has value in terms of individual responsibility and a shift from blaming or trying to change others, it is missing the core need to have a redeemed relationship with God. The primary goal of Bowen theory is increased maturity in relationships, rather than seeking God's will and kingdom purpose. A person can recognise a pattern from their family of origin and through their own effort try to change, or they can take it to Jesus to ask for help to change and submit their sensitivities to his redeeming transformation. For example, a person comes to see the impact of worry about finances and patterns of bankruptcy in previous generations of their family through exploring their family diagram. They can be assisted to use this information to understand how they are also prone to lose perspective about managing money, and then be encouraged to consider how casting this care upon the Lord can be core to reducing their anxious controlling behaviours in this aspect of their life.

Conclusion

In summary, Bowen's observations about intergenerational patterns require some reinterpretation through Christian eyes. When a psychological theory reduces human life struggles to mechanistic patterns, it distorts the truth that all humans are actors who are "consciously or unconsciously seeking to live autonomously from the Creator and Redeemer" (Powlison, 2003, p. 197). With the human sin problem removed, the family systems approach turns to evolution and patterns of survival to make sense of family relationship strengths and weaknesses. A biblical worldview reinterprets Bowen's discoveries about human relating and generational transmission of immature patterns. It understands these generational family symptoms and challenges as the outworking of both sin and the anxious ramifications of a broken relationship with God, that is, a human rebellious bent to live without fear of God—"We all, like sheep, have gone astray, each of us has turned to our own way; and the Lord has laid on him the iniquity of us all" (Isa 53:6)—as well as all the anxious ramifications of this confusion and groaning in a fallen world:

> We know that the whole creation has been groaning as in the pains of childbirth right up to the present time. Not only so, but we ourselves, who have the firstfruits of the Spirit, groan inwardly as we wait eagerly for our adoption to sonship, the redemption of our bodies. (Rom 8:22-23)

This paper has presented a case for the value of generational family research and use of the family diagram as an information generating tool—a tool that may broaden a person's view from simplistic cause-and-effect individualistic thinking. It has also presented aspects of investigating family history and family patterns that are compatible and can add extra knowledge within a biblical framework, while also cautioning against the use of these as a tool for linear thinking about human problems. The expansive view of generational transmission of family patterns is consistent with biblical narratives and genealogies. Bowen's use of multigenerational research can contribute insight into the deep influence of the families that have gone before us. The need for a biblical reinterpretation of Bowen theory is highlighted in the ways that intergenerational family patterns have been used as an explanatory framework for understanding the context of human problems.

Bowen theory's attention to family generational patterns provides details about people in family or social groups, beyond what is found in the Bible. Hence there is benefit in understanding Bowen's science of relationships while continuously applying the effort to "think the way Jesus thinks [in order to] rightly align all that [we] can learn from other sources" (Powlison, 2010, p. 254). Each of us can learn from the legacies of our families and be attuned to ways that family patterns, and our part in them, make us more vulnerable to particular sins. A biblically aligned counselling approach that draws on these good lessons will direct people to bring their challenges, hurts, and maturity gaps, not just to their self-awareness and self-effort, but to their Lord Jesus. The information about generational family symptoms and associated relationship patterns can add to a person's conscious and prayerful efforts to live lives worthy of their calling through God's grace. The sanctifying work of the Holy Spirit through the wisdom of God's word is central in the work of growing a person in freedom from generational afflictions and in developing godliness. This is the people-changing process that goes well beyond the limitations and scripts of our earthly family heritage.

References

Bowen, M. (1978). *Family therapy in clinical practice.* Jason Aronson.

Friedman, E. (1985, 2011). *Generation to generation: Family process in church and synagogue.* Guilford Press.

Guerin, P.J. (1976). *Family therapy: Theory and practice.* Gardner Press New York.

Harrison, V. (2018). *The family diagram & family research: An illustrated guide to tools for working on differentiation of self in one's family.* Center for the Study of Natural Systems and the Family. www.csnsf.org

Kerr, M. E., & Bowen, M. (1988). *Family evaluation.* WW Norton & Company.

McGoldrick, M., Gerson, R., & Petry, S.S. (2008). *Genograms: Assessment and intervention.* WW Norton & Company.

McGoldrick, M. (1997). *You can go home again: Reconnecting with your family.* WW Norton & Company.

Powlison, D. (2003). *Seeing with new eyes.* P&R, Phillipsburg, NJ Chapters on Ephesians.

Powlison, D. (2010). A biblical counselling view, Ch. 6 in *Psychology and Christianity: Five views.* Ed. Johnson E. J. InterVarsity Press.

Powlison, D. (2007). Cure of souls (and the modern psychotherapies). *The Journal of Biblical Counseling, 5, 14.*

Thompson, R. (2007) Humanism. Chapter 5 in *A spectator's guide to world views.* Ed. Smart, S. Blue Bottle Books.

Titelman, P. (Ed.). (1987). *The therapist's own family: Toward the differentiation of self.* Jason Aronson.

Chapter 4

ANXIETY AND DIFFERENTIATION IN THE EPHESIAN CHURCH

Peter Frith

Timothy was appointed by the apostle Paul and the "elders" (1 Tim 4:14) as the lead pastor of a first century church in the thriving city of Ephesus, located in what is now modern Turkey. Young, timid Timothy (1 Tim 4:12; 2 Tim 1:7) found himself set in the midst of a somewhat fractious congregation, evidenced by Paul's references to various interest and pressure groups[1], and it is plausible that Timothy had considered abandoning his post as a result (1 Tim 1:3). The two letters which Paul wrote (c. 65-67 AD), reveal his attempt to help Timothy respond to these challenges with levelheadedness and poise rather than to cut and run.

---

[1] For example, there were the myth promoters (1 Tim 1:4; 2 Tim 2:23), the false teachers and ascetics (1 Tim 1:6-7, 4:1-5), the legalists, the promiscuous and unrepentant (1 Tim 1:6-10, 5:20), contentious men and indecorous women (1 Tim 2:8-10), the wealthy (1 Tim 6:17-19), and predators (2 Tim 3:6-7).

This paper attempts to introduce Bowen family systems theory (here on in referred to as Bowen theory) as a conversation partner in the reading of the text and as a commentator on the Ephesian church as an emotional system, particularly with reference to differentiation and anxiety.

The central idea for this paper is contained in Paul's instruction to Timothy, "But you, keep your head in all situations"[2] (2 Tim 4:5), advice which bears an uncanny resemblance to the key concept of the differentiation of self in Bowen theory. But, instead of keeping his head, Timothy appears to have been overwhelmed by the "situations" he faced, and to have responded to them anxiously. Murray Bowen understood anxiety as "the response of an organism to a threat, real or imagined" (Kerr & Bowen, 1988, p. 112) and as being evidenced by certain emotional reactions manifested in behaviour. Anxiety of this type seems to have been experienced not only by Timothy, but by Paul and the Ephesian congregation as well and this is depicted in the reported behaviour[3]. However, before exploring this further, it is important to address three hermeneutical issues with regard to using Bowen theory as an interpretive tool.

Hermeneutical issues with regard to using Bowen theory as an interpretive tool

Firstly, some may object to the use of a secular, psychological theory to comment on the biblical text, deeming it unwise

---

[2] The Greek word translated here as "head" (νῆφε) means to be "sober", "circumspect", "vigilant" (Mounce, 1993).

[3] Note: the material in Paul's letter to the Ephesians was not included in this study because it is widely accepted that Ephesians was a circular letter sent to many churches and contains more generic material. It does not contain the parochial detail of 1 and 2 Timothy.

or even dangerous. Indeed, caution is advised, but it must be acknowledged that every reader approaches a text with their own set of presuppositions. Background, language, education, and experiences all influence who the reader is, what they bring to the text, and how they interpret what they read. It is an inescapable process for any reader as they view the text through their own cultural lens. Bowen theory simply furnishes the reader with a different but legitimate lens through which they can conceptualise the human drama.

Secondly, Bowen theory adds a vocabulary for reframing pastoral questions that the reader may bring to the text. For example, an inexperienced pastor, struggling with what to do as the leader of their first church, might ask questions of content such as, "what does Paul tell Timothy to do?". Such a question might lead them to focus on instructions like "preach the word…" (2 Tim 4:2) or "command and teach these things…" (1 Tim 4:11), both essential pastoral duties. But, approaching the text with a Bowen mindset, one might ask questions of process such as, "what sort of person did Paul want Timothy to be?", or "how was Timothy expected to function under pressure?".

Thirdly, Bowen did not invent the emotional processes that his theory describes. He merely recognised their existence and labelled them. Although words such as "differentiation" or "triangling" do not appear anywhere in the Bible, their absence does not disqualify their usefulness for describing the social interactions reported in the Bible. Adopting words in this way is, in fact, a recognised hermeneutical practice. For example, the word "trinity" never appears in the biblical corpus, yet it is a commonly accepted term to signify a spiritual truth. If a word does not appear in the Bible this does not necessarily mean that the concept to which it refers is not biblical. The same is true with the use of Bowen theory terms. Human emotional processes have existed since the dawn of time and it doesn't matter what label is ascribed to them because "a rose by any other name would smell as sweet" (Shakespeare, 1975, 1020)[4].

Paul's anxiety

In Paul's first letter to Timothy, his personal greeting quickly gave way to a pressing issue: "As I urged you when I went into Macedonia, stay there in Ephesus" (1 Tim 1:3). Paul had urged Timothy on at least two separate occasions, once in Macedonia and again in this letter, to remain in Ephesus. It appears that Timothy had considered, for some length of time, abandoning his post there and Paul seemed anxious about a number of possible scenarios developing:

1. If Timothy departed, the church would surrender its apostolic-based leadership and the vacuum created by Timothy's departure would be filled by false teachers and myth promoters who would undermine authentic gospel ministry (1 Tim 1:3-4; 2 Tim 2:17-19).

2. Viral groups had infiltrated the congregation and threatened the church's wellbeing; for example, the Jewish genealogists (1 Tim 1:3-4) and the ascetics (1 Tim 4:1-3). Some of these groups had already targeted vulnerable members of the church (2 Tim 3:6) and Paul was worried about their teaching, their domineering style (2 Tim 3:3-7), and their eroding influence[5]. Other internal issues also concerned Paul, such as church order, morality, the appointment of

---

[4] William Shakespeare, *Romeo and Juliet* (Act II, Scene II).

[5] Paul's description of them is remarkably similar to Edwin Friedman's depiction of parasitic, non-self-regulating types who hold "the whole system hostage by their oppressive behaviour" (in Steinke, 2000, p. 59).

leaders, the treatment of widows, and autonomous teachers who were bypassing Timothy's leadership.

3. Timothy's own personal development would be impeded. For example, Paul's call for Timothy to attend to his own "life and doctrine" (1 Tim 4:16) and to "fight the good fight" by pursuing "righteousness, godliness, faith, love, endurance and gentleness" (1 Tim 6:11-12), reveals Paul's concern for Timothy's personal growth. Fleeing Ephesus might reduce Timothy's stress but it would not help him build resilience and character.

4. Paul's absence meant that Timothy worked alone and Paul was concerned that Timothy ministered in an isolated situation, and so he longed to reunite with Timothy. "Recalling your tears, I long to see you, so that I may be filled with joy", he wrote touchingly (2 Tim 1:4). However, his longing was not just for a personal reunion but included Paul's desire for Timothy to, once again, partner with him in ministry and, together with him, bear its associated suffering (2 Tim 1:8, 2:3, 4:5). In the meantime, Paul wrote to inspire Timothy with some examples of others who had endured hardship for the gospel, namely, Paul himself (2 Tim 4:6-7, 16-18), and Jesus (1 Tim 6:13) and reminded him of the indwelling presence of God's Spirit (2 Tim 1:3-7) and Christ's protection (2 Tim 4:17-18) in an attempt to alleviate Timothy's feelings of aloneness and impotence.

5. Paul feared that Timothy might become a ministry casualty like others who had failed in the ministry (1 Tim 1:20; 2 Tim 1:15, 4:10). His call for Timothy to care for himself (1 Tim 5:23) and his warning about those who had already shipwrecked their faith (1 Tim 1:19) are evidence of his concern for Timothy's emotional, spiritual, and physical wellbeing.

6. Paul seemed aware of his own imminent death, as noted in his second letter which he probably penned in Rome (2 Tim 4:6-7). If this eventuated, he was concerned for the continuation of gospel ministry under a new generation of faithful leaders such as Timothy.

Timothy's anxiety

1 and 2 Timothy contain seven key pieces of evidence that Timothy had experienced anxiety and that it resulted from both his ecclesial circumstances and his personal disposition.

1. Timothy appeared to have been a reclusive type of person. Paul knew that Timothy possessed a thin skin and wrote, "for the Spirit God gave us does not make us timid, but gives us power, love and self-discipline" (2 Tim 1:7) in an attempt to motivate him to become more daring. Together with Timothy's temptation to flee Ephesus, this insight depicts an individual who tended to retreat in the face of hardship.

2. Timothy's timidity may have partly sprung from his family of origin (2 Tim 1:5). There is no mention of Timothy's father in this reference and it is a glaring omission worth noting. Did Timothy lack a paternal role model as a child? Having been reared by his mother Eunice and grandmother Lois (see 2 Tim 1:5), the absence of a father figure might indicate that his father may have been a disinterested unbeliever, or was deceased, or had been absent from the home during Timothy's upbringing. Given the patriarchal household structure of the first century, it is likely that an attending, believing father would have played a role in his child's upbringing and, therefore, would have rated a mention. Furthermore, Paul, on a number of occasions, referred to Timothy as his "son" (1 Tim 1:2, 18; 2 Tim 1:2, 2:1). Coupled

with Paul's personal interest in, encouragement of, advice for, and longing to reunite with Timothy, this could suggest that he had assumed the role of a surrogate parent. These two letters certainly resonate with a familial tone. For instance, Paul's urging of Timothy "to fan into flame the gift of God, which is in you through the laying on of my hands" (2 Tim 1:6) sounds like a fatherly encouragement, as if to say, "I believe in you son, you can do it".

3. Timothy possibly felt abandoned and stranded. He had been left alone in Ephesus to defend his post without Paul. It seems that their parting, over which Timothy shed tears (2 Tim 1:4), was particularly grievous and the lack of frequent contact or news from Paul may have left Timothy feeling somewhat forsaken. Richardson wrote that the feeling of abandonment is a high anxiety generator (Richardson, 1996, p. 44). This is not to suggest that Timothy had been abandoned in reality, only that it is reasonable to suppose that he felt that way.

4. Ministry presented Timothy with some difficult challenges, such as defending the gospel against superstitious and mythical doctrine, internal conflicts, gender role disputes, and justifying his youthful authority. But Timothy somewhat lacked the courage to challenge erroneous doctrine and caustic behaviour in the church or to endure its consequential adversity. Hence, Paul urged him to face these challenges with single-minded focus, like that of a soldier and with bravery to share the hardship that ensued (2 Tim 2:3-4).

5. Timothy's desire to depart Ephesus, coupled with Paul's admonishment for him to remain, would have engendered within Timothy a moral dilemma causing some anxiety.

6. By the time Paul wrote these letters, the Ephesian church was around ten years old. Some were critical of Timothy's leadership, saying he was too young and inexperienced for such a role (1 Tim 4:12). The lack of confidence in his leadership, together with his timid nature could have unnerved him.

7. Timothy was prone to frequent illnesses (1 Tim 5:23), including stomach complaints. The origin of his illnesses is unknown but the symptoms are consistent with stress-related causes. It is possible that Timothy's situation together with his timid disposition could have contributed to some sort of psychosomatic condition.

Anxiety in the Ephesian church

One gets the feeling that life in the Ephesian church was anything but calm. Paul's description of the factions and their associated behaviour patterns suggests a highly agitated church and the following list proposes some possible anxiety-inducing triggers in the Ephesian church:

1. The role of men and women in leadership and teaching (1 Tim 2:8-15)
2. Leadership issues: aspirants to leadership, their qualifications, selection, maturity, and moral integrity (1 Tim 3:1-12) and complaint protocols (1 Tim 5:19-20)
3. Contentious teaching: Paul and Timothy versus the genealogists, ascetics, and myth promoters (1 Tim 1:3-6)
4. Timothy's youth (1 Tim 4:12), lack of self-confidence (2 Tim 1:6-7, 2:15), and ill-health (1 Tim 5:23)
5. The tension between the social and gender classes, e.g., slaves and masters (1 Tim 6:1-2), the wealthy (1 Tim 6:17-19), men and women (1 Tim 2:8-15)

6. The care of widows and the exploitation of the church by those who neglected their own relatives (1 Tim 5:3-16)
7. Gossip, anger, disputes, and quarrels (1 Tim 2:8, 6:4, 20; 2 Tim 2:23). For example, those who "worm their way into homes" (2 Tim 3:6) to teach their myths and fantasies, some of whom were autonomous women and who had bypassed Timothy's leadership and authority[6]. Triangling, a key indicator of anxiety in Bowen theory, is evident through a number of disputes
8. Narcissistic behaviour (2 Tim 3:1-5)
9. Coalitions gathered around false teachers (2 Tim 4:3-4).

It is not possible for the reader to observe peoples' reactions, their facial expressions, gestures, posture, or inflections, but it does not follow that emotion cannot be revealed in the text at all. Chronic anxiety can only be deduced from long-term observation, which is not possible here, but there are enough signals to at least discern a level of acute anxiety in Paul, Timothy, and the congregation at the time of Paul's letters. There is also evidence of low differentiated activity among poorly self-regulated individuals who were secretive, who triangled, and who transgressed the boundaries of decency. In Bowen theory, these are symptoms of anxiety in the system.

---

[6] The controversial passage of 1 Timothy 2:11-14 contains Paul's prohibition for women to teach or have authority over men. Some understand Paul's reference to the Adam and Eve story as suggesting his argument was *ontological*. That is, there is something built into the DNA of men and women that makes this male/female order timeless. Others understand this creation story *typologically*, suggesting that Paul chose a quintessential Old Testament narrative that corresponded to the type of situation in Ephesus. Women in the church had bypassed Timothy as their leader. They autonomously visited households and imposed their false ideas on unsuspecting and vulnerable people (1 Tim 5:13; 2 Tim 3:1-6). By circumventing Timothy, they repeated the sin of Eve who similarly bypassed Adam, the sole human bearer of God's word, and acted independently. The point is that this issue would have raised the emotional temperature in the Ephesian church, as it does today in modern churches.

Differentiated leadership at Ephesus

Paul's instructions in these two letters were partly directed towards Timothy's self-management and this provides a unique insight into the Pauline correspondence. He wanted Timothy not only to remain at Ephesus, but to also reinforce his personal convictions (1 Tim 1:19; 2 Tim 3:14-15), assert himself as leader (2 Tim 1:13), and expand his capacity to weather criticism and opposition. All of this was to be motivated by love which demands connection with others (1 Tim 1:5). In other words, Paul wanted Timothy to become a more highly differentiated leader.

In Bowen theory, differentiation of self refers to the individual's ability to distinguish thinking and feeling and how this influences the individual's capacity to connect to others while maintaining a distinctive self. Higher differentiated individuals can think reasonably and rationally while holding their emotions in check. Conversely, lower differentiated individuals confuse and fuse thinking and emotion, rendering them indistinguishable. The line in the song *Love is All Around* by British band The Troggs (1967), "My mind's made up by the way that I feel", captures succinctly how emotion can overrule rationality among low differentiated people. Bowen illustrated these polarities in his scale of differentiation[7] which, if applied to Timothy, reveals responses that approximate lower differentiated functioning.

Paul's challenges for Timothy to progress, confront crucial issues in the church, and to face the backlash, imply that Timothy's response up to that time had been one of fear and withdrawal, culminating in his desire to flee Ephesus.

---

7 See below Bowen's scale of differentiation in Figure 1, adapted by the author.

Figure 1

Bowen's Differentiation of Self Scale

High differentiation (100):

Thinking and feeling are disentangled. Reasoned, thoughtful responses are not sabotaged by emotion. Person is characterized by:

- Less anxiety, relationship enmeshment, and thinking/emotional fusion
- Better decisions and relationships and fewer life problems
- Less determined by others peoples' opinion
- Life is lived from a solid sense of self which is shaped by convictions and beliefs.

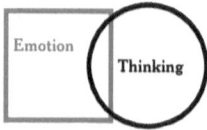

100 is hypothetical only

75-95
- Can listen without reacting
- Able to assume responsibility for oneself
- Not preoccupied with placement in the hierarchy

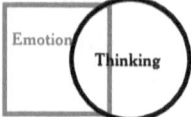

60-75
- Less emotionally reactive & less chronically anxious
- Able to choose between closeness and goals
- Can extricate themselves from high emotion situations

50-60
- Aware of the difference between thoughts & feelings
- Still sensitive to others' opinions
- Hesitates to say what they believe lest they offend

25-50
- Lives in a feeling world
- Borrows beliefs and convictions from others
- Quick to imitate others to gain acceptance
- Energy goes into loving and being loved
- Little energy for goal directed activity
- Addicted to comfort
- Can react as authoritarian, compliant, or rebellious

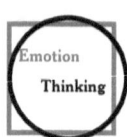

0-25
- Makes major life decisions based on what feels right
- Responses range from compliance to rebellion
- Narcissistic statement dominate e.g. "I want" or "I hurt"
- So sensitive to other's opinions that functioning is governed by reactions to the environment
- Immersed in a feeling world

Low differentiation (0):
Thinking and emotion are fused and confused.
Automatic, instinctive reactions overwhelm cognitive objectively.
Characterized by:

- More anxiety, relationship enmeshment, emotion/thinking fusion, and life problems
- Poorer decision making, more relationship trouble, and focused on others' opinions
- Life is lived from a pseudo-self which is shaped by others.

Timothy had allowed people to disrespect his youth, so Paul challenged him to dissuade them from doing so[8]. Paul also urged Timothy to replace feebleness with boldness, self-protection with love and self-discipline (2 Tim 1:6-7), and to accept his share of suffering for the gospel because Timothy had struggled in these areas (2 Tim 1:8, 2:3). However, Paul's method was wiser than to impose a list of imperatives. He wanted Timothy's conduct to spring from his gospel-centred convictions (1 Tim 1:19), so Paul reminded Timothy of his faith heritage, which was strongly rooted in his family of origin (1 Tim 4:6; 2 Tim 1:5-6), and in the models of other servants of God who had endured similar opposition (2 Tim 1:12; 1 Tim 6:13). His advice to Timothy centred on strengthening the inner man, out of which a more courageous and loving functional style would emerge. It would seem that Paul knew about differentiation even before the term was invented.

Richardson has proposed a graphical way to visualise a person's functional style using the parameters of togetherness/individuality to plot their level of enmeshment with others on the one hand, and of differentiation/fusion to plot their level of maturity on the other (Richardson, 1996, p. 101). Paul's desire for Timothy to move from lower to higher levels of differentiation can be theoretically plotted using Richardson's graph (see Figure 2)[9]. Initially, it would appear that Timothy functioned more in Quadrant 4, a position of fused isolation. Timothy's instinctive reactivity had overshadowed calm reflection to the point of cutting loose from the church. He had chosen to distance himself; however, he was still emotionally fused with the church because his reactions were determined by

---

[8] An implied contrast behind Paul's exhortation "don't let anyone look down on you because you are young" (1 Tim 4:12), suggests that Timothy had been doing just that.

[9] A generic form of this graph appears in Richardson's *Creating a Healthier Church*, (1996, p. 101).

it. Paul encouraged him to move towards Quadrant 1, a position in which Timothy could draw from a solid self[10] and, less anxiously, remain connected to the church.

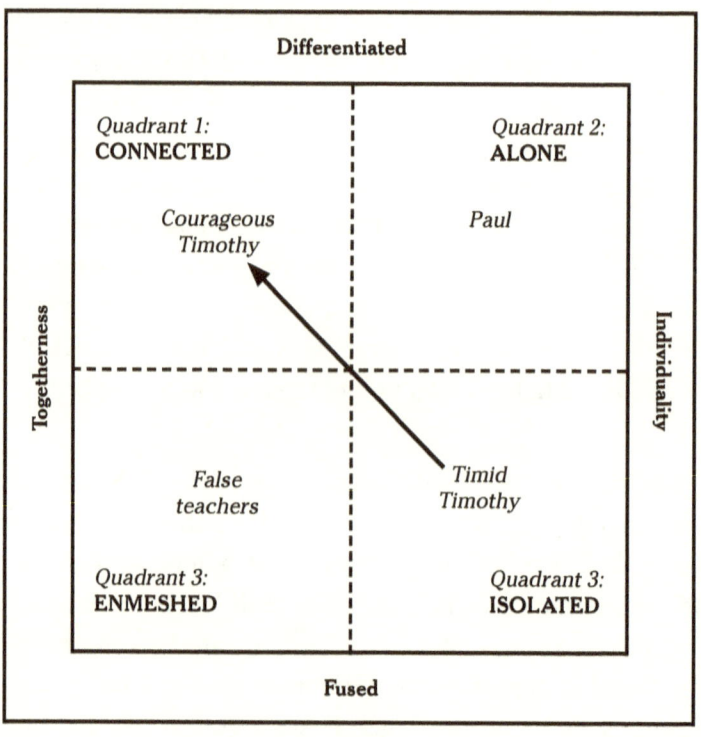

Figure 2 – Richardson's functional style graph

Paul, on the other hand, appears to be located in Quadrant 2 because he seems to be more highly differentiated but alone. As Paul approached the end of his life and after years of opposition and suffering due to his defence and proclamation of the gospel,

---

10 The *solid self* is Bowen's term to describe the self that is "made up of clearly defined beliefs, opinions, convictions, and life principles" that can say, "'this is who I am, what I believe, what I stand for, and what I will do or will not do' in a given situation" (Bowen in Gilbert, 2008, pp. 20-21). The *pseudo self* is a self that is borrowed from others.

many of his friends and associates had distanced themselves from him (2 Tim 4:10, 16). Unlike Timothy, however, Paul's isolation was not a chosen reaction but had been consequentially imposed upon him.

The false teachers have been placed in Quadrant 3 because they seem to be emotionally fused to members whom they could assimilate into their own likeness. Emotion appears to have dominated their thinking as they huddled together in groups that discouraged difference. They would "worm their way into homes... are swayed by all kinds of evil desires" and "are men of depraved minds"(2 Tim 3:6-8). They disregarded appropriate social boundaries and coerced people to think like them in a way that approximated Bowen's "undifferentiated ego mass" (Bowen, 2004, p. 122)[11].

Richardson proposed that differentiation is "the basic requirement for good leadership in the church and the major marker that distinguishes better and poorer leaders" (Richardson, 1996, p. 86), and he believed that a higher level of differentiation enables a person to:

- perceive more accurately the reality of a situation
- identify his/her own opinions, beliefs, values, and commitments
- think clearly and wisely about possible options for action
- act flexibly on one's opinions, beliefs, values, and commitments.

These abilities appear to resemble those that Paul urged Timothy to cultivate[12].

---

[11] A phrase coined by Murray Bowen to refer to a lack of individuation.
[12] See 1 Tim 1:5, 1:19, 4:6-8, 4:12, 4:14-16, 5:1-3, 6:11-12, 6:20-21; 2 Tim 1:8, 2:15, 2:22-25, 3:10-15.

Richardson also identified four reactive responses that emerge from a combination of high anxiety and low differentiation: compliance, rebellion, power struggle, and emotional distancing (Richardson, 1996, p. 93). Paul did not advise Timothy to capitulate to the behaviour of the anxious church, nor to rise up in rebellion. It could be perceived, however, that Paul did instruct Timothy to engage in power struggles. For example, "Command certain people not to teach false doctrines", Paul wrote (1 Tim 1:3). But Paul did not endorse power struggles per se, the goal of which is often dominance, but rather instructed Timothy to stand strong for truth, the goal of which is love (1 Tim 1:5) and which would invariably invite opposition. Furthermore, Paul cautioned Timothy explicitly to avoid quarrels, disputes (1 Tim 4:7; 2 Tim 2:23), and "godless chatter" (1 Tim 6:20; 2 Tim 2:16). But avoidance should not be confused with emotional distancing. Rather, a differentiated individual sets defining boundaries around "what is us" and "what is not us" and avoidance, in this instance, was to be a deliberate and calculated response by Timothy to de-triangle himself from contentious factions[13].

Paul was undoubtedly unaware of the modern insights of neuroscience, but he knew that Timothy would be the one person in the Ephesian church who would need to exercise the higher, reasoning part of his brain and wrote, "But you, keep your head in all situations..." (2 Tim 4:5). Paul was aware of those who possessed a "corrupt mind" with whom Timothy had to contend and whose conduct revealed their lower levels of differentiation. But Paul expected better things of Timothy. If Timothy learned to operate more from a "clear conscience" and put more distance between his thinking and emotion, he could offer a calm and rational

---

13 Literally, περΐίστημι, translated "avoid", means to "stand around"; not to stand in or among (Mounce, 1993). In this sense it would be possible to engage with one's opponents but not adopt their beliefs.

presence (1 Tim 1:5, 18-19; 2 Tim 2:22-23). He would be able to more accurately perceive the reality of situations, think clearly and wisely about strategies, and act flexibly and responsibly.

Arthur Boers (2002) observed that when leaders are confronted with difficult behaviour, they can react with "hardball" or "softball" responses, neither of which are healthy. Hardball, or "fight" mode responses include blame, retribution, hostility, and counterattack. Softball, or "flight" mode responses are more indirect, non-confrontational, passive, sentimental, placating, or appeasing. Both these responses do more harm than good, Boers wrote[14]. 1 and 2 Timothy contain no evidence that Paul directed Timothy to either hardball or softball responses. In fact, he encouraged Timothy to move beyond his softball responses of withdrawal and desertion. He urged Timothy to remain in contact with his congregation and to expand his repertoire of responses to include commanding, teaching, setting an example, exhorting, managing complaints, avoiding, and so on. He was to do this "without partiality" or "favouritism" (1 Tim 5:21), both of which are characteristics of less differentiated leaders who are motivated by the need to "fit in" or gain a following. Paul's instructions are consistent with Bowen's concept of balancing the definition of self with maintaining a vital connection with others. He wanted Timothy to lead and influence them, not be absorbed by them, and to maintain a non-anxious presence in the community[15].

Conclusion

This paper has proposed that Timothy had considered resigning as leader of the Ephesian church and Paul had written on two

---

14 Boers' description of hardball and softball responses closely resemble Bowen's concepts of *overfunctioning* (hardball), *distancing*, and *cutoff* (softball).

15 Bowen's term for a differentiated and connected individual in an anxious system. This author, however, prefers the phrase "low-anxious presence" because he believes a non-anxious state to be a virtual impossibility.

occasions urging him to adopt a different strategy, that of remaining and building his resilience. Using Bowen family systems theory as a way to conceptualise the situation at Ephesus, evidence was presented which suggested that Timothy, Paul, and the church experienced anxiety over a range of issues. Their anxiety appears to have been amplified by poorly differentiated individuals who had imposed upon and exploited vulnerable people with false doctrines and immoral conduct.

In such a culture, Timothy's feelings of inferiority, impotence, and fear (1 Tim 4:12-14; 2 Tim 1:6-7, 2:15) had caused him to lose perspective and the ability to think calmly and reasonably (2 Tim 4:5). His withdrawal and intention to sever his ties with the church suggests that he had over-focused on the congregation's responses. Paul's letters reveal his attempt to urge Timothy to build a more solid self by drawing on a good conscience and sincere faith (1 Tim 1:5, 19), reflecting on his family heritage (2 Tim 1:5-6, 3:14-15), fixing his mind on Jesus (2 Tim 2:8), not on the congregation, bravely engaging in the battle for truth, fighting the good fight of love (1 Tim 1:18, 6:12), and preparing himself to suffer the consequences (2 Tim 2:3). By reinventing himself via a process of differentiation of self, Paul hoped Timothy would learn to "keep his head" (2 Tim 4:5), remain in Ephesus, and offer a more poised, calm, connected, and courageous style of leadership.

References

Boers, A. P. (2002). *Never call them jerks: Healthy responses to difficult behaviour.*

Bethesda MD: The Alban Institute.

Bowen, M. (2004). *Family therapy in clinical practice.* New York: Rowman & Littlefield Publishers, Inc.

Gilbert, R. M. (2008). *The cornerstone concept: In leadership, in life.* Virginia: Leading Systems Press.

Kerr, M. & Bowen, M. (1988). *Family evaluation: An approach based on Bowen theory.* New York, NY: Norton

Mounce, W. D. (1993). *The analytical lexicon to the Greek New Testament.* Grand Rapids, Michigan: Zondervan. Accessed from 2017 Accordance Bible Software Version 11.2.5. Altamonte Springs, Florida: Oaktree Software.

Richardson, R. W. (1996). *Creating healthier congregations: Family systems theory, leadership and congregational life.* Minneapolis, MN: Fortress Press.

Shakespeare, W. (1975). *The complete works of William Shakespeare.* New York: Gramercy Books.

Steinke, P. L. (2000). *How your church family works: Understanding congregations as emotional systems.* New York: The Alban Institute.

The Troggs, (1967). *Love is all around.* Lyrics retrieved from www.songfacts.com on Monday, 17th September 2018 at 6:17pm.

Chapter 5

"A NEW TEACHING— AND WITH AUTHORITY!"
A Theological Reflection on Bowen Theory

Andrew Errington

"What is this? A new teaching—and with authority!"
According to Mark's Gospel (1:27), this was the reaction that the crowds had on first hearing Jesus' teaching. Not infrequently, it also describes the way that people react when they encounter Bowen theory. For a Christian, this ought to be disconcerting. What does it mean for some new teaching, unrelated to the gospel, to come with authority? Should we not be deeply suspicious of something like that? Can it be anything other than a false gospel, a misleading claim about where humanity's problem, and its salvation, lies? This short essay reflects theologically on the place and significance of Bowen theory. It argues that the nervousness described just now should be taken seriously by advocates of Bowen theory, but that it need not be decisive, precisely because of the kind of teaching that Bowen theory is, at its best. Bowen theory should be understood, theologically, in connection with the doctrine of creation. It reflects a kind of wisdom, and as such, need not be finally opposed to the good news of Jesus Christ, even though there are real dangers inherent in the theory.

What follows proceeds in three sections. The first, and longest, draws on the book of Proverbs to introduce the biblical concept of wisdom, and to show how it creates space for Christians to welcome sources of insight into human life from outside the Bible, and outside explicitly Christian teaching, while also asserting the limits of such insight. The second section then suggests a number of reasons why it might make sense to think of Bowen theory in such terms. The final section considers the limits and dangers of Bowen theory, when seen from this perspective. Sections two and three enter into dialogue with one important text for Bowen theory: Kerr and Bowen's *Family Evaluation* (1988). The comments about Bowen theory made here are intended to be exploratory, aiming to open up possible lines of reflection for those more familiar with the theory.

Authority, creation, and wisdom

How should we understand Bowen theory theologically? A good point from which to begin is with the observation, made above, that Bowen theory often seems to have some kind of authority.[1] That is to say, aspects of it seem, at least to some people, to be insightful, to get something right, and say something true. Yes, that's right, we react. This is by no means to say that everyone who is introduced to Bowen theory has this reaction, or has this reaction to every part of it—that is certainly not the case. But some people clearly do have that reaction. It seems to them that there is some kind of disclosure, here, of how things really do stand. Were this not the case, then the theory would probably already have vanished.

Now, one explanation for this might be that those who have this reaction are simply mistaken. We are all capable of being mistaken, and that could well be the case here. Christians, especially, ought

---

[1] The account of authority here depends on the work of Oliver O'Donovan (2013, 2014). I have explored O'Donovan's thinking about authority in detail in Errington (2016).

to be alert to this possibility: "See to it that no one takes you captive through hollow and deceptive philosophy, which depends on human tradition and the elemental spiritual forces of this world rather than on Christ" (Col 2:8).

Shouldn't we be wary of the feeling that some other teaching, apparently unrelated to Christ, seems to show us something true? We should certainly be cautious; but this does not mean such a feeling is automatically mistaken. To say that would commit us to saying quite a lot more than most of us are comfortable saying. We would have to renounce all such experiences of authority, from the explanation of a complex mathematical theory to the demonstration of how to operate a forklift. The skilled gardener who tells me that what is wrong with my orange tree is that it has citrus canker would have to be distrusted just as much as the persuasive university lecturer whose theories challenge my Christian faith.

It is immediately obvious to most of us that this is a bit silly; and that is a clue. For what it makes clear is that not all authoritative teaching is necessarily "captivating." There is a great deal of teaching-with-authority that aims not to make us captives, but simply to show us how things are. Quite often, when we experience some teaching or explanation as a kind of disclosure of how things stand, we are right; that is just what it is.

The Reformer John Calvin agreed. "Shall we," he writes in *Institutes* 2.2.15–16, "say that the philosophers, in their exquisite researches and skillful description of nature, were blind?"

> Shall we say that those who, by the cultivation of the medical art, expended their industry in our behalf were only raving? What shall we say of the mathematical

sciences? Shall we deem them to be the dreams of madmen? Nay, we cannot read the writings of the ancients on these subjects without the highest admiration; an admiration which their excellence will not allow us to withhold. (Calvin, 2002 [1536])

It was critical, Calvin thought, "not to reject or condemn truth wherever it appears." "If the Lord has been pleased to assist us by the work and ministry of the ungodly in physics, dialectics, mathematics, and other similar sciences, let us avail ourselves of it, lest, by neglecting the gifts of God spontaneously offered to us, we be justly punished for our sloth."

But how far does this go? In particular, does it extend to teaching about how we should live? Can we expect truth to appear in relation to questions such as these? At least to some extent, Calvin thought we could. He included, among his examples of places where truth has appeared, "those ancient lawgivers who arranged civil order and discipline with so much equity." But aren't we on dangerous ground there? At what point do we cross over into the captivating philosophy about which the apostle warns? This is the crucial issue for something like Bowen theory. For, in its own way, Bowen theory concerns the successful living of human life; how we may conduct our relationships in ways that work. It is, in a sense, a set of ideas and teachings about what the ancient world thought "ethics" was about, namely, how to live your life so that it turns out well.[2] Let us ask more carefully, then, how we could understand such a thing theologically. Why, from a Christian

---

[2] Much ancient ethics began from the assumption that all human beings desire *eudaimonia*. That word is often translated "happiness" in English. However, *eudaimonia* relates to a wider set of considerations than we tend to think about with the term "happiness". When Aristotle, for instance, said that all human beings desire happiness, he meant something like that all human beings want to make a success of their lives; we want our lives to turn out well. On these issues, see Spaemann, 2000.

perspective, might we think it is right, within certain limits, to welcome teachings that seem to disclose something true, even about issues relating to how we should live our lives?

The answer, I think, lies in the doctrine of creation.[3] The Bible tells us that God has made the world in such a way that it is hospitable to human life. The world is a good world, and good not only in the sense of being beautiful and interesting, but good in the sense that it is good *for us*; it is a good world *to live in*. One important way the Bible expresses these ideas is through the concept of *wisdom*. God, the Bible says, made the world "by wisdom."[4] "By wisdom the Lord laid the earth's foundations, by understanding he set the heavens in place" (Prov 3:19). The wisdom and understanding that are in view here have to do with skillful action. "By wisdom a house is built," Proverbs tells us later (24:3). Wisdom is about knowing how to do things well. God, the Bible tells us, made the world skillfully and well, so that the final product—the world we live in—is a place that is truly good, and good for us. As the stunning poem about wisdom in the eighth chapter of Proverbs puts it:

> When he gave the sea its boundary so the waters would
> not overstep his command,
> and when he marked out the foundations of the earth.
> Then I [Wisdom] was constantly at his side.
> I was filled with delight day after day,
> rejoicing always in his presence,
> rejoicing in his whole world and delighting in mankind.
> (Prov 8:29–31)

---

[3] The following discussion draws on my doctoral thesis at the University of Aberdeen (Errington, 2017).

[4] This idea occurs a number of times in the Old Testament, outside the book of Proverbs. See Psalm 104:24; Jeremiah 10:12, 51:15. Job 28:25–27 expresses the same kind of idea in different language.

The consequence of God's making the world by wisdom is that the world has a certain shape and character. It is a world that has been wisely made. What this means is that there are good and bad ways of living and acting. There are ways of operating that make sense—that work—and there are ways that don't. In the book of Proverbs, *wisdom* and its opposite, *folly*, have to do with these different ways. In fact, the language of "ways" and "paths" is central to the book. Wisdom is about ways of acting that work, "straight paths," "paths of life" (Prov 2:19, 4:11); folly involves trying to act in other ways, "dark" and "crooked" paths, which lead to disaster and failure (Prov 2:13–18).

The book of Proverbs also makes clear that these good ways of acting and living are not in principle beyond the reach of our knowledge. On the contrary, the world that God has made opens itself to our knowledge. Wisdom, Proverbs tells us, *calls*.

> Does not wisdom call out? Does not understanding raise her voice? At the highest point along the way, where the paths meet, she takes her stand... "To you, O people, I call out; I raise my voice to all mankind." (Prov 8:1–4)

Wisdom calls. That means that the created world God has made is hospitable to our wise action, and to our knowledge. God did not create a world that is out to make it difficult for us. We are not working *against* nature when we try to work out and express how the world is, and how we may live in it and understand it.

This does not mean that all our efforts to understand the world will be successful, or that our attempts at living well will mostly be right. The truth, according to Proverbs, is sadly the opposite. Wisdom calls, but her call is generally refused, so that we wind up making a mess of things. Here is how Wisdom speaks at the beginning of Proverbs:

> Since you refuse to listen when I call and no one pays attention when I stretch out my hand, since you disregard all my advice and do not accept my rebuke, I in turn will laugh when disaster strikes you; I will mock when calamity overtakes you. (Prov 1:24–26)

The idea of God's creation by wisdom does not authorise any great optimism about our capacity to see how we should live. In a thousand ways, we fail to see and to stick to the paths that lead to life. Nevertheless, the point is that such failures are *folly*; they are infuriating, stupid, and unnecessary. Because in and of itself, the world we live in is a world that can be lived in successfully, like a house that is made well and furnished to make a home (see Prov 24:3–4).

Teaching that carries authority is possible partly because of this reality. The book of Proverbs emphasises the significance of instruction. Alongside wisdom's calls, the opening chapters are full of parents urging their children to listen to their instructions about how they should live. "Listen, my son, to your father's instruction and do not forsake your mother's teaching" (Prov 1:8). Sometimes, it sounds like the instruction in view is the law of Israel, God's revelation of how to live. Other times, however, the instructions in question are much more mundane: don't join a violent criminal gang (1:10–19), don't sleep with someone else's wife (6:26–29). Moreover, the opening chapters prepare the way for chapters ten to thirty-one. These are full of instructions that are not simply drawn from God's revelation to Israel, but are proverbial observations on life and how things work. They are little moments of authority, shafts of light breaking through to us and disclosing how things stand.

These proverbs, of course, are for Christians Holy Scripture, meaning that they are more than simply observations drawn from experience of the world. They are indeed more; but they are not less. These proverbs, like most proverbs, represent the wisdom of tradition, insights into the world gained over time and formulated with care. This should suggest to us that, while these pieces of traditional instruction hold a special authority, we should expect to find wisdom elsewhere, too. For the world is the kind of world that makes that possible: it is a world full of the wisdom of God, which calls out to us, though so often we fail to listen.

We have several hints in this direction within the book of Proverbs. Wisdom literature existed not only in Israel, but throughout the ancient world. This wider wisdom teaching was known in Israel—a fact that should not surprise us, given the stories that depict King Solomon sharing his wisdom with "the whole world" (1 Kgs 10:24)—and there are indications that it was taken seriously. Foreigners speak in Proverbs (see Prov 30:1, 31:1). More strikingly, in chapters twenty-two and twenty-three of the book, there is a passage that almost all scholars agree depends on a wisdom tradition from Egypt called *The Instruction of Amenemope* (see e.g., Murphy, 1998, pp. 290–294). "By me kings reign, and rulers issue decrees that are just" says Wisdom in Proverbs 8:15. The clear implication is that this is true of *all* rulers, not only those of Israel. As David VanDrunen concludes, in a discussion of how Proverbs contributes to a biblical theology of natural law, "Proverbs recognises that genuine wisdom exists outside the bounds of Israel and indicates that God's people should learn from the wisdom of others" (2014, p. 397).

If what we have said so far is right, this should not surprise us. God's creation by wisdom opens up the possibility of human insight and understanding about many things, by all kinds of people. Although we so often fail to appreciate it, the fact is that this is a world that is *open to* our living our lives successfully, and understanding how to do so. It is a world in which wisdom calls out to us, and this is why we may encounter teaching that shows us something true about how the world works. This does not mean that we do not need to be careful with such a thought, or that such teaching does not have its limits. As we will see, both these things are true, and important. First, however, we need to consider why this might help us understand Bowen theory, specifically.

Bowen theory and wisdom

There are a number of reasons to think that this account of creation and wisdom is an illuminating viewpoint from which to understand what is going on with Bowen theory. To begin with, it is important that we notice the way Bowen theory is explicitly grounded in what we could call the natural realities of human life. Bowen himself repeatedly emphasised, and was frustrated at being ignored on this point, that Bowen theory draws deeply on theories of evolution and sociobiology (see e.g., Kerr & Bowen, 1988, pp. 10, 21–26, 359–360). While at first sight this may seem unnerving to Christians, the key underlying point can actually be welcomed: human beings are *creatures*, "a part of all life," as Kerr puts it (p. 21). A Christian should, in fact, have no difficulty affirming that in many respects human beings are just like other animals. Indeed, the book of Proverbs invites us to think along such lines, deliberately drawing similes between the life of animals and that of humans.[5] Well before the behaviour of "army ants" was seized on to illustrate the idea of emotional units (Kerr & Bowen, 1988, pp. 30, 38–44, 50, 89), Proverbs had already called us to "Go to the ant… consider its ways and be wise…" (Prov 6:6–8; cf. 30:24–28). This is not to say that everything Bowen theory draws from natural science should be accepted. It is simply to affirm the basic point, "that much of the human's competent as well as dysfunctional behaviour is a product of that part of man he has in common with the lower animals" (Kerr & Bowen, 1988, p. 20). For a Christian, who believes that human beings, while different from

---

5 As well as the references cited below, consider Proverbs 30:18–19, 29–31.

the other animals, are also very much like them, this should not be problematic to affirm. Bowen theory is a theory that is explicitly anchored in aspects of life human beings have in common with other creatures. That is a way of thinking that the book of Proverbs, and indeed other parts of the Bible,[6] can be taken to lead us to expect will be fruitful, at least in some limited respects.

This focus upon the creatureliness of human beings may explain why there are numerous, fascinating points of contact between Bowen theory and the book of Proverbs. The opening chapters of Proverbs pulsate with the fundamental realities of family life of special interest to Bowen. They consist chiefly of passages of parental advice, appeals by fathers and mothers to "listen, my son!" (see the opening verse of the first seven chapters). They are full of the anxiety of parents and the struggle of young people to make their own way in the world.[7] What is particularly striking about these dynamics, from the point of view of Bowen theory, is that the parents who speak never simply call their children to family loyalty, or to closeness. Rather, they call them to *wisdom*. The father's teaching is important not simply because he is the father, but because, "I instruct you in the way of wisdom and lead you along straight paths" (4:11). There is an appeal to reality here that is, I think, very close to the way Bowen theory emphasises getting beyond feeling-interpretations to an objective perspective, a view of the world "more as it is than as [one] wishes, fears, or imagines it to be" (Kerr, in Kerr & Bowen, 1988, p. 111).

One also hears echoes in Proverbs of central principles of Bowen theory. One saying encapsulates the dangers involved in triangling: "Like one who grabs a stray dog by the ears is someone

---

6 Consider, for instance, Job 12:7–12, or Psalm 104.

7 The significance for Proverbs of the "liminal threshold" between adolescence and adulthood has been explored by Leo Perdue (1981) and Raymond VanLeeuwen (1990).

who rushes into a quarrel not their own" (26:17).[8] In another we are reminded of the dangers of distancing: "Like a bird that flees its nest is anyone who flees from home" (27:8). Others could be taken to support the interconnection of biological, psychological, and social realities that is so basic to Bowen theory: "A heart at peace gives life to the body, but envy rots the bones" (14:30).

A final reason to think about Bowen theory in terms of creation and wisdom is that it is a theory that is grounded in practical knowledge. Wisdom in Proverbs, as we have seen, fundamentally has to do with action: it is about the way the world God has made opens up paths of life in which we may walk. From the start, Bowen theory was grounded, not simply in a theory derived from speculative principles, but in the observation of the actual functioning of families. The theory seems to have emerged partly through Bowen's taking seriously how certain ways of acting were helpful (see, for example, Bowen's observations about the way he learnt about the use of language in the care of people suffering from schizophrenia, in Kerr & Bowen, 1988, pp. 359, 363). It developed partly through trial and error, through the testing of theory in practice, and improvisation when things were not working (see, for example, Bowen's comments about the way he modified the frequency of therapy sessions in response to success, in Kerr & Bowen, 1988, p. 378). Bowen *theory* is derived, at least in part, from a fundamentally *practical* purchase on the realities of human life. And that, I think, is why it makes sense to think of it in connection with the biblical idea of wisdom.

The limits of Bowen theory

Framing Bowen theory in these terms gives the Christian a way to appreciate its insights. However, it will also lead us to be wary

---

8 See the essay in this book by Lauren Errington for further reflection on this proverb.

of certain aspects of it. "The fear of the Lord is the beginning of wisdom," says Proverbs (9:10). Bowen theory, on the other hand, might claim quite seriously that the beginning of wisdom is the *differentiation of self* (e.g., Kerr & Bowen, 1988, p. 385). The two are not mutually exclusive: the fear of the Lord can be a form of the differentiation of self, in the sense that reverence for God and the desire to shape one's life around him can make one less susceptible to surrendering oneself to others' emotions and agendas. That is one reason a Christian perspective can accommodate many of Bowen theory's insights. However, the two are also not the same. The fear of the Lord cannot be reduced to the differentiation of self. And that is why, from a Christian perspective, Bowen theory presents certain dangers.

Certain tendencies within Kerr and Bowen's *Family Evaluation* (1988) illustrate these dangers, even if they are not central to the book. One of the assumptions that appears to accompany this text is a deep confidence in historical progress and human potential. The emergence of Bowen theory is placed within a history of human progress going back to the Big Bang, and celebrating such moments as the Ionian Greeks, Copernicus, and Galileo (see pp. 14–17, 25–26, 351–352). In his concluding epilogue, Bowen speaks of his "deep belief in the future" (p. 381), and of how "the future is limitless" (p. 385). The emergence of the concept of differentiation of self, Bowen writes, was "for the benefit of all people" (p. 365). The book concludes with a thrill at the possibility that through differentiation of self, "the human" will become able to "control his own evolution through the control of his emotional system" (p. 386). "When the human believes he can do something," Bowen writes, "it will be done" (p. 386).

These are heady thoughts that stand in striking contrast to other, perhaps more prominent, aspects of Bowen's thought. In other respects, Bowen theory is far from optimistic about humanity. "The human is a narcissistic creature," he laments, preoccupied with "his own square inch of real estate" (Kerr & Bowen, 1988, p. 385). Moreover, Bowen theory tends to have very modest expectations about *individual* progress within any one lifetime. It seems, however, that such sober judgments can go hand in hand with much freer, more mesmerising hopes about humanity in general.

Such hopes can lead us astray, because they can suggest a kind of privileged access to the truth about reality. One may not be able to achieve a much higher level of differentiation within a lifetime; but one can *know* about differentiation and its significance, and so see things in a new light, from above the messy realities of human life and suffering.[9] Within *Family Evaluation* (1988) there are a number of troubling hints of such a perspective. There is an ugliness and indifference in the summary judgments of how the "street people" "avoid and are avoided by others because of the problems generated by human relationships" (p. 75), or the dismissive references to the immature and poorly differentiated— "fairly typical no-selves"—as almost beyond hope (pp. 100-102). It would not be fair to see these moments as representative of the overall tenor of the theory; they are somewhat jarring and out of place. Yet they illustrate a temptation in thought that opens once differentiation of self is seen as holding the promise of the future. This is a way of seeing things, however, that a Christian can have no time for whatsoever. For such "no-selves" are, nevertheless, known to and precious to God. "It is not the healthy who need a doctor, but the sick. I have not come," Jesus said, "to call the righteous, but sinners" (Mark 2:17). There are points, that is to say, at which the Christian faith may need to stand in clear opposition

---

9 Such a pattern, where salvation lies in a kind of transcendence through theory of the day-to-day reality of life, is a persistent temptation of modernity, perhaps best illustrated by Spinoza's *Ethics*. See Hampshire (1977).

to Bowen theory, and proclaim, "Has not God made foolish the wisdom of the world?" (1 Cor 1:20).

Conclusion

To frame Bowen theory in terms of wisdom and creation is to offer an alternative (theological) framing to that offered in the original formulations of the theory itself. That is a bold thing to do, of course. Yet, there are reasons to think it is the right thing to do. For unless insights into the nature of the world such as those of Bowen theory can be absorbed within a wider perspective that will constrain them and put them to work in limited, modest ways, they can indeed become captivating, holding out a promise of salvation that they cannot deliver, because, as the apostle recognised, they "depend… on human tradition and the elemental spiritual forces of this world rather than on Christ" (Colossians 2:8). Reflecting on the way the early days in the formation of the theory took shape, Bowen spoke of how "A powerful force guided the entire operation" (Kerr & Bowen, 1988, p. 370). Instead of thinking of this force as a kind of historical necessity, it might be better to think of it as the call of wisdom: God's creation extending its hospitality to human life in one particular way, allowing something true and important to be grasped about human life. But it was only creation; it was not the Messiah.

References

Calvin, John. (2002 [1536]). *The institutes of the Christian religion*. Translated by Henry Beveridge. Grand Rapids: Christian Classics Ethereal Library.

Errington, Andrew. (2016). Authority and reality in the work of Oliver O'Donovan. *Studies in Christian Ethics* 29/4: 371–385.

——————. (2019). *Every good path: Wisdom and practical*

reason in Christian ethics and the book of Proverbs, T&T Clark: Edinburgh.

Hampshire, Stuart. (1977). *Two theories of morality.* Oxford: British Academy.

Kerr, Michael E. and Bowen, Murray. (1988). *Family evaluation: An approach based on Bowen theory.* New York and London: W. W. Norton and Company.

Murphy, Roland E. (1998). *Proverbs.* Word Biblical Commentary 22. Nashville: Thomas Nelson.

O'Donovan, Oliver. (2013). *Self, world, and time. Ethics as theology 1: An induction.* Grand Rapids: Eerdmans.

——————. (2014). *Finding and seeking. Ethics as theology 2.* Grand Rapids: Eerdmans.

Perdue, Leo G. (1981). Liminality as a social setting for wisdom instructions. *Zeitschrift für die alttestamentliche Wissenschaft* 93/1: 114–126.

Spaemann, Robert. 2000. *Happiness and benevolence.* Translated by Jeremiah Alberg. Notre Dame: University of Notre Dame.

VanDrunen, David. (2014). *Divine covenants and moral order: A biblical theology of natural law.* Grand Rapids: Eerdmans.

VanLeeuwen, Raymond. (1990). Liminality and worldview in Proverbs 1–9. *Semeia* 50: 111–44.

Section 2

APPLYING BOWEN THEORY IN
DIFFERENT MINISTRY CONTEXTS

Chapter 6

CHURCH UNITY AND ANXIOUS TOGETHERNESS FORCES
Discerning the Difference

Jenny Brown

Bowen theory proposes that when tension increases in a relationship, so does the force for *togetherness*. The observation Bowen made is that stress between people in relationship initially triggers the effort towards achieving sameness. This sameness functions as a dampener to the perceived threat of disharmony. While connection and togetherness is an essential positive force in relationships, an anxiety-driven togetherness is the fuel of *fusion*, where people give up their individuality for the sake of group security. When I work with people who are trying to tease out how their Christian faith relates to Bowen theory, I am often asked about the togetherness force:

> Isn't being united always a good thing for a Christian? After all, doesn't the Bible call us to be of one mind—to be one in Christ? And what's this idea of *differentiating*? Where does that fit in with the call to love others and deny self?

This chapter will explore the tension between ideas about unity and togetherness in the Bible and in Bowen theory, and bring out the distinction between anxious, "people-pleasing" togetherness versus mature efforts to cultivate unity in Christ. The common confusions and criticisms from Christians about Bowen theory's views of group unity will be discussed. The chapter will then apply Bowen's concepts of fusion and differentiation to a hypothetical ministry team relationship. Lastly it will present a case example drawing on the author's own family of origin influences that illustrates how patterns of relating with parents can translate into a drive for pseudo-harmony in church relationships.

The call to biblical unity in the church and Bowen's ideas about anxious togetherness

Certainly, the unity of believers is central to the biblical theology of the church:

> Therefore if you have any encouragement from being united with Christ, if any comfort from his love, if any common sharing in the Spirit, if any tenderness and compassion, then make my joy complete by being like-minded, having the same love, being one in spirit and of one mind. (Phil 2:1-2)

Jesus himself prayed for such oneness over separateness for future believers, "that all of them may be one, Father, just as you are in me and I am in you. May they also be in us so that the world may believe that you have sent me" (John 17:21). Alongside this is the call to sacrifice self-interest as a follower of Jesus: "Whoever wants to be my disciple must deny themselves and take up their cross daily and follow me" (Luke 9:23). Self-serving autonomy is to be laid aside for the sake of others' good.

Bowen warns of too much connection between people that removes distinctiveness amongst individuals. Less mature (less differentiated) people are more prone to "fuse into each other in close relationships" (Bowen, 1978, p. 424). The more mature (more differentiated) person has increased capacity "to function separately from the emotional system even in intense feeling states" (Bowen, 1978, p. 424).

On the surface it is easy to assume that Bowen's warning about losing individuality sounds at odds with the call of Christ. Bowen theory equates less differentiation/maturity with too much togetherness and more differentiation/maturity being displayed in clearer boundaries with others, thus raising the potential dilemma I often hear:

> We're called as Christians to be unified and here is Bowen theory saying that fusion is synonymous with low maturity and a lack of differentiation of self!

When one places the biblical call to unity in the context of the New Testament letters to the churches on how this looks in practice, it is clear that being unified in the gospel of grace will often involve times of taking a position of disagreement and concern:

> Instead, speaking the truth in love, we will grow to become in every respect the mature body of him who is the head, that is, Christ. (Eph 4:15)

It is relationally complex to maturely apply this injunction wisely; to take action that asks us to tolerate a period of tension in a relationship is part of the unifying process. This same imperative to include admonishment in working for church unity is reflected in theologian Mark Dever's example of a church membership commitment:

> We will work and pray for the unity of the Spirit in the bond of peace. We will walk together in brotherly love, as becomes the members of a Christian Church; exercise an affectionate care and watchfulness over each other and faithfully admonish and entreat one another as occasion may require. (Dever, 2001)

Having laid out some of the biblical dilemma, this paper will now proceed to explore if Bowen's theory offers any biblically compatible assistance in this complex relationship process; a process that is necessarily challenging for us repentant and forgiven yet struggling sinners seeking to live peacefully in obedience to Jesus.

Bowen theory and fusion (anxious togetherness)

It is imperative firstly to investigate what Bowen means when he refers to fusion or loss of differentiation of self. A lack of differentiation of self is where we set aside thinking our own thoughts, and adopt the thinking of others in order to join in with the group. When they are anxious, people instinctively "fuse into taking sides in the emotional issues of the system" (Bowen, 1978, p. 486). The unity of the group is enhanced by an "us against them" posture. This serves to reduce tension and hence to preserve harmony, both for the group and the internal harmony within an individual. We humans ease our discomfort, and that of others, with the push to join in the shared harmony of "we all think the same way and agree on the same matters." Additionally, in the face of another's angry protests, we are prone to give in for the sake of peace. This can be expressed in a parent's unwillingness to hold a position in the face of a child's defiance or by a member of a ministry team setting aside what they think in order to avoid conflict or upset. To avoid confusion about Bowen's link between stress and the togetherness force, it is useful to briefly clarify Bowen's concepts of fusion compared to cutoff. In Bowen theory, fusion (heightened togetherness) and cutoff (distancing/avoiding) are inextricably linked; one flows out of the other. Bowen's concept of emotional cutoff particularly describes the breaking of relationship between the generations. He is referring to the degree to which each person moves away from the generation before them (their parents), without having genuinely defined themselves in that relationship. The more that distance is utilised to leave home and launch into adult life, the more prone one will be to seek intense togetherness in new relationships. Hence people can be propelled towards needing harmony but at the same time primed for distance because of their intolerance for disharmony:

> Distance seems to be the safety valve of the emotional system. Yet at the same time distance leaves people primed for closeness... [with] greater vulnerability to intense emotional processes in current relationships. (Papero, 1990, p. 63)

What is Bowen theory proposing about togetherness and separateness?

According to Bowen, the engine room of human patterns of relating is the dynamic of the two life forces of togetherness and separateness. These drives are viewed as biologically embedded and necessary to survival—put simply, we all need protective nurturing attachments but, as adults, equally need to be able to make decisions and carry out duties without being dependent on others. The process of development from infancy to adulthood is that of gradually increasing autonomy to a level of balance with connection with others. The problem occurs when tension gets injected into these biological drives. Thus, enriching mutual attachments can shift to incorporation/suffocation (fusion) if there is sustained tension. However, Bowen theory does not devalue human togetherness; rather it distinguishes mature connections from relationship bonds that simply serve to reduce tension. An anxiety-driven togetherness process is "characterised by people's pressuring one another to think, feel and act in specific ways" (Kerr & Bowen, 1988, p. 256). The subsequent loss of individual thinking and responsibility can result in symptoms for members of a group as they lose their capacity to function for themselves or they become overburdened by their overfunctioning for others.

Since Bowen theory points to the traps of this reactive togetherness, there may be a potential risk for the student of this theory to overvalue individualism. Bowen may appear to prescribe caution about too much compassion. Such caution could be indicated in some of his writing about the togetherness force:

> ...emotional forces overlap and bind together, assigning positive value to thinking about the other before self, being for the other, sacrificing for others, considering others, feeling responsible for the comfort and wellbeing of others, and showing love and devotion and compassion for others. (Bowen, 1978, p. 218)

In writing this, I suggest that Bowen is not denouncing these forces of compassion. He does not say that caring for others leads to immature fusion, unless it is at the expense of a counterbalancing differentiating force. That is, maturity is seen when one assumes responsibility for self rather than expecting others to meet one's needs, as would be the case in a fused relationship. It is all too easy to take quotes from anyone's writing and remove them from the clarifying context of the surrounding text. Bowen writes of the value of a differentiating force operating alongside the togetherness force, where a person in the group is willing to:

...define principles and [...take...] action in terms such as "This is what I think or feel or stand for" and "This is what I will do or not do." The responsible "I" avoids thinking that tends to blame one's own unhappiness, discomfort, or failure on the other. It avoids the posture of the irresponsible or narcissistic "I" who makes demands on others. (Bowen, 1978, p. 218)

It is important to recognise that in Bowen theory the force of differentiation is not towards rugged selfish individualism. Rather it is a mature autonomy that brings more responsibility to relating constructively with others. Kerr clarifies this in writing:

Giving up some togetherness does not mean giving up emotional closeness. It means that one's functioning becomes less dependent on the support and acceptance of others. (Kerr & Bowen, 1988, p. 107)

A hypothetical ministry example of the togetherness and separateness forces

As previously mentioned, Bowen observed that there is an inevitable tension generated by the drive for both togetherness and autonomy. The back-and-forth of these drives generates two types of anxiety: separation anxiety when connection seems under threat; and what Bowen called *incorporation anxiety* (I call this *suffocation anxiety*) when one's individuality is perceived to be threatened. The following is a simple illustration of how these forces might play out over time in a ministry relationship. See if you can recognise the process:

Two people start a ministry project together. Person A is a new church planter, and Person B is a good friend from college days who shares the vision and agrees to come on board with this ministry project. They know each other well and share a similar worldview. Their efforts go towards developing an equal but complementary working partnership. In the early days, as they're planning for the beginning of their project, B understands A, A understands B, and it proceeds as an energising togetherness (not dissimilar to a courtship). Both hold the same view, thinking "This person gets me, this person understands me, and we're on the same page."

How sustainable is this degree of togetherness? Inevitably it's not going to take long for one of the parties (let's say it's Person A) to start thinking, "I need a little bit more space just to myself, and I'd like to work on this project more autonomously." Person A doesn't say anything in particular to convey this to Person B, but they just slightly remove themselves. Now Person A is sometimes closing their office door where previously it had always been open. Person B's stress (separation anxiety) is now activated in response to this distancing. This leads to a ramping up of the togetherness force that propels Person B's efforts to pursue Person A in order to restore the comfortable harmony of their early working relationship. Person A thus experiences an increase in Person B asking them questions and eliciting their wisdom on their joint ministry project. This then triggers some slight feelings of guilt in Person A about their negative distancing. They respond by reversing this pattern and restoring the balance of harmony (this can be described as a return to homeostasis or equilibrium).

Can you see how this back-and-forth movement to and from togetherness and separateness will be repeated in various versions over time? It could be a continuance of the distancing-and-pursuing cycle, which can develop into a positive, "caretaking" pursuing and the other responding with increased neediness, or it might translate into a critical cycle of pursuing that pressures the distancing one to be more accountable, which in turn triggers a defensive counter-response. Sometimes one party will defer in order to restore comfortable harmony. As the pattern increases in negative tension it is inevitable that each party will vent their frustrations to third parties who will sympathise with their complaint. This is when a triangling process is utilised to deal with anxiety generated by the disruption to the original relationship togetherness. It's important to note that the ebbing back-and-forth between togetherness and separateness is all very normal; problems occur when tensions are raised and are dealt with immaturely.

If this escalating tension in the working relationship is to be resolved it will require one (or both) of the parties to focus away from the immediate drive to restore harmony and address their part in the problematic pattern. They must consider if they can manage their discomfort without

- pursuing a sameness
- distancing and avoiding
- triangling in a third person/ally
- giving up their responsibility
- trying to rescue/fix the other.

This responsible management of discomfort is what an effort towards differentiation looks like. The patterns of anxious togetherness described in this hypothetical are illustrative of most of the patterns of managing tension that Bowen describes in his theory: fusion, over- and underfunctioning, conflict and distance, and triangling in allies.

The change goal of Bowen theory in relation to togetherness: from self in *reaction* to others to self in *relation* to others

In Bowen theory, the goal in assisting people to contribute to flourishing relationships is to invite more thoughtful representation of the individual within the togetherness of a relationship or group.

> The primary effort goes into helping people distinguish feeling states from intellectual functioning and helping them dare to develop firmer opinions, beliefs and convictions, in spite of pressure from the relationship system to retain the former level of amorphous "no-self." (Bowen, 1978, p. 424)

Bowen is clear that the goal is not to eradicate the togetherness force that is part of life. Rather the goal is to rise up a little out of the anxious fusion force. The differentiating effort requires thoughtful planning and action from an individual without seeking the consent of others. In this way it is an effort to reduce the human drive towards people-pleasing. It does not cut off from genuine contact with others but listens to others' perspectives and thoughtfully responds to others' requests. It avoids "mind reading" others and replaces this with invitations for others to explain themselves. Rather than fusing with others, the effort is for two people to be genuinely known to each other. Bowen described this as a "person to person relationship" (Bowen, 1978, p. 498). I often explain this to people as moving from "self in *reaction* to others to self in *relation* to others".

How relationships in my family of origin have played out in a church context

The following section is my personal reflection on my tendencies to fusion in my church systems. The reflection looks at my primary triangle with my parents in my growing up years. It considers how this awareness assists in shedding light on the way I have fallen into fusion in relationships at church:

In my teenage years, my mother and I moved into a very strong alliance: a close insider position. My father was distant from that relationship, although this did not generate conflict for my parents. My sense is that my father was relieved to have me take the position of my mother's confidant because this calmed his discomfort about not meeting his wife's expectations of him for emotional closeness.

A strong thread in the narrative of my parents' marriage was that my mother was a church-going Christian, and my father was a nominally religious doubter. I understand that my father had made an agreement prior to marriage that he would always go to church with his wife and family. I surmise that this was made overt to alleviate concerns about the partnership from my maternal grandparents who were a clergy couple. In the latter stages of his life my father expressed his sense of inadequacy in his faith. He would say, "I could never have the faith of your mother." It's interesting for me to reflect that when a person gives up their own investigation of faith and accommodates to another's beliefs to keep harmony in a system it leaves them with less of a self in this life arena. It left my father with a degree of emptiness in not having an autonomous journey about matters of faith. This pattern of one spouse putting individual development of beliefs aside in service of harmony (Bowen refers to this as *de-selfing*, 1978, p. 265) was part of the story in my parents' marriage. Neither my mother nor father caused this to happen. Rather, this pattern grew out of the way differences were navigated in the families they each grew up in. There were both costs and benefits in the family arising from this arrangement.

As a second daughter, who developed a personal faith at age 13, I became someone my mother could identify with and talk to about church and Christianity. She was a very central person in the church and community and clearly valued involving me in discussions about church relationships as well as matters of faith. As this alliance grew during my adolescence, my mother proceeded to extend her scope of confiding by unburdening her worries about each of my brothers and sisters.

I wonder if you can predict the impact this had in shaping my emotional patterns? How might it now affect what relationship situations I'm most comfortable with and what relationships I gravitate towards as an adult? How much has this shaped my career path as a "helper"?

My elevated position as my mother's ally positions me towards more high-status/insider relationships in any organisation I'm part of. In a church I was prone to gravitate towards togetherness with leaders and their families. I would be most comfortable in a "helper and confidante" role in these relationships. (Of course, I will also be comfortable in any helper and advice-giving postures in church and non-church relationships). These stances in church relationships were outside of my awareness and happened instinctively.

I have come to see through my study of family systems theory that a togetherness force that gets injected with my automatic anxiety positions of my family of origin can easily become detrimental. As I look back over earlier ministry relationships, I see that being an insider with influential people at church has not always fostered Christ-honouring unity. The close confidant relationships can have a guise of Christian unity but can actually become a veil for a loss of integrity. The particular sign for me of this type of togetherness is when I start listening to gossip about other church members (just as I listened to my mother's concerns about other family members).

My primary triangle has primed me to borrow a sense of importance, through listening to peoples' anxious worries about others. My father's comfortable distance was as much fuel for this as my mother's closeness. When this has been out of my awareness it has been automatic. While it is not a deliberate choice it certainly can lead to sinful relating for myself and the others I relate to in generating gossip and a lack of honesty about self. It has led to examples of unhealthy fusion in previous church relationships where I have borrowed a sense of specialness and closeness from being an insider with key ministry team members and their spouses. Any of my vulnerabilities are masked in such relationships as I draw security from words of approval and the sense of being in the "inner group". It's not a pretty picture.

Bowen said in his own observations of himself and his workplace that gossip is a key indicator of fusion in an emotional system. He writes, "This 'fusion' into the emotional system operated most intensely with those most involved in the gossip system at work" (Bowen, 1978, p. 485). As I have worked to address my areas of reactively-driven fusion I have carefully looked out for my part in gossip triangles. I ask myself before opening my mouth, "Would I be sharing this information about a third party to another if that third party was standing behind my shoulder? Would I be comfortable saying it with them listening in?"

And as a Christian, I recognise the wrong of triangling gossip: "A gossip betrays a confidence, but a trustworthy person keeps a secret" (Prov 11:13). Listening to personal information about an absent party displeases God and needs to be confessed and avoided. Bowen theory has assisted me to see the subtlety of this process and to see the way it undermines relationships with and distorts perceptions of the absent third parties.

Family of origin patterns and their influence on relating styles

Thinking about family of origin can shed some light on how we can automatically gravitate to relationships that replicate the equilibrium we were most accustomed to in our family. The most formative relationship is the primary triangle we are in with our caregivers. It has interlocking connections to triangles with siblings, with grandparents and with people in the community. However the relationship that we have with our parents is central in shaping these broader interconnections. Bowen writes that this is the "most important triangle in life, and the one in which a person develops the triangle relationship patterns that remain relatively fixed in all relationships" (1978, p. 531). This core triangle may not always be with biological parents; for example, it can be a parent and a grandparent who were central caregivers. In separated households the triangle may include a parent that is absent from one's life. If a father left a mother early and a child has a relationship with the mother around the story of the "abandoning" father, this will be a powerful shaping primary triangle.

Predictably, there are two versions of the way that fusion is acted out in groups such as a church community. One way is, if we were in a comfortable, validating fusion in our family of origin, we will tend to replicate that somewhere in our church. On the flip side, if we were in an uncomfortable, more negative fusion in our family of origin, perceiving a parent as favouring a sibling or being overly critical, we may look for a replacement parent figure in our church to reverse our sense of invalidation. The first process is one that is inclined towards overfunctioning, and the second to underfunctioning and inviting caretaking from others to meet our neediness. At this point, it's worth a reminder that these relationship experiences are not caused by a parent; they are contributed to by the reactions and counter-reactions of all parties.

The effort to step out of automatic and self-serving relationship togetherness starts with recognising the reactive patterns we find ourselves replicating from our original families. Bowen theory has much to offer here. The theory also sets a realistic expectation that changing one's part in unhealthy or immature patterns will not come easily and requires a long-term responsible effort to do things differently (perhaps with the assistance of a family systems coach). It is a challenge to lift oneself out of fusion, since:

> The togetherness forces are so strong in maintaining the status quo that any small step towards differentiation is met with vigorous disapproval of the group... Without help the differentiating one will fall back into togetherness to get emotional harmony for the moment. (Bowen, 1978, p. 371)

As Christians, however, we are not left to our own efforts in growing our godliness/maturity. We have the Counsellor, the Holy Spirit, to call on in the work of regeneration—to become more like Jesus. And part of this sanctifying work includes reducing each Christian's deeply embedded, people-attuned sensitivities.

Conclusion

This chapter has explored Bowen theory's descriptions of fusion and anxious togetherness with a careful check that it is not at odds with the call to self-sacrificing unity in Christ's church. The discussion has endeavoured to make a clear distinction between unity generated by gospel priorities and harmony fuelled by inadvertently seeking our own comfort. Anxious togetherness that leads to fusion functions to reduce relationship tension and garner acceptance from others. It is essentially "people-pleasing":

> For am I now seeking the approval of people, or of God? Or am I trying to please people? If I were still trying to please people, I would not be a servant of Christ (Paul, in Gal 1:10).

The examples presented from a hypothetical ministry partnership and from the author's own family of origin and church relating have aimed to assist the reader to identify the difference between the unity that derives from being "in Christ", and anxious togetherness that creates a pseudo-connection in relationships. These distinctions and the comparison of fusion and people-pleasing deserve ongoing critical attention. It is hoped that the reflections in this chapter provide a platform for more reflections, discussion, and biblically informed scholarship about the traps of an immature push towards harmony in churches. Can one recognise anxiously driven accord that avoids disagreements, that distances from people who are different, and fosters gossiping/triangling about others? Being able to discern the patterns of reactive togetherness and to address one's part in them provides an important pathway for one to contribute to more godly ways of relating in the system that is the body of Christ.

For further reflection:

How does one identify the difference between the unity that comes out of being "in Christ" and the drivers of anxious togetherness that create fused relationships?

To help answer this question, ask yourself:

- What is the energising force, or the fuel of it?
- What are the markers?

- How could we recognise the markers of fusion compared to the distinctive attributes of Christian unity?
- What are the outcomes or the fruits of each?

These reflection questions may be useful in identifying one's fusion vulnerabilities from family of origin:

- How was my relationship with one or both of my parents validating me?
- How might I gravitate towards similar comfort in church relationships?
- What aspects of my relationship with one or both of my parents did I distance from?
- How might I try to create with others what I cut off from or viewed as a deficit in my parents' relating?

References

Bowen, M. (1978). *Family therapy in clinical practice.* NY & London: Jason Aronson.

Dever, M. (2001). *9 Marks of a healthy church.* Booklet. Fourth Ed. PDF (CCR).

Accessed 20/9/18 at https://cn.9marks.org/wp-content/uploads/2014/10/Nine-Marks-of-a-Healthy-Church-Booklet-4th-Edition-PDF.pdf

Kerr, M. E. & Bowen, M. (1988). *Family evaluation.* New York: W. W. Norton & Company.

Papero, D. (1990). *Bowen family systems theory.* Needham Heights, Massachusetts: Allyn & Bacon.

Chapter 7

APPLYING BOWEN THEORY TO PASTORAL CARE
From Rescuing Pastor to Coaching Pastor

Tara Stenhouse

Michelle was really struggling in life.[1] She was often depressed and anxious. Work was hard. She felt isolated from friends and had difficult relationships with her family. At times she felt so bad she just wanted to disappear. We'd meet once a fortnight to talk and pray. I felt really sad for her, wishing I could just take her pain away. I did a lot of listening, but also a lot of thinking. I tried to work out the cause of the depression and anxiety. I asked her a lot of questions about what she was feeling. I tried to work out what to do to make her feel better. She'd ask me for help, so I'd give her some advice. Sometimes I'd sit at home in the evening wondering if I'd said the right things that day, feeling quite burdened. I'd worry about her safety. It even got to the point where I'd wake each morning wondering how she was going. I'd think about what I should say that day when we caught up. I often felt overwhelmed and helpless, losing some of the joy I previously had in this pastoral care role.

---

[1] Michelle is a fictitious character, with scenarios describing a conglomeration of pastoral experiences.

As you can see, I got pretty stuck in my relationship with Michelle, so I sought professional supervision from a counsellor who works within a Bowen theory framework, which I was familiar with, but not actively applying. What followed was the beginning of my journey in understanding and applying Bowen theory from a biblical view in the area of pastoral care (gained from professional supervision, my own observations and practice, as well as some reading and listening, e.g., Ferrera, 1990; Brown, 2007).

I am hoping you will see that Bowen theory has provided some wonderful wisdom, revealing my "rescuing" tendencies and encouraging a more principle-directed, self-differentiated approach to pastoral care.

A chronic rescuing pastor!

Bowen theory has grown me in self-awareness, through three key observations.

Firstly, I observed that I naturally use a linear individual "cause-and-effect" perspective, thinking that the problem or symptom lies purely within an individual. I seek to diagnose the problem (with a label), and try to find a cause within the person. I try to work out why they are struggling, focusing on questions about how they are feeling, and why they are feeling the way they are. Bowen theory, however, looks at the overall relational system and the emotional process at work in the interconnections with others, which led to the further two observations about myself.

Secondly, I observed that if someone shares with me their pain and difficulties, or even a dilemma, I experience great anxiety. I find it difficult to see someone else in pain, or to see them wrestling with difficult decisions. I feel bad for them. I want to get rid of the pain for them, so that they do not have to go through that pain anymore (and so that I will not feel anxious anymore!). They usually want to get rid of it as well and want me to do something to help.

Thirdly, in order to relieve the anxiety of caring for someone like Michelle, the predictable automatic pattern that I have observed in myself is *overfunctioning*, or being the "rescuing pastor." I do not deliberately set out to rescue someone (I know in my head that I cannot rescue anyone), but my automatic reactions "kick into action", in an attempt to calm my anxiety by trying to rescue them. I do anything to reduce their pain, by functioning for them, thinking for them, feeling for them, doing for them, or giving them advice. In this way I am "giving up self" to the other person, and "taking self" from them. Bowen theory helps show that my desire and efforts to help someone are not so much a wonderful Christian other-person-centred desire to love them, but instead a desire to reduce the anxiety I am feeling.

What is the impact of being a chronic rescuing pastor? There is a *perceived positive impact*. I feel pretty good about myself when I am needed, and when I can offer some rescue and advice. I feel like I am doing my job. The other person also thinks I am doing my job and says thank you. They have received a short-term solution for their problem. So at first, my anxiety and their anxiety is decreased, which feels great.

However, Bowen theory shows the *negative impact* of my rescuing pattern on those I am supposedly caring for. Where there is overfunctioning there is the reciprocal pattern of underfunctioning—each side reinforces and consolidates the other posture. When I become a rescuer, giving someone advice, accepting their invitation for me to solve their problem, this reinforces the idea that they are helpless, that they cannot solve the problem, that they need my help, that they are the problem-person and I am the rescuer—and so their functioning goes down (since I am functioning for them). Roberta Gilbert puts it this way: "The other one takes on anxiety as a result of this arrangement and, eventually, develops symptoms. *The dominant one gains self from the other, who loses it*" ([Emphasis added] 2006, p. 13). This is what happened with Michelle. Although her anxiety decreased a little, this was just for a time, and her functioning got worse, as she became more dependent on me and my advice.

There is also an eventual negative impact on the overfunctioner. Caring as a rescuer leaves me more overwhelmed and stuck, feeling quite burdened by my pastoral role, wearing the anxiety of the suffering of others in a way that lingers after I have left work. As Roberta Gilbert says (in the context of a discussion about marriage and symptom development in one spouse), "The overfunctioner is just as caught in this relationship process as the underfunctioner. Often overfunctioners, though they may lead productive lives much of the time, may themselves be subject to sudden physical illness or 'burnout' because of the stress involved in taking responsibility for two people" (1992, p. 68).

Some of the other negative impacts of being an overfunctioner are: pride (I feel like I am a better person than the other person who is struggling), an avoidance of addressing areas of one's own life (my focus is on them, not myself), and a one-way relationship (I am not seeking to learn from them, and I am not going to be honest and share my struggles). These may leave the overfunctioner isolated and burdened. Overfunctioning in particularly difficult pastoral situations may also lead to a neglect of caring for others you are responsible for, or a neglect of other responsibilities in life.

In all of these ways Bowen theory helps me recognise my anxiety-driven rescuing pastor tendencies, and the negative impact of these—but it also helps reveal a different approach to pastoral care, that of a principle-driven, alongside "coaching" pastor.

The journey towards being an alongside, coaching pastor

The Bowen theory concept I have found helpful in understanding a different approach is that of a coach. It is used in a clinical setting, referring to the role of a counsellor as they meet with a client (Brown, 1999). A counsellor-coach stands alongside someone, coaching them to do their own thinking, so that they work out how they will respond to their own situation, with some support along the way. The coach needs to manage their own emotions (especially the discomfort of seeing someone suffer), to listen to the other person, holding back on thinking for them and giving advice, and to be patient, not automatically rescuing them. The coach recognises that this person is capable and has many resources to work things out for themselves. The coach gives some input and encouragement to work through things, but the person themselves comes up with a plan, then seeks to put their plan into practice in real life. At the next session they talk through how things went, what they observed about themselves and the situation, what went well, what didn't go well, and come up with another plan. The goal of this coaching (for the coach and the person coached), then, is not relief of anxiety, but rather differentiation of self—the maturity of self.

The following table seeks to communicate what an alongside "coaching" pastor looks like, in terms of their role, goal, and methods, especially compared to a "rescuing" pastor. In seeking to understand and apply Bowen theory, and pull together what I have learnt in various seminars, books, and articles, I found it valuable to separate the various specific ideas from each other. Slowing down and noticing the differences in the two approaches has helped me see the specific ways I am being a rescuer—but also to learn practically how to move towards an alternative way of pastoring. I have also found the comparison table helpful in clearly communicating the differences.

"Rescuing" Pastor	Alongside "Coaching" Pastor
Seeking to rescue someone from their suffering/pain; trying to reduce their distress; trying to fix them	Standing alongside someone, encouraging them through their suffering/pain; allowing them to experience their distress
Overfunctioning for the other person (them underfunctioning)	Each having a responsibility for our own self; working out my role in pastoral care and being clear about that; allowing them to struggle and find their own way through it
Anxiety-driven helpfulness; trying to reduce my own anxiety by reducing their anxiety	Care arising out of my Christian principles (principle-directed helpfulness); managing my own anxiety; working on my own emotional maturity/differentiation of self; coaching myself to sit with their anxiety and let them work on their own dilemmas
Looking down on them, viewing the other person as helpless and me as the helper	Standing alongside them; viewing them as a capable person, who has been given resources by God; inviting them to use their own coping strategies; me seeking to learn from them in a real way; genuine two-person relationship
Problem/rescue approach	Encouraging a research/observation approach
Focusing on their symptoms/problems; labeling them	Relating to the whole person; focusing on their functioning
Focusing on the content of the problem	Focusing on patterns or process of relationship
Feeling for the other person	Recognising my own feelings as I care for them
"I feel your pain. Let me help"; taking on their problems	"I feel your pain. What ideas do you have about what you can do next? What could you try differently?"; inviting them to take their own responsibility

Focusing on their feelings; usually ask "How are you feeling" questions	Encouraging them to focus on observing the events that have been happening; encouraging them into their heads; offering them a "place to think"
Thinking for the other person	Inviting them to think for themselves; respecting their autonomy as a capable person, even in the midst of their struggles
Looking for a cause and effect; usually asking "why" questions	Asking questions that focus on the facts and helping them observe the patterns in their relationships; e.g., what, when, who, where questions; what have you found has worked in the past; what hasn't worked; what could you try differently?
Advice-giving; telling them what to do	Listening to them; asking good questions; only giving advice once they've done some good thinking; then sharing my own perspective/experience, what I've found helpful, how I've approached things; my Christian wisdom in this situation
Blaming others; side-taking; thinking others need to change	Acknowledging everyone is contributing in some way, including myself; managing self and encouraging them to manage themselves; what can they do?
Trying to change them	Working on changing myself and my part in the relationship; trusting the Holy Spirit to change me and them; praying for change
"Doing for" the other person; "I will be all things to you"	Acknowledging my own limitations to myself and to them
Focus is on the rescuing happening in our time together	Focus is on the work happening as they live life in the real world, making their own observations, then me as "coach" touching base at their initiative to see what they've discovered; encouraging them to keep going; being a sounding board

Caring for Michelle looked different when I started to apply this "alongside coaching perspective" on pastoral care. Rather than responding out of my own anxiety, seeking to rescue her from her pain, my role now is to stand alongside her through her suffering, loving and supporting her, caring for her as a sister in Christ, and gently pointing her to Christ. I aim to listen to her genuinely, and to ask questions that help her think for herself, that help her observe what is working and what is not working, and that encourage her to come up with something different to try. Rather than going into a panic about her suicidal desires and seeking to persuade her not to take action, I instead ask her to reflect on God's perspective, and what ideas she has about keeping herself safe. I encourage her to draw on her relationship with God—on what she's read in God's word, on what she's praying for, and on what it looks like for her to glorify God in her current difficult situation. In the past Michelle asked me what the Bible says about her struggles, and I'd answer as best as I could, but now I ask her what she's read in God's word, where she would go to find some of these answers, and encourage her to spend a little time over the next week reading and come back to discuss it together. In that context I might share one verse that I've found helpful for me as I've wrestled with these issues in the past. I also ask her to pray for me in one of the struggles I might be currently experiencing, as well as ask her for any of her wisdom, seeking to learn from her. What a different approach this is to being a rescuer!

Learning how to ask good questions has been vital for me in making the transition from rescuing pastor to coaching pastor—questions aimed at managing my own anxiety and my role, at inviting someone to be a good observer of themselves and to do their own problem-solving. As a rescuing pastor I asked "why" questions focused on looking for cause and effect, as well as questions focusing on how they were feeling, and drawing this out. Bowen theory teaches us to ask questions that invite someone to think for themselves, helping them observe the patterns in their relationships; that is, questions that invite them to draw on the resources God has given them, to be researchers of themselves in their relationship systems—the what, when, who, and how questions. Questions like, What thinking have you been doing? What has worked in the past to help manage your emotions? Can you see any alternative ways of relating? Are there any unhelpful reactions you have had? What do you think is your responsibility? What have you brought before God with this difficulty? What does your Bible reading reveal about how God views this difficulty? (Brown, 2007).

It takes a big effort for me to think as a coach rather than a rescuer. My automatic patterns to rescue (formed in my family of origin) are powerful, especially when life is busy, overwhelming, tiring, and when the symptoms are serious. I have found it helpful to take time before our meeting to reflect on what my goal is and what my approach should be, even writing down some questions that will help me respect them as a capable person and invite them to use the resources God has given them. Although making these kinds of changes is incredibly difficult, Bowen theory teaches that even small changes make a significant impact (Brown, 2012, p. 222).

In little ways I have found that when I do relate as an alongside coaching pastor, it does make a difference in me, as well as in the person I am meeting with. I am less anxious, I am clearer about what my role is, and I am more confident of what I am trying to do. I have come away refreshed and encouraged—I have not aimed to solve their problem, rather to listen, acknowledge their pain, and ask good questions. As for the other person, I have seen them become calmer and grow in their motivation and confidence to work things through for themselves. One person invited me to do the thinking for them (that is why they asked to meet with me), but with an alongside coaching approach they came away more encouraged and empowered that they could work on things for themselves, which surprised and delighted them.

Biblical worldview on "rescuing pastor" versus "alongside coaching pastor"

This idea of being an alongside coaching pastor, rather than a rescuing pastor, resonates biblically, grouped here as five principles:

1. God as the ultimate rescuer and refiner (often through suffering)

God is the ultimate rescuer, heart-changer, and refiner, not us (Eph 1:1-15, 2:4-8; 2 Cor 4:6; Col 1:9-14). As a pastor I cannot change anyone or their circumstances—only God can. One day God will completely remove all sin, pain, and suffering (Rev 21:1-5), but until then God, in his wisdom and grace, works through our suffering to grow us to be more like Jesus, testing our faith (Rom 8 esp. vv. 28-30; 1 Pet 1:6-7; Jas 1:2-3). God does not remove all suffering from our lives, but works through it to grow our trust in him, teaching us to long for Jesus' return. My desire as a rescuing pastor to get rid of the difficult things in someone's life will rob them of an opportunity for them to trust God to be at work in growing them.

2. God's glory and maturity in Christ being the goal of pastoral care

So our goal in pastoral care is not first and foremost to bring relief from suffering or to reduce anxiety (others' or our own), but rather God's glory and our maturity in Christ (1 Cor 10:31; Col 1:28). We want to point people to God so that they entrust themselves to him, seeking his glory and honour (1 Pet 2:21,23). We want people to turn to God, to listen to him, to cry out to him, to cling to him (not to us).

3. Pastors as under-shepherds

Jesus is the good shepherd (John 10:11-18; 1 Pet 5:4), but God appoints leaders to shepherd God's flock among them (1 Pet 5:2-

3; Acts 20:28-31), or what I would call *under-shepherds*. Under-shepherds are firstly to submit to the good shepherd, aware of their own sin and responsibility to grow to be more like Christ (e.g., Acts 20:28, "keep watch over yourselves"). It is easy to focus on the sin and the growth of the person being cared for, rather than our own sin and growth.

How does an under-shepherd keep watch over God's flock? By teaching God's word (in public and private, see Acts 20:20-21, 27, warning them about the false teachers/"wolves" Acts 20:29-31), caring for their salvation (1 Thess 2:7-9), and being an example (Acts 20:33-35; 1 Pet 5:3; 1 Thess 2:10-12; 1 Tim 4:12). There is genuine love and concern for each person (including personal sacrifice and tears, see Acts 20:19, 24, 34-35), but the goal is not the removal of their pain or difficulty—rather, to encourage them to rely on Jesus, drawing comfort from his word, turning to him in prayer, entrusting their situation to him, and putting their hope in the sure future found in him.

Under-shepherds rely on God, entrusting each person to the good shepherd—through constant prayer and patience, as well as "time out": rest and sleep. Our Lord Jesus taught and urged people, and cared with genuine compassion—but he also took time out to pray, to rest, and to sleep (he wasn't available to be summoned 24 hours a day! See Luke 4:42, 6:12, 9:18, 28-30, 11:1, 22:41-46). The apostle Paul followed Christ's example, shepherding the flock with tears and suffering, considering his life worth nothing to him—but he was in constant prayer, entrusting each person to God's sovereignty and grace (Phil 1:3-11; 2 Thess 1:11-12, 2:13-14, 16-17).

4. Our equality as those created by God
We stand alongside those we care for as those equally bearing the image of God (Gen 1-2), equally sinful (Gen 3, Rom 3), equally

saved (Rom 3), as well as equally resourced to live as followers of Jesus in this world. We have each been resourced with the Holy Spirit (Gal 5:16-25; Eph 6:18; Col 1:9-10; Rom 8:26-27), with God's precious word (Ps 19:10, 119:72, 127; 2 Tim 3:14-17; Heb 4:12), with spiritual gifts (Rom 12:3-8), and with the fellowship of the body of Christ (Gal 6:1-2; 1 Cor 12:7, 12-26; Rom 12:10, 13, 15). God is with all those who trust Jesus, wherever we go, and he is caring and powerful (Heb 13:5; 1 Pet 5:6-7). He has also given us a mind that is capable of applying God's will to our lives, of observing ourselves, and learning from our mistakes.

It is easy for the "carer" to be seen as the responsible one, who is able to "help", who "has it all together"—and the "cared for" as lacking responsibility, "helpless" and needing our help. However, there is equality and mutuality between the carer and the cared for as those made in God's image and accountable to God for our response to him. The under-shepherd is also one of the sheep. We're all in need of being cared for, as well as all responsible to care for others. The carer doesn't have extra special resources unavailable to the cared for. God has given each of us his wonderful resources.

We are to respect one another, and learn from one another (Rom 12:16; Col 3:16). Paul had genuine two-way relationships with other believers, longing to be mutually encouraged and refreshed (Rom 1:11-13, 15:32).

5. All Christians are to care for others

It is not only the under-shepherds who are responsible to care for and love others—all followers of Jesus are to love one another (Rom 12:10; 1 John 3:11, 4:7, 11-12), care for one another (2 Cor 13:11), respect one another (Rom 12:16), teach and admonish one another (Col 3:16), speak the truth in love to one another (Eph 4:15), pray for one another (Jas 5:16), serve one another

(Gal 5:13), and bear one another's burdens (Gal 6:2). We are to be humble, patient, kind, and compassionate (1 Pet 5:5; Gal 5:22; 1 Thess 5:14; Eph 4:32).

Pastoral carers serve within a context of mutual Christian relationships—they are not the only ones doing pastoral care. The under-shepherd is to equip all of God's people to build each other up in love (Eph 4:11-13; 1 Thess 5:11). Sometimes part of the "burden" of the pastoral care role is because we are not encouraging everyone to care—pastoral care is often reliant on one person.

Conclusion

It can be seen, then, that these five biblical principles are consistent with an alongside coaching view of pastoral care, and not a rescuing pastor view.

The possible limitation of the coaching pastor view and the language of coaching is that it may lead to a "distant", "uncaring" view of pastoral care, especially in light of the biblical teaching on laying down your life for others. Nevertheless, it is a helpful corrective to the rescuing pastor tendencies of most pastoral care. A shepherding metaphor could be used; however, this is often interpreted with rescuing pastor tendencies. Using the term under-shepherd may be better (albeit sounding clumsy), as it emphasises a reliance on the Chief Shepherd (for the carer and the one being cared for), as well as genuine care and compassion. This under-shepherd is also a fellow sheep, expressing the mutual alongside nature of pastoral care. This mixing of metaphors, while perhaps confusing, highlights the complexity and richness of the biblical worldview, which enriches the Bowen theory principles.

My journey of applying these Bowen theory principles from a biblical worldview is far from over. Fighting my anxiety-driven rescuing pastor tendencies is difficult. However Bowen theory reveals a different approach to pastoral care, that of a principle-driven alongside coaching pastor. The table comparing the different aspects of these two alternative approaches to pastoral care, along with the tool of asking good questions, has provided me with practical ways of persevering as an alongside coaching pastor.

References

Brown, J. (1999). Bowen family systems: Theory and practice, illustration and critique. *Australian & New Zealand Journal of Family Therapy.* 20(2), 94-103. Retrieved May 31, 2018 from http://www.thefsi.com.au/wp-content/uploads/2014/01/Bowen-Family-Systems-Theory-and-Practice_Illustration-and-Critique.pdf

Brown, J. (2012). *Growing yourself up: How to bring your best to all of life's relationships.* Wollombi, NSW, Australia: Exisle Publishing.

Brown, J. (2007) Family systems and implications for ministry, especially for pastoral care. [CD audio recording]. Neutral Bay, NSW Australia: Family Systems Institute.

Ferrera, S. (1990). What is help? A theoretical and personal perspective. *Family Systems: A Journal of Natural Systems Thinking in Psychiatry and the Sciences.* 5 (1): 44-55.

Gilbert, R. M. (1992). *Extraordinary relationships: A new way of thinking about human interactions.* New York: John Wiley & Sons.

Gilbert, R. M. (2006). *Extraordinary leadership: Thinking systems, making a difference.* Falls Church, VA: Leading Systems Press.

Chapter 8

QUARRELSOME OR CAUGHT IN A QUANDARY?
Triangles and the Complex Position of the Ministry Spouse

Lauren Errington

"It's so hard to be gracious to you when I know what a pain you are!"

Kate was describing the thoughts that had run through her head when, at church on Sunday, she had found herself talking with a woman whom she knew had been complaining to Kate's husband, the minister, about the level of noise during the church service.

In a nutshell, this is what an emotional triangle is. My friend Kate had nothing to do with the actual problem, but here she was, slumped back in the lounge looking frazzled and exhausted trying to explain it to me and trying to work out how to reduce noise levels during the service. How is it that Kate had become the person most affected by the issue, while her husband and the congregation member managed to continue on fairly normally in their church interactions?

In this case, Kate had been "triangled" into the conflict between her husband and the congregation member. *Triangling* is when the tension between two people becomes too much for that relationship to handle, and so a third person is brought in as a way of diffusing the anxiety. The presence of the third person means that the original problem, while unresolved, doesn't feel as stressful anymore because there is another person (often keen to help or be supportive) sharing the emotional load. The problem is still a problem though! And the third person now carries the emotional weight of the problem until they find a way to alleviate their own anxiety.

Sometimes the consequence of the share of anxiety for the third person is of fairly low intensity, like feeling awkward over a cup of tea with someone after a service. But sometimes it can, over time, become very emotionally intense and extreme alternatives are sought as a way of relieving the discomfort. This was the case for Kate, who ended up attending a different church to her minister husband.

In her research, Thomas (2012) found that sixty percent of church planting wives in her control group reported exhaustion, ministry burnout, anxiety disorders, and a variety of other physical ailments they had not previously experienced before church planting. Eighty percent reported suffering from depression. These are confronting statistics, but sadly, unsurprising. A systems perspective helps us understand how it is that such a high number of ministry spouses end up carrying the emotional weight in church relational systems.

In this article, I want to highlight the way in which ministers' spouses, by virtue of their relationship to the minister, are frequently triangled in to the emotional processes that occur in congregational relationships. Drawing on personal experience, anecdotal evidence, and the Scriptures, I will primarily be talking about ministers' wives, but the relational process is just as applicable to spouses or partners of others in ministry capacities. Some readers may find it useful to adjust the label "spouse" to ministry wife or husband as fits the context they are reflecting on.

What is an emotional triangle?

Briefly, the emotional triangle is a concept in Bowen theory that describes how people draw on a third person in their surrounding relationships to relieve tension that exists between an original twosome. The involvement of a third person helps the relationship between the original twosome to not "overheat", by having another set of relationships available to share or diffuse the stress. The three-person triangle can contain more heat overall because the triangle is made up of interconnected relationships, creating pathways or circuits for the anxiety to shift around between the relationships without any one relationship getting too "hot". While the original problem still exists, and may be exacerbated by more people being involved over a longer period of time, the triangling ensures that no one relationship feels the anxiety of the problem for long enough to exceed the threshold for discomfort.

Triangles are made up of two "insiders" and an "outsider" (Kerr & Bowen, 1988). In calm periods, triangles still exist but might seem invisible, such as in Figure 1 where the two top insiders maintain a sense of harmony in their relationship and the outsider is a relatively happy outsider. However, when anxiety increases, the relationship between the insiders gets more uncomfortable, at which point the outsider is brought in to relieve the tension (Figure 2). The outsider, often eager to be involved, responds quickly to the invitation and the triangle is activated. A common pattern is that the conflict is then relocated between the outsider and the second insider (Figure 3), and the original twosome regain some harmony.

Figure 1   Figure 2   Figure 3

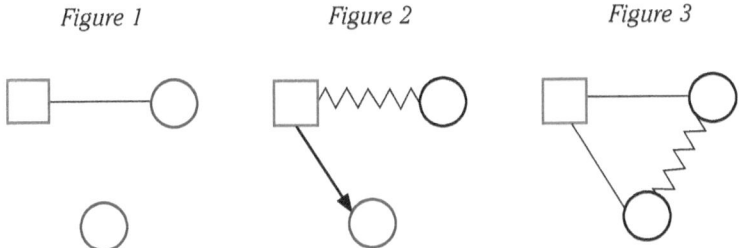

Anxiety is contagious and can move quickly through relationship systems that are under stress. If a third person in a triangle complains to someone else, for example, another triangle is activated and what we then have is a series of interlocking triangles. The anxiety continues to be shared through the relational emotional processes rather than resolved.

The precarious position of the minister's spouse

Often it is not a deliberate move by the original twosome to involve a third person in the tension. The third person can actively get involved and want to "fix" things, or become involved by the invitation of a person seeking help or emotional support, or simply by having the problem "overflow" onto them by hearing gossip or someone well-intentioned sharing their concerns.

Here enters the minister's spouse. If the third person is a competent, generous, intelligent, energetic, and personable person, like most of the ministry spouses I know, they are often all too ready to be involved. Attuned to others' emotional needs, present at countless church events, keen to help, and with a vision to serve the church, the spouse is perfectly positioned to be triangled in to endless relationship problems that are not their own. Here are a few of the triangles in which I have observed spouses involved as the third person:

- The tension arising from transitioning to a new minister from a previous minister
- The frustration between the assistant minister and senior minister over leadership
- The discontent between a church minister and a congregation member
- The conflict between the minister and the music director
- The exhaustion of barracking for the minister in the new church plant to congregation members
- The gossip over morning tea by a congregation member about another congregation member
- The complaints by a group leader about the underfunctioning of another group leader
- The conundrum of problems being raised by one church member about another
- Being "in the know" about a person's otherwise confidential mental health or marital problems.

In my experience, there appears to be two main contributing factors to a spouse's vulnerability to being triangled. Firstly, the ambiguous nature of the spouse's position in the church may mean they are easily susceptible to getting involved in other people's problems. That is, they are not officially employed by the church, but often very actively involved; and they are known by many in the congregation but not quite sure who their own friends are. In his research on clergy families, Lee (1988, in Thomas, 2012) suggests that ambiguity is endemic to ministry: "To the clergy family, the system is not clear. All members of the family participate either directly or indirectly in the church. There is some role expectation of the congregation, which must be fulfilled by the minister, his spouse, and even his children. This level of ambiguity causes high levels of stress for clergy spouses."

Secondly, a minister's spouse is typically interested in and committed to her partner's work in a beautiful but sometimes problematic way as she navigates her own sense of self in an intense interpersonal environment. She often shares a Christian vision and her partnership and investment in gospel ministry is important to her personally, while simultaneously having a position by affiliation which often carries a physical and emotional investment. She will have also often made significant changes to her own life—location, friends, houses, and work—in order to support the family's ministry decisions. These things on their own can carry a significant amount of stress[1]. Thomas states that of all her ministry training, nothing prepared her for the level of stress she would soon learn to live with as if it was ordinary:

> [The wife] often has less access to information or hears the problems but is not involved in the resolution. Women ask, "How much should my husband tell me? I realise I am his primary support, but it's hard to love people well when I know how they have hurt him." (Thomas, 2012)

Herein lies one of the key challenges of these triangles—when a ministry spouse is triangled in to her partner's relationship dilemmas, it inevitably affects the way he or she is able to relate to others in the church community.

A systems view of triangles helps us understand how it can be that, as Thomas (2012) found, the church planter's wife often lives with even higher levels of stress than the planter. When the

---

[1] In her research about stress faced by church planting wives, Shari Thomas (2012) states that "major life stress such as change of residence and culture, finances, increased marital arguments, loss of close friends and the like, will highly tax the most capable person…The added strain of being the primary and often only caregiver of the children during the early planting years, the lack of a recognised position of power equal to her ministry responsibility combined with higher levels of ambiguity regarding her role compound the already stressful life of planting."

ministry spouse is the one who is the bearer of anxiety; when they are triangled in as the third person to relieve the tension between her partner and another person; then, over time, Bowen would suggest, the compounding anxiety will either cause or exacerbate emotional and physical symptoms. One reason for this is that "the person most prone to becoming symptomatic is the one who makes the most adjustments in his or her own thoughts, feelings, and behaviour to preserve relationship harmony" (Kerr & Bowen, 1988, p.172).

What do we do with anxiety?

Anxiety is uncomfortable. I am referring to the stress arousal that every human experiences when perceiving threat and challenge. It may not necessarily be experienced as mental health anxiety symptoms. When stress undermines our feeling of emotional wellbeing, we act, mostly not even consciously, in ways that will reduce the anxiety (Kerr & Bowen, 1988).

There seem to be two main ways a minster's spouse responds to the anxiety she feels when she is triangled in to her partner's concerns: she either gets overly involved or she distances herself. These responses look very different: one situation has the spouse very present and involved at church, while another is noticeably absent; one seeks to know a lot about everything and everyone at church, while another might seek refuge in alternative occupations or relationships outside of church. But Titelman (1998) suggests that being overly involved or distancing are two sides of the one coin. Joining in the togetherness of anxiety, or trying to distance or cut off from it, are both efforts to manage the high degree of anxiety or emotional intensity in the relationship system.

While our previous relationship experiences, particularly in our families, mean we might be wired to do one or the other of these things (that is, getting overly involved or distancing), we often do whatever it takes to try and get ourselves in the most comfortable position we can. A friend of mine described two of her church experiences while her husband was an assistant minister—in the first church, she knew everything that was going on about her husband's conflictual relationship with the senior minister, which led to her finding it very difficult to know how to relate to the senior minister herself. After that experience, in their second church, they agreed that the husband would not share any difficulties he had with the ministry team with her, in the hope that it wouldn't affect her relationship with them. She distanced herself from knowing about interpersonal tensions, but over time when there were disagreements, her husband was quiet and distracted at home and they then found it difficult to talk about it. In both cases, the wife was equally involved in the emotional process, even though in the first instance she was very present, and in the second, more distant.

Most of the time when relationships make us anxious, we opt for short-term solutions which help to relieve the anxiety of the moment, rather than considering what might be most useful in the long run. A key element in triangles is side-taking. We look to others to relieve our anxiety and provide for our wellbeing, and give in to one another by saying things and doing things that aim to reduce each other's anxiety. We choose someone who will take our side and reassure us, and we feel better for it. This makes us feel comfortable and keeps relationships in harmony for a little while... until the tension rises again. The problem is, each time we do this we might not be clear about what we actually think but go along with others to keep the peace, which, if done repeatedly over time, means we are being less of our own "self" in the relationship. We keep giving ourselves over to keep others happy rather than thinking about what might actually be best for the relationship and for each person, ourselves included, to grow and mature.

Whose anxiety is it anyway?

God knows that we desperately want to fix things ourselves. He knows our tendency to want to get involved in other people's problems and sort them out. He knows it, and he warns us not to do it:

> Like one who grabs a stray dog by the ears
> is someone who rushes into a quarrel not their own.
> (Prov 26:17)

The writers of Proverbs have a remarkable way of finding stark illustrations to reveal our follies. It's pretty clear that yanking a random dog's ears is a foolish thing to do, provoking the dog to anger and aggression. Just as foolish, we are told, as getting involved in a problem between two people that does not belong to us.

Some brief observations about this proverb: firstly, the person *rushes* in to get involved. The person is hasty in their involvement, and immediate in their response. The person does not wait, but very quickly becomes part of the interaction. Secondly, the quarrel is *not* their own! This is a problem between two other people, and this third person is unnecessarily getting involved. Thirdly, the third person gets *emotionally* involved. Some translations (ASV, ERV) describe this person as "vexing" themselves with "strife that does not belong to him." His meddling means he is now also emotionally vexed. Lastly, we might assume there are *consequences* for the third person getting involved. Grabbing a dog by the ears gives the impression of a person wrangling with an angry canine—we can only imagine what the implications of this could be for the person, and wonder how it relates to getting involved in a quarrel. One consequence, we might think, is the third person being troubled by the issue unnecessarily. The third person in this proverb could well be described as triangling themselves in to the tension that belongs between the two others.

This proverb cautions us about getting involved in problems that are not our own. It is essentially a lesson in self-control, and as such, teaches us that staying out of other people's affairs is an effort of restraint. Proverbs continually exerts the need for godliness to be characterised by self-control and patience (e.g., Prov 16:32, 21:23, 25:28, 29:11,18), exhortations which are carried through to the New Testament (Gal 5:22-23; 2 Peter 1:5-9). The man in this proverb is not quick to listen, slow to speak, or slow to become angry (Jas 1:19); instead, he is quick to speak and become vexed. In Proverbs we are told that "a person's wisdom yields patience; it is to one's glory to overlook an offense" (19:11). There is wisdom in being patient, in taking things slowly, and exercising self-control in our responses to anxiety, sometimes overlooking them altogether.

Under the auspice of helping, we can be quick to become involved in other people's affairs unnecessarily. We see strife between others, and we are hasty in our intervention: a smiling interruption to break the tension, a quick word after church, a follow up phone call or email to see that things are okay. The difficulty with triangling is that these interventions are often welcomed—no one likes tension! But are they necessary? Often, our efforts to help others are actually actions that make *us* feel less worried about something. If I do something to help, it makes *me* feel better about the situation. But what if our "helping" actually inhibits the other person from finding the resources themselves to solve the problem? What if my attempts to help are more about me than them? Our best efforts to love others in our community might be to be self-controlled and restrained in our attempts to try to fix things for other people. These efforts are the ones that can encourage others toward emotional maturity as they encourage others to take responsibility for their own problems, and, perhaps, dig deeper in their relationship with God as they do this.

At the heart of triangling ourselves in to other people's problems, I suspect, is the pride that tells us that people *need* us to be involved and a fear of what will happen if we are not. People may *want* us to be involved, and we may be invited in as a third person in a triangle to other people's quarrels, and most of the time we justify it as helping. But, in fact, it is the opposite. It is an act of humility to slow down and observe the way others can manage their own problems. It is adopting a posture of love to be alongside people but not overfunctioning for them. It is trusting God when I feel anxious for other people that he will continue a good work in them, and that he does not always need me to be a part of that.

The art of detriangling

Despite good intentions by the third person to help "fix" the problem, such a move can distract the twosome from the original problem, and by taking on a share of the anxiety, functioning in such a way that the problem is never resolved. Bowen suggests that a problem between two people can be resolved without the well-intentioned efforts of a third person to fix it. Although this goes against the grain of what we (overfunctioners like myself) like to think, trying to help fix someone else's problem may not actually be the most useful thing for them[2].

Bowen's idea is that when a person can have an emotionally mature response and *detriangle*, the problem is more likely to be contained and less likely to spill over into other interlocking triangles. It is impossible to be completely removed from a triangle, but detriangling describes the efforts of one person to take a different

---

2 It is important to remember that triangles are not problematic in themselves. In fact, Bowen (1978) describes triangles as being more stable than a two-person system, because a two-person system can tolerate little tension before involving a third person. Triangles inevitably exist, and systems are made up of any number of interlocking triangles. Side-taking and triangling is an inevitable part of human relationships, and the main effort of detriangling from a destructive system is in the process of recognising it and working out how to back out of it.

position; to do things differently. What detriangling requires is that the third person be in *adequate emotional contact* with the other two and able to remain *emotionally separate* from them.

So what might this look like? We might remember that there are two main responses to anxiety—distancing, and getting overly involved. Detriangling correlates to both of these: instead of distancing ourselves from others, we need to be in adequate emotional contact with them; and instead of getting emotionally involved, we need to remain emotionally separate to them. Detriangling efforts might involve intentional efforts to have contact with each person in the triangle, even though these interactions might be awkward. Even though it is difficult at times, the challenge is to stay connected with the individuals, even in simple ways. For example, I am struck by a pattern that I see emerging where there ends up being distance between the assistant minister's wife and the senior minister. Part of the challenge here is for the assistant minister's wife to have her own contact with the senior minister, and not vicariously through her husband.

Remaining emotionally separate in the triangle is the other challenge, especially when others want you to take their side! Part of detriangling in this way is for me to manage my own anxiety, because how I manage my own anxiety will either calm things down or rev things up. Trying to be a non-anxious presence in a system can help the spread of calm. Refusing to take on the anxiety and working to leave the responsibility for the problem with the person who owns it can actually help the tension to be properly resolved rather than circulating anxiety through a system by continuing to bring others in to help. Moreover, if I work to keep from being emotionally involved in other people's affairs, I can gently encourage others to take responsibility for what they are able to, thus encouraging them to grow in their own emotional maturity. In practice, this means being curious about the facts of a situation (What happened exactly? Who was involved? What did the person do after that?), rather than joining in speculation (Why?) or giving in to subjective assessments of the event. Objectivity can help dampen the anxiety process, whereas subjectivity can fuel it.

While detriangling is an opportunity for us to work on our emotional maturity, and to encourage others in their own emotional maturity, it also gives us an opportunity to develop disciplines to grow us in spiritual maturity. I think the Christian art of detriangling prompts us in three particular areas of growth: patience, love, and trust in the living God.

The Christian art of detriangling

Firstly, the biblical texts discussed above from Proverbs encourage us toward patience. Things are often not as urgent as they seem or as our anxiety tells us they are. Patience may mean working on understanding our own anxiety—what triggers it, what it feels like, what we are prone to do when feeling anxious—which help us identify times when we are anxious and, by engaging our cognitive faculties in these observations, help us slow down our immediate reactions and choose how we respond. When David is anxious in the Psalms, even when others accuse him falsely, he chooses to resist the temptation to turn inward on himself and instead chooses to turn toward the living God and pray for patience:

> Teach me your way, Lord; lead me in a straight path because of my oppressors.
> Do not turn me over to the desire of my foes, for false witnesses rise up against me, spouting malicious accusations.
> I remain confident of this: I will see the goodness of the Lord in the land of the living.
> Wait for the Lord; be strong and take heart and wait for the Lord. (Ps 27:11-14)

Secondly, the Christian art of detriangling requires love, not just knowledge. Friedman (1985) suggests that "the most triangled position in any set of relationships is always the most vulnerable, but when the laws of emotional triangles are understood, it tends to become the most powerful"(p. 39). Knowledge of the emotional process of triangles will help to identify times when we are getting unnecessarily involved with other people's problems. But knowledge on its own is not enough, because we need a vision of the love that God has for his people to work to truly love each other and prompt each other to emotional and spiritual maturity.

I learnt this when I was, classically, triangled in to the conflict my husband was having with our senior minister. I knew of their differences but it wasn't until I witnessed an argument between them that my own immaturities came to light, whereafter I fed my husband my own opinions which affirmed a view of how unfair the senior minister was being. The thing about this particular situation was that all three of us knew about triangles! Recognising that my relationship with the senior minister was deteriorating, in one of my detriangling attempts I met with him and we talked explicitly about triangles. But the knowledge was not enough to make change. At the time I was aware of my own emotional reactivity but was reluctant to work on it—in the same way that when sin confronts us we may find ourselves resisting the need for repentance and the slow, hard work of becoming more Christlike. But managing and working on self takes more than puffing up with knowledge; it takes humility, commitment, endurance, and building up love for others. "Knowledge makes arrogant, but love edifies" says the apostle Paul in 1 Corinthians 8:1 (NASB).

Finally, the Christian art of detriangling prompts us to trust God, not the assurances of man. When I am anxious, I am quick to seek out reassurance from others. When I feel badly done by, I want others to know, and I want them to take my side. One of the challenges in the face of anxieties or seeming injustices is to turn toward God and to trust him with them, and to ask ourselves—is it enough that God knows?

John Piper asks this question in a podcast about the challenges in forgiving others, and goes on to say:

> Our great need, my great need, is that God be more real to me than other people are... Is it enough for God to know our sorrow, for God to know our pain, for God to know our disappointment, our frustration? Can we hand our cause entirely over to God? Can we move forward treating others better than they treat us, even if it means only God knows and nobody else? That is how real God has to become to us. (Piper, 2015)

It may be that no one will ever know as we do this: we won't get the verbal reassurances, or the validation we desire. But the God who knows the number of hairs on our head will know. He knows when we choose to try and return good for evil, when we try to manage our anxiety and refuse to badmouth or gossip about others, and when we try to love our adversary. He knows it, and sees that we are trying to obey him (Luke 6:27–28). And, as Piper goes on to describe, God delights in it. We are pleasing God at that moment when we are trying to be a little more like Jesus. "When they hurled their insults at [Jesus], he did not retaliate; when he suffered, he made no threats. Instead, he entrusted himself to him who judges justly" (1 Pet 2:23).

It is my experience, and my hope for others, that systems thinking about triangles in relationships may not only provide us with knowledge to do what is truly helpful to encourage others to emotional and spiritual maturity, but that God will give us hearts that enable us to put managing ourselves into practice as we pray for patience, seek to love others and trust the living God.

References

American Standard Version. (1901). Excerpt taken from website https://biblehub.com/asv/proverbs/26.htm on September 26, 2018 at 8:08pm.

Bowen, M. (1978). *Family therapy in clinical practice.* Jason Aronson: New Jersey.

English Revised Version. (1885). Excerpt taken from website https://biblehub.com/erv/proverbs/26.htm on September 26, 2018 at 8:08pm.

Friedman, E. (1985). *Generation to generation: Family process in church and synagogue.* The Guilford Press: New York.

Kerr, M. & Bowen, M. (1988). *Family evaluation: The role of the family as an emotional unit that governs individual behaviour and development.* W.W.Norton & Company: New York.

New American Standard Bible. (1995). The Lockman Foundation.

Piper, J. (2015). The major obstacle in forgiving others Extract taken from www.desiringgod.org/interviews/the-major-obstacle-in-forgiving-others on March 18, 2018 at 4:30pm.

Thomas, S. (2012). A summary of research findings on church planting spouses. Extract taken from www.parakaleo.us/research on February 22, 2014 at 2:30pm.

Titelman, P. (1998). *Clinical applications of Bowen family systems theory.* The Haworth Press: New York.

Chapter 9

CAN BOWEN THEORY HELP US AVOID BURNOUT?
Bowen Theory and the Practice of Sustainable Pastoral Ministry

Anna Moss

Burnout amongst ministry workers is a well recognised phenomenon in Australia, with the National Church Life Survey (Saundercock-Brown, 2008) reporting 23 percent of Protestant pastors experiencing burnout. A further 56 percent were classified as "borderline to burnout" and deemed potential candidates for burnout if current issues were not resolved (Saundercock-Brown, 2008). This paper will argue that Bowen theory has a valuable contribution to make in fostering the practice of healthy and sustainable ministry and therefore serving as a protective factor against burnout. It will consider the ways in which Bowen theory can contribute to the practice of sustainable pastoral ministry within the local church. The specific nature of the church will be discussed alongside an exploration of the church as an emotional system. As part of this work, the author interviewed a group of ministry workers in order to ascertain the ways in which they used their knowledge of Bowen theory to manage themselves in the complexity of ministry work and relationships. Comments from these interviews are used as illustrations throughout the paper.

Bowen theory has been applied in some American ministry contexts with the view to encouraging ministry workers to grow their understanding about how they manage themselves better within the complexities and challenges of church ministry. It is interesting to note however that most of the current literature which applies Bowen theory to the church context does so largely without articulating the theological purpose and role of the church.[1] These works provide valuable insights into the ways Bowen theory can assist the ministry of the local church; however foundational questions regarding the theological nature of the church remain essentially unanswered. This paper will attempt to make a contribution to this domain of thinking, beginning with a discussion of ecclesiology, followed by practical applications of the theory to ministry life. Three key areas of ministry leadership will be addressed: the importance of understanding self and others, managing conflict, and anxious overfunctioning.

The nature and role of the church

As Richards and Hoeldtke (1980) state, "Our understanding of the tasks of human leaders and their ministries must grow out of our understanding of the church as a living organism in which leaders play a significant part" (p. 24). A theological understanding of the church needs to form the basis for any discussion regarding the practice of healthy and sustainable ministry. It is not possible to include an exhaustive ecclesiology here; however, some observations are made to help shape our thinking about the church, before applying Bowen theory to the practice of pastoral ministry within that context.

---

[1] Richardson (1996), Richardson (2005), Steinke (1996), Steinke (2006), Galindo (2009), and Friedman (1985) are examples of such works.

Our understanding of the church needs to encapsulate the functional model of what the church *does,* but also needs to grapple with something deeper and more basic about what it *means* to be the church (Van Gelder, 2000, p. 24). The Bible is rich with varied pictures of the church. The church is a royal priesthood, a holy nation, a people belonging to God (1 Pet 2:9). It is the bride of Christ (2 Cor 11:2; Rev 21:9), the family of God (2 Cor 6:18; Eph 2:19), the temple of God (1 Pet 2:5; 1 Cor 3:16), God's household (1 Pet 4:17), and a community indwelt by the Holy Spirit (John 20:22; 1 Pet 4:13-14). A central picture of the church is the body of Christ (1 Cor 12:12-30; Eph 4:12), where Christ is the head (Col 1:18; Eph 4:15). This image teaches that believers are all united under Christ (Rom 6:5; Eph 4:13). In Christ, we who are many form one body, and each member belongs to all the others (Rom 12:5). However the oneness and unity of the church does not equate to homogeneity and the dissolving of selves. First Corinthians pictures one body made up of many parts, whose distinctness and diversity of roles are essential for the body's life. Romans 12 envisages a multiplicity of gifts and responsibilities. Volf (1997) states:

> The many who are incorporated into Christ are accordingly constituted not only in their unity, but also each in his own personhood by the same relationship between the Son and the Father, just as in Christ himself. (p. 86)

Healthy and sustainable ministry will therefore uphold and foster both unity and diversity within the church family. Clowney (1995, p. 15) helpfully exhorts us to remember that, "a doctrine of the church that does not centre on Christ is self-defeating and false." As we ponder healthy and sustainable ministry in the local church, we must be clear about the object and purpose of that ministry.

This will shape our priorities and what we deem to be the greatest needs of those we minister amongst. The role of church leaders is not to build the self-esteem of church members. It is not primarily focused on helping people to improve their relationships with others. Healthy and sustainable church ministry will always seek to encourage peoples' relationship with Christ. Their self-esteem and confidence must be centred in Christ and rooted in his saving work.

One of the great challenges of church ministry is the frequent feeling of disconnect between these biblical descriptions of the church and the reality of how churches function on the ground. As Horton (2011, p. 843) observes:

> Lodged by the Spirit between "this age" and "the age to come", the church has an existence and visibility that are at present ambiguous: "already" and "not yet"... [Christ] has already experienced the exaltation and glorification that is our hope together in him, while we are still subject to decay, death and sin.

The biblical models of the church are true and right, yet our experience of them is marred by sin. As we live in community as redeemed, yet broken sinners, a knowledge of self and others can assist us in learning to live out who we are as God's people. Bowen theory has much to teach about understanding self and others, and in this way serves as a useful tool in the practice of healthy and sustainable ministry in the local church.

A leader in healthy and sustainable ministry

Bowen describes people being in relationship with one another as an *emotional system* in which people respond and react to one another more instinctually and automatically than they may realise. As the gathering of God's people, the church can be viewed as an emotional system made up of emotional processes (Steinke, 2006, p. xiii). There are positive aspects to these processes—friendship, mutual encouragement, and joy. However, a key observation of Bowen theory is that all emotional systems are inherently anxious and are thus prone to certain predictable, maladaptive relationship patterns (Kerr & Bowen, 1988, p. 32). This section will explore some key ministry issues in light of Bowen theory and the Bible, which may help ministry leaders develop healthier and more sustainable patterns of ministry as they learn more about how they and others function in relationships within the church community.

Understanding self and others

Differentiation of self is the ability to remain an autonomous, inner-directed individual while staying meaningfully connected to significant others. Simply put, it is emotional maturity. One's level of emotional maturity is best assessed when the emotional system is anxious and under stress. Pastors and teachers are exhorted to build up the body of Christ in unity and maturity (Eph 4:12-16). Ephesians 4 links unity and maturity as processes. Spiritual and emotional maturity will lead to unity in the church family. It is an authentic unity that is envisaged here, not one that is based on superficial sameness driven by people-pleasing and approval-seeking. Green (2013, p. 189) states, "The shepherd-teacher needs to have as a constant question, 'is the goal of my ministry that people will be encouraged, resourced and trained for what they have to do, or will they just admire me for the skill with which I do what I have to do?'"

As pastors better understand themselves and their roles, and address their personal insecurities, they will forsake the building up of themselves in order to see others matured, trained, and equipped, and ministry multiplied. People will be placed above programs and a meaningful seeking of others' maturity will override the desire to see one's own programs succeed. If growth in emotional and spiritual maturity is a key goal of ministry, then pastoral workers must be prepared to speak the truth in love. This will involve a readiness to have difficult conversations that address the presence of sin in one another's lives. It will require an ability to refrain from rescuing others from their own discomfort and refraining from relationship postures that alleviate discomfort and distress in ourselves and others.

There are unique challenges and stressors for people involved in church-based ministry, such as complex relational demands, working in team contexts, being connected to one's colleagues as well as the spouses of one's colleagues, ministering to single congregation members as well as those who are married, as well as the dual relationships[2] that often exist in ministry roles. One's level of emotional maturity will impact the ways in which a person is able to manage the relational demands they face. Acknowledging the variation in people's emotional maturity levels and being aware of the gaps in one's own emotional maturity can be helpful in addressing the complex nature of church community. In particular, understanding that personal growth is a lifelong process can encourage an approach to relationships that is humble, curious, and willing to learn from setbacks and conflict scenarios.

Increasing one's level of self-awareness is a key step in growing emotional maturity. The way a leader functions arises out of who the leader is: "being and functioning are twin to each other" (Steinke, 2006, p. xi). When I spoke with ministry workers about the ways in which Bowen theory shaped their approach to relationships and work, one pastoral worker stated: "What I like about family systems is that it makes you focus on yourself

---

2 For example, someone may be in a leadership position over someone they consider a friend or over someone whose children are in close friendship with their own.

but in a helpful way rather than in a negative way. [In difficult pastoral situations] it was helpful to realise that sometimes the strength of my reaction is because it's me. It touches on my own experience."[3] Effective ministry is aided by the leader's ability to perceive their own role in the system and what they themselves contribute to the issues at play.

Church communities commonly present ministry leaders with a variety of competing demands and priorities. Amongst congregations there is likely to be a mixture of preferences and ideas about how ministry should be done. For leaders, managing oneself calmly in the face of competing relationship pressures will involve a "readiness to define who you are from within, rather than adapting to please others or defining yourself over against others" (Steinke, 2006, p. 44). It will also involve grace and humility. "Humility starts with our view of ourselves... and humility inevitably involves how we treat others" (Green, 2013, p. 165).

Growing in self-awareness through looking thoughtfully at one's own family of origin is a key coaching process in Bowen theory. This approach challenges the individual to observe their own emotional reactivity and work on increasing their emotional maturity in the context of close relationships. The ministry of pastoral workers will inevitably be affected by their unresolved emotional attachments[4] within their own families. Emotional attachment has less to do with major traumatic events and more to do with the ongoing daily patterns and "emotional grooves" that are shaped over long periods of time (Richardson, 2005, p. 14). This

---

3 Transcript from interviews undertaken with vocational pastoral workers in local church contexts.

4 Unresolved attachment is the fused aspect of one's life that is carried from the family of origin into one's adult life.

is evidenced in the following reflection by one minister: "So if my parents saw things in a certain way I used to think I had to conform to their ways but then I sat down to think about it, 'Am I serving the people God's way or am I just being very directed by my parents and my cultural upbringing?'"[5] Local church ministry inevitably involves intimate work with both individuals and families. Unresolved issues with one's own family of origin impacts the way leaders approach helping others as they will be drawn to either getting involved or avoiding particular relationships and issues.

Growing one's identity in Christ is imperative to the growth of emotional maturity and differentiation of self. In a seemingly ironic statement, Jesus teaches that in order to gain life and self we must be willing to lose it (Matt 16:24-25). Jesus calls us to deny the false selves we have previously clung to, in order to know our true selves in him. Differentiation of self requires that one first establishes an authentic self. As Christians, our personal identity is rooted in who we are in Christ. As we develop a more solid self in Christ we will be less dependent on external aspects such as personal achievements or the approval of others in order to maintain self.

Maintaining a solid sense of self can be particularly challenging for women in ministry roles who are working in complementarian ministry contexts[6] whose main responsibilities may be largely unseen by the wider congregation. This can contribute to a lack of self-definition for women in this role. "Some of the factors that contributed to [burnout] was definitely a poor view of self…that's tied to my understanding of myself as a child of God as well as family of origin issues. There was lots of work going on in terms

---

5 Ibid., 3

6 Complementarianism posits that God created men and women equal in being but assigned different—and equally valuable—functions. (Duncan & Hunt, 2006, p. 32)

of understanding my own personhood. Working out who I was, what does this look like, how does that work. Knowing that you are doing your job well in ministry is hard... So much of what we do is unseen. At least for the guys they preach once a week, but nobody sees the work that we do. Working self out has been a life long journey for me."[7] The process of finding self in Christ provides the firmest foundation from which to relate to others in mature and healthy ways.

As we consider our identity in Christ, and the role it plays in forming a solid sense of self, it is interesting to reflect upon our status as children of God and the seemingly paradoxical way in which this truth enables us to live emotionally mature, adult lives. Henri Nouwen (2006) writes:

> Developing your identity as a child of God in no way means giving up your responsibilities. Likewise, claiming your adult self in no way means that you cannot become increasingly a child of God. In fact the opposite is true. The more you can feel safe as a child of God, the freer you will be to claim your mission in the world as a responsible human being. (p. 159)

A strong sense of self which is rooted in Christ will assist the kind of ministry that seeks to equip and train up others. It will support a readiness to see others shine in the service of God's kingdom, rather than attempting to build up a sense of self by being seen as competent, capable, and busy.

As one seeks to understand their own contribution to the relational patterns in which they participate, they will grow in understanding of others too. Seeking to understand other

---

7 Ibid., 3

people by adopting a calm, broad view of the emotional system is a key concept in Bowen theory. A key goal of ministry is to nurture others in Christ, which requires clarity about what their genuine and deepest needs are. Doing this, while perceiving the simultaneous relational and emotional processes that are at work, is challenging. As one female worker stated, "It's easy in ministry to just want people to be happy and to be happy with you, rather than letting them see the consequences of their sin and not rescuing them from it. It's interesting to think about the ways we accommodate each other in the church family, in ways that aren't always helpful and don't help people to grow in their own maturity."[8]

Healthy, mature, and sustainable ministry will be shaped by the willingness to ask self-reflective questions. Examples of other self-reflective questions might include:

- What drives me in my work and relationships?
- How much of my ministry is self-directed, and how much is driven by family or cultural influences?
- Am I seeking to alleviate my own anxieties in unhelpful ways?
- What is behind the reactions that I have towards other people?
- What relational sensitivities do I bring to my ministry context?

Managing conflict

Bowen theory suggests that when relationship intensity gets too much, people react in two main ways: emotional withdrawal and distancing behaviours; or an anxious fusion where people seek to

---

[8] Ibid., 3

be extra-connected and often give up self and compromise their values for the sake of harmony and cohesion.

Pastoral workers usually live close to the actual church building and within the same community as many of their parishioners. The close proximity of these relationships can be both a joy and a challenge for pastoral workers. The temptation to reactively withdraw, attack others, or give up self in times of conflict is strong, yet the ability to remain calm, curious, objective, and constructive is vital to healthy ministry. One pastor commented, "Bowen theory has been helpful too in conflict, trying not to get angry or defensive or withdrawn. Trying to avoid those three responses or even if I do have one of those responses, then working out what is the rational voice in all of that."[9] Friedman (1985, p. 208) notes that church leaders are like "transformers in an electric circuit"; that is, anxious energy feeds back from them into the congregation at a higher voltage. The way in which leaders manage conflict within the church system is crucial to the health and sustainability of their ministry.

Bowen calls the pull to be connected to others the *togetherness force* (Kerr & Bowen, 1988, p. 59). An awareness of this temptation can help leaders to become more observant of their tendency to seek approval, to comply, and to compromise their principles and values in times of conflict. Being sensitive to the approval of others, giving way to others' goals rather than defining one's own goals, avoiding conflict, and putting off difficult conversations are perhaps common experiences for many. In times of conflict and heightened anxiety, it is helpful to slow down and think about the role one is playing in the relationship dynamics.

---

9 Ibid., 3

On the flip side of the togetherness force, Bowen describes the temptation to separate oneself from the relationship system as a pull toward the *individuality force* (Kerr & Bowen, 1988, p. 59). Again, awareness of a desire to distance oneself can enable a pastoral leader to gain awareness of their tendency to reactively withdraw or emotionally cut off from others in seasons of conflict. As one pastor commented, "Differentiation of self appealed to me too, because it's about staying in your own skin... It's about being yourself, not bowing to pressure from others or running away and withdrawing when there's conflict."[10]

Effective ministry will be enhanced by an ability to remain calm, to be curious rather than defensive, and to be appropriately flexible and open rather than rigidly enforcing one's own views. In times of conflict it is helpful to consider to what extent one seeks to gain a sense of self over and against others, rather than seeking to express oneself with clarity and humility. An ability to remain connected and non-defensive, to be goal-directed and consistent, yet not rigid, in the face of disagreement with others is valuable in establishing a healthy and sustainable ministry.

Reflective questions for exploring one's role in the system include:

- Am I willing to engage with others who are different to me and to discuss issues with those who may not readily agree with my views?
- In leadership, do I gather together people who are the same as me or am I willing to work alongside a diversity of opinions?
- Is the unity of the church based merely on homogeneity and sameness?

---

10 Ibid., 3

- Am I comfortable enough in my own skin that I can sit with the strong reactions of others without prematurely acting to alleviate their anxiety as well as my own?
- Do I personalise others' responses and feel I have lost solidarity with them when they disagree with me?
- Do I fail to take a stand when I fear other people's reactions?
- Have I taken time to clarify my own goals and priorities rather than allowing the goals and priorities of others to shape my actions?

Overfunctioning and underfunctioning

Bowen theory emphasises the reciprocal nature of relationships within an emotional system and encourages individuals to consider their own role and contribution within it. As one understands the automatic, emotionally reactive ways in which they tend to respond to relationship tension, it becomes more possible to exercise calmer, more mature, and less reactive ways of interacting. One example of the reactive interplay between people is the notion of *overfunctioning* and *underfunctioning*:

> The overfunctioning person is typically one who feels responsible for the emotional well-being of others and who works to compensate for perceived (real or imagined) deficits in their functioning. The underfunctioning person, on the other hand, feels dependent on the overfunctioning one to do things that they feel reluctant or unable to do themselves. (Kerr & Bowen, 1988, p. 56)

For people in pastoral roles, the temptation to overfunction is a very real one. As a "helping" profession, pastors may be tempted in their helping efforts to take responsibility for other people's decisions, experiences, thoughts, and feelings: "Overfunctioning is a really big concept for me… in terms of the church context, where I feel like I'm not doing enough. But I've been challenged to ask myself, 'Is that a valid belief or is it your own expectations of yourself and are you overfunctioning?' Maybe people don't see you that way, or they shouldn't see you that way but you have taken it upon yourself."[11]

Perceived and real expectations from church members can compound a pastoral worker's tendency to overfunction. In managing the expectations of other people and oneself, it can be helpful to consider that personal expectations are often linked with one's experiences growing up in one's family. Our family background shapes the way we manage others' expectations of us and also influences the kinds of expectations we have of self and others. Individuals will therefore vary in the level of sensitivity they have in interpersonal expectations. Understanding these variations and the part that family background plays can help those in pastoral ministry to be less reactive to expectations and can encourage a more observant, thoughtful consideration of the various factors that may be at play in these interactions and perceptions.

One minister commented, "I think church family expectations contribute to [burnout], and particularly as a single person some people thought nothing of ringing me at six o'clock in the morning when a kid was sick or they needed something to happen. They wouldn't ring the senior pastor because he has his own family."[12] Another worker added: "That's been a new thing for me, not giving everyone everything. Actually thinking, no, they need to stand on their own feet and they need to work things out…so now, I consider what is in this person's best interests, because I've invested a lot in a lot of people, and they haven't shown much response, so I need

---

11 Ibid., 3
12 Ibid., 3

to be careful [my motivation is] also not coming from laziness or tiredness."[13] Managing expectations and demands from church members were a significant issue for all those interviewed and particularly so for those who were single.

The tendency to measure one's success on outcomes that are bound up in other people's choices can cause pastoral leaders to overfunction in their role and to assume responsibility for the attitudes and actions of others. As one pastor said:

> The Bible calls us shepherds and we will be held to a higher standard and so you have to balance that off with what you are responsible for and what people are responsible for. So when they are not wanting to meet with me or when they are rejecting the gospel, it's not about me, it's about their relationship with Jesus, it's not about my performance as a ministry worker. I had a very large sense of over-responsibility, so thinking about differentiation of self really helped with that, in not taking responsibility for others and that took years of practice... It was really helpful in me being responsible for myself, my responses and my emotions, my reactions and allowing other team members to be responsible for themselves too.[14]

The perception of one's own efficacy and success in ministry can easily become linked to the way other people respond to Christ and whether or not others appear to be maturing in their faith: "It's tempting to judge the efficacy of your job by outcomes that are largely out of your control... did this person become a Christian? Is this person still attending Bible study?... It's tempting to think

---

13 Ibid., 3
14 Ibid., 3

it's your own fault and that someone else could be doing a better job."[15] Leadership maturity involves an ability to trust God for his outcomes and to expect that real life change will come from the power of God's word through the Spirit, rather than from one's own hard work, capabilities, and skills.

Healthy and sustainable ministry will require a commitment to knowing self and others. Helpful questions for leaders to ask themselves might include:

- What am I getting out of my helping role?
- Am I able to sit with others' discomfort or do I rush in to rescue and alleviate their (and my own) distress?
- Is my involvement with this person helping or hindering their ability to take responsibility for themselves and to make mature, authentic decisions?
- Am I more invested in this person changing than they are?
- How do I define my own success in my ministry?
- Am I looking to outcomes that are out of my control in order to define my success or usefulness?

Conclusion

This paper has explored the ways in which Bowen theory, and more specifically how the concept of differentiation of self, can be usefully applied to assist with the practice of healthy and sustainable ministry in the local church. As pastoral workers who are broken sinners ministering to and with people who are also broken sinners, there is likely to be a frequent sense of disconnect between the biblical models of the church as a place of love, unity, and service and the functional reality that we observe day

---

15 Ibid., 3

by day on the ground. Burnout is sadly a common experience for ministry workers as they struggle to manage the complex realities of local church ministry. Differentiation of self involves ongoing self-reflection and a willingness to confront the gaps in one's own maturity, and the repeated work of seeking to manage oneself differently in relationships. As is the case with spiritual maturity, emotional maturity is a lifelong project and one that, thankfully, is undergirded by the precious truth of the gospel—we are broken, flawed sinners who are immensely loved, wholly accepted, and thoroughly forgiven by God through the death and resurrection of the Lord Jesus, and transformed by the sanctifying work of the Holy Spirit as we seek to serve him.

References

Bowen, M. (1978) *Family therapy in clinical practice.* New Jersey: Aronson.

Clowney, E. (1995) *The church: Contours of Christian theology.* Leicester: Intervarsity Press.

Duncan, J. L. and Hunt, S. (2006) *Women's ministry in the local church.* Wheaton, Crossway Books.

Friedman, E. (1985) *Generation to generation: Family process in church and synagogue.* New York: Guildford Press.

Galindo, I. (2009) *Perspectives on congregational leadership: Applying systems thinking for effective leadership.* New York: Educational Consultants.

Green, C. (2013) *The message of the church.* Nottingham: InterVarsity Press.

Horton, M. (2011) *The Christian faith: A systematic theology for pilgrims on the way.* Grand Rapids: Zondervan.

Kerr, M.E & Bowen, M. (1988) *Family evaluation*. Ontario: Penguin Books.

Nouwen, H. (2006) *The dance of life: Weaving sorrows and blessings into one joyful step:* Notre Dame: Ave Maria Press.

Richards, L. and Hoeldtke, C. (1980) *A theology of church leadership.* Grand Rapids: Zondervan.

Richardson, R.W. (1996) *Creating a healthier church.* Minneapolis: Fortress Press.

Richardson, R.W. (2005) *Becoming a healthier pastor: Family systems theory and the pastor's own family.* Minneapolis: Fortress Press.

Saundercock-Brown, H. (2008) *To burnout or not to burnout?: An examination of burnoupreventionstrategieswithAustralianministers.* Availableat australianclergyfamilies.com/clergy resources.

Steinke, P. (2006) *Congregational leadership in anxious times.* Maryland: Rowman and Littlefield.

Van Gelder, C. (2000) *The essence of the church.* Grand Rapids: Baker Books

Volf, M. (1997) *After our likeness: The church as the image of the Trinity.* Grand Rapids: Eerdmans.

Section 3

WORKING IN CHRISTIAN MINISTRIES
DURING ANXIOUS TIMES

Chapter 10

CONFLICT RESOLUTION IN THE WORKPLACE
A Case Study on Using Bowen Theory in Collaboration with the Bible

Craig Foster

Introduction

This paper investigates the effectiveness of using Bowen theory and the Bible in seeking to resolve difficult relationships in the workplace. It draws on a personal experience and records my efforts to use Bowen theory and the Bible to help resolve some difficult workplace relationships. I experienced these difficult relationships while working in a Christian organisation. In seeking to resolve these difficulties I developed seven steps guided by my understanding of Bowen theory. I also sought to ensure that these steps sat under the authority of God's word. It is hoped that this paper will demonstrate how Bowen theory can be helpfully used alongside the Bible in seeking to resolve workplace conflict.

The development of seven steps used for growing in difficult relationships

Conflict is part of every organisation—Christian and secular. Prior to joining this organisation, I had not experienced any significant workplace relationship difficulties. However, things were to change for me in this Christian organisation. I would describe the organisation as having a strong hierarchical and non-consultative approach to decision making. I was at the middle management level and began to experience some difficult relationships. As time progressed I sought to put on my Bowen theory hat and try to understand what was going on in the relationship systems of the organisation. In the process I developed a set of steps derived from Bowen theory that assisted me to manage myself more maturely in the midst of workplace tensions.

Resolving relationship conflict was always going to be more complex than following a nice neat seven-step process. But for the purposes of helping myself, I developed the following seven steps in seeking to manage myself in these difficult relationships. Unfortunately, I was not always able to follow them as closely as I would have liked, but they became a helpful guide for me nonetheless.

Step 1 – Thinking through difficult relationships

Roberta Gilbert, in her observations of organisations and groups using Bowen theory, says:

> Watching for process is complex but fascinating. It involves watching for as many parameters and patterns of functioning of the self and others in the system as possible—over as much time as possible… as one observes thoughts, feelings, and behaviour as they move

in a group of related people, and even within the self, one can often see repetitions. (Gilbert, 1992, p. 33)

Gilbert observed how when a group is relatively calm, hierarchical behaviour is less evident and individuals treat each other more as equals; rank being less obvious and important to the group. In the heat of a battle, however, hierarchical rank often becomes very important (Gilbert, 2006, p. 57). I noted that things were never stable or calm for long in this organisation. Things were always changing and those lower down the hierarchy experienced what was referred to as "change fatigue".

To begin to understand my work system better I began to gather information about the hierarchy above me. I did this so that I could seek to better understand them and be less reactive to them. Over time I became curious about different aspects of my colleagues' lives and functioning: family sibling position; triangles evident in relationships at work; relationship patterns at work (such as *cutoff, distance, triangles, conflict, under/overfunctioning*); high stressors for these people; and new projects and priorities for different leaders. This may sound intrusive, but my goal was to better understand and empathise with those I worked for. From my own self-observation using a Bowen theory lens, I knew that these things could help me understand the type of leadership and functioning a person adopted at work.

This information enabled me to also see more clearly the relationship patterns that were operating amongst the senior leadership of this organisation. It also enabled me to see how those relationship patterns were impacting upon those further down the hierarchical line. Hence, I could reflect on my own responses to these patterns and shift from negative judgments about leaders to seeing the system and patterns that all were a part of.

Biblical reflection

The Bible is a book that is intimately interested in relationships. We have a Trinitarian God of eternal relationships who created humanity in his image, male and female. God related with humanity and humanity related with each other and it was all "very good" (Gen 1:31) before sin entered the world and made relationships difficult. The great danger of Bowen theory from a biblical perspective is that one may seek to improve difficult relationships from a purely selfish motive—it is good for me! Thus, the Bible provides a helpful corrective to this, as it tells us to put others before ourselves, to seek the good of the other and to even love our enemies. The Bible not only provides us with a helpful corrective but provides us with God's definition of love: "This is love: not that we loved God, but that he loved us and sent his Son as an atoning sacrifice for our sins" (1 John 4:10). This is obviously a fundamental truth and a great starting point for Christians, as we seek to be a blessing to the organisations and the relationships of which we are a part.

Step 2 – Thinking through negative feelings – moving from subjective to objective thinking

Bowen theory argues that the emotional system is counterbalanced by the intellectual system in a human. When an individual is threatened, the emotional system tends to override the intellectual system. Being a differentiated person refers to the ability to distinguish thoughts from feelings and to choose between being guided by one's intellect or one's emotions. In contrast, a poorly differentiated person tends to be more emotionally reactive, finding it difficult to maintain calm in response to the emotionality of others. They tend to make subjective decisions based on what "feels right"; in short, they are trapped in an emotional world (Kerr & Bowen, 1988, p. 320).

With this understanding, I found it helpful to give expression to my feelings and try and move my thinking more towards objectivity. The way I went about this was as follows:

i) Subjective feelings in the relationship

I observed that repeated patterns had occurred in each of my difficult relationships. I had a feeling of no input into decisions that were directly impacting me and my area of responsibility; I had a feeling that my view was not being heard or valued; I had a feeling that some decisions were not fair and reasonable; I had a feeling that favouritism was being used in decision making; and I had a feeling that my theology and belief priorities were different to some of those I reported to.

ii) Seeking to be more objective about my feelings

Next, I wanted to explore if those feelings were a reality or if they were my imagination at work. What I learnt as I explored these feelings was that these people had said "no" to several of my ideas and suggestions and I did seem to have different theological views and priorities to these people. Thus, there did seem to be some objective facts behind my feelings, although it was still hard for me to know for sure how accurate my feelings were.

iii) Some preliminary conclusions about my feelings

I wanted to analyse the situations further to consider if the feelings were driven by deeper factors. From my research it did appear that different theological priorities were causing clashes for me. These differences in theological priorities became more evident in times of business stress, where the decisions made, and the money spent, showed me where a person's real priorities appeared to lie.

This step was considered helpful for my thinking process. However, it was still explorative, and I wanted to think through specific examples in detail before I could make any concrete conclusions.

Biblical reflections

Relationships and emotions were "very good" in the beginning of creation. However, as sin entered the world (Gen 3), relational and emotional breakdown occurred at every level. In a post Genesis 3 world, our emotions are a mixture of good and bad. So, it becomes important for us to look behind our emotions and study the facts as well to know what is really going on. Back in Genesis 3 when Adam and Eve sinned for the first time, God did not ask them how they were feeling. He asked them about the facts: "What is this you have done?" (Gen 3:13). To me, this indicates that God wants us to look at our actions and consider how we have sinned against him and others. This is not to say that our feelings and emotions are not important, but it's important to get beyond our feelings to the facts—"The purposes of a person's heart are deep waters, but one who has insight draws them out" (Prov 20:5). Thus, Bowen theory's encouragement of objectivity about situations aligns itself well with the Bible's approach where finding the truth is a priority.

Step 3 – Thinking through specific examples

It is one thing to say that objectivity is important, but it is still a challenge to get behind the emotions to the real facts. Sometimes we are aware that our thinking has been altered by feelings and emotions, but often we are not (Kerr & Bowen, 1988, p. 60). Kerr (1988) states:

> The human intellect is capable of observing nature objectively, but the intellect is vulnerable to losing that objectivity. While the capacity for objectivity is theoretically always present, it is often acutely and even chronically overwhelmed by emotional and feeling process. (p. 32)

With this understanding of Bowen theory, I decided to list specific examples of the difficulties I had encountered with these people and how I had responded. I wanted to make sure that I was not imagining things and that there were specific examples of difficulty. As I analysed specific examples, I sought to consider the relationship and communication patterns at work in these examples. I was encouraged to ask questions such as: What was the situation? Where did it take place? How did things start? What happened next? How did I react? What did I do? How did they respond? Where did things end up? What thoughts did they have about their part in it?

In these examples I was trying to work out what Bowen theory relationship patterns were observable at work in these difficult relationships (e.g., cutoff, fusion, distance, triangles, under/overfunctioning). Through these questions I was able to pinpoint more clearly what was making these relationships difficult. For example, I discovered that in each case I had allowed distance to grow in the relationship. Although this distance helped alleviate the emotional intensity for me in the short term, it intensified it over the longer term. I was learning that it was far more helpful to deal with the little conflicts along the way than to wait to deal with the bigger conflicts they grew into down the road.

Biblical reflection

The unhealthy relationship patterns Murray Bowen observed in families through his decades of research (distance, fusion, under/overfunctioning, triangles, distance, and conflict) are all at work in Genesis 3. In Genesis 3, as sin enters the world, humanity hides from God and cover up from each other (distance), man blames woman (fusion, triangling, and underfunctioning), the woman blames the devil (fusion, triangling, underfunctioning), bearing and raising children has become cursed (all patterns operating), the husband/wife relationship becomes difficult (all patterns), and mankind is sent from the garden away from God's presence (distance and cutoff).

Thus, much of the relational and emotional patterns of dysfunction addressed in Bowen theory are understood as outworkings of the fall in Genesis 3; that is, the problem of forfeiting the conditions of relationship with the creator, God. However, as Bowen theory does not see rejection of God (sin) as humans' fundamental problem, it may lead to dangers such as viewing intergenerational family history as the source of our problems or seeking to resolve broken relationships for purely selfish reasons (i.e., to make me feel better) rather than because God requires it of us (Matt 22:37-40).

Step 4: Consider what they are dealing with in me as well as what I am dealing with in them (see the co-contribution)

In relationship difficulties individuals often push each other to the limits. One person feels rejected or not listened to, while the other is oversensitive to disharmony or confrontation so they withdraw or at least show no surface reaction to interactions with this person. This pursuing and withdrawing pattern can intensify until the one who feels rejected and ignored finally explodes. Kerr observes that:

> Helplessness and bossiness feed on each other, pushing two people in a relationship to extreme positions neither really wants. Even though the bossy overfunctioning person is often perceived by himself as "strong" and the helpless underfunctioning person as "weak", both people seek emotional support and acceptance with about the same intensity. (1988, p. 122)

At this stage of my research, I was becoming clearer on what the issues were. I had managed to regulate the strength of my feelings and emotions. I had come a long way along the path of objectivity. In this step I wanted to take a further step back and consider what I was bringing to the situation and what they were bringing to the situation. This step involved some hard personal thinking for me which resulted from answering the following two questions:

i) **Observation of "self"—What are they dealing with in me?**
What is my possible sin in this? What is my possible emotional immaturity in this? What kind of people do I generally conflict with? What are my natural response patterns when dealing with those I disagree with (cutoff, distance, conflict, over/under function, triangle with a third party, etc.)?

What I found especially fascinating and humbling was that I seemed to be having difficulties with a certain type of personality and often responded to them in a predictable manner. The people I tended to struggle with were: strong authoritarian people who had been an eldest or an only child in their families, who were perhaps used to getting their way. What was interesting for me was how my difficult relationships in the workplace were replicating the difficult relationship patterns I experienced in my own family of origin while growing up. In my family, I struggled to deal well with a strong authoritarian parent in my pre-teen years and a sometimes-bossy older sibling. I would either distance myself from them or blow up at them when they pushed me too far.

ii) **Observation of "other"—What may they be bringing to the situation?**
With this knowledge I began to explore the same questions for the other person: What appears to be their contribution to the relationship angst? What is their particular expression of self-interest and pride? What kind of people do they generally conflict with? What are their probable standpoints in these situations? What are their natural response patterns when dealing with these people?

This was helpful as it gave me a genuine appreciation for where they were coming from and it helped take the edge off my emotions and angry judgments. I also observed that I was not the only one who had a difficult relationship with these people. This highlighted to me that there are always two sides to a relationship difficulty. I noticed that some of the leaders would distance from their difficult relationships and form triangles with others to gain strength. This demonstrated to me the distancing and triangle patterns that were at work amongst the senior leadership of the organisation, which made it difficult for those lower down to be heard. I could see more clearly how the strong hierarchical structure of this organisation was contributing to me being "done in" by the system. However, I could also see that my sensitivities and distancing pattern contributed to me being more done in than was necessary.

Biblical reflection

The Bible is particularly useful at this step as one of the characteristics of God's word is that it helps reveal our sin (Rom 7:7). The Bible enables us to analyse our thoughts and heart at a deep level and consider if they are righteous or sinful. Many Bible passages encourage such an analysis of our heart. James chapters 3 and 4 is very challenging and confronting with respect to our inner motives:

> For where you have envy and selfish ambition, there you find disorder and every evil practice. But the wisdom that comes from heaven is first of all pure; then peace-loving, considerate, submissive, full of mercy and good fruit, impartial and sincere. Peacemakers who sow in peace reap a harvest of righteousness. (Jas 3:16-18)

These verses challenge us to consider the envy and selfish ambition that may be at work in our own heart. Jesus also warns us about the danger of being hypocrites and to take the plank out of our own eye before taking the speck of sawdust out of our brother's eye (Matt 7:3-5). Although Bowen theory is a great tool to help identify unhelpful relationship patterns it does not encourage one to look at the underlying sin behind our unhelpful relationship patterns. The Bible leads to the deepest change possible, as it commands us to repent of our sins if we are to experience true forgiveness and peace with God, and assures us of the Holy Spirit's work in changing us as we turn to Jesus Christ in repentance and faith.

Step 5 – Reflecting upon differentiation of self in difficult relationships

Bowen theory's concept of differentiation of self "involves the ability to remain emotionally present, engaged and non-reactive in emotionally charged situations, whilst simultaneously expressing one's own goals, values and principles" (Wright, 2009, pp. 29-41).

This is a constructive posture to aim for in the face of conflict. Roberta Gilbert (2006) uses the terms *separate*, *equal*, and *open* to help explain what differentiation of self looks like in practice. Here is a summary of Gilbert's points:

- Being separate emotionally from the other, where there is no need to take responsibility for the other's emotions, since each is responsible for self. However, the relationship is not without sensitivity and awareness of the other's state.
- Being equal in postures towards the other, where each person does not overfunction or underfunction for the other. However, equal partners accommodate each other

and may divide up labour or tasks according to interests and ability.
- Being open in communication with the other, where there is nothing people can't talk about. It is based on integrity and honesty, often referred to as *transparency*. Remembering that you are not seeking to change the other, only to share your experiences and perspective and encourage a more open communication about them. (Gilbert, 2006, pp. 81-83)

To grow in differentiation of self and become separate, equal, and open in our relationship difficulties may seem like an impossible task. However, Bowen theory points out that although differentiation of self probably changes little over a lifetime, any change in one person will eventually be matched by others. This means that even a small amount of change dramatically affects relationships. This was a liberating discovery for me working in a large organisation full of change and stress—that as the self modifies its part, the other will modify their part. To be a calm self in one part of the system can have a helpful impact on the entire system. To put it visually: it can have a "gentle ripple-like effect of a pebble thrown into a pond", or aromatically: "the pleasing aroma of freshly brewed coffee wafting down the office hallways."

Biblical reflection

One of the potential dangers with Bowen theory for the Christian is equating differentiation of self with godliness. This is because there may be some people who have high differentiation of self but who are also highly arrogant towards God and others. Thus, Christian practitioners of Bowen theory need to be wary of inadvertently turning differentiation of self into a mark of godliness. As with all psychological systems apart from God there is a danger of making self an idol and seeking change for selfish reasons rather than for God's glory.

Bowen theorists are not unaware of the danger of selfishness in applying Bowen's theory. Kerr helpfully warns:

> Everybody proclaims the importance of being a "self", but much of what is done under that rubric is selfish and fails to respect others. Many so-called "I positions" are really attempts to get others to change or are attempts to pry oneself loose from emotionally intense situations. (Kerr & Bowen, 1988, p. 108)

Step 6 – The conversation plan

Bowen theory reminds us of the importance of staying in contact and not distancing from those we are having difficulty with, as an important way of working on oneself. Roberta Gilbert (1992) has this to say about meaningful contact in relationship difficulties:

> The range of possibilities for contact open to human beings is extremely large, ranging from conversations that can last hours to something as brief as a pull on a pigtail. However, just a small attempt to make contact with the other person on a regular basis can put a distance back on track. (p. 59)

Unfortunately, I had let distance and tension creep into my difficult relationships. So, I resolved to address this pattern by initiating special meetings with these people to connect and try to resolve things. This was not easy for me and produced significant stress in me before the event; however on each occasion, it was a very helpful meeting. The relationship ideas raised in Step 5 around the markers of differentiation of self were functionally achieved in those meetings. Next time, my goal is to make sure I don't let distance build for too long, as I discovered the extent to which it had increased the tension over time!

Conflict Resolution in the Workplace

For the meetings organised I went to the trouble of constructing a conversation plan, as I wanted to make sure I was clear in my thinking. I wanted to ensure my emotions would not take over and I remain objective. Thus, I developed the following conversation scaffold:

- Pray, Pray, Pray
- Connect warmly and lovingly with this person
- Express my own experience and perspective (I position)
- Summarise the important thing I wanted to make sure I communicated
- Acknowledge that I had contributed my part
- Value being able to hear their perspective
- Seek to be separate, equal, and open throughout the conversation
- Consider what good and bad conversation directions may look like and how I would like to respond in each case.

Biblical reflection

Jesus in his Sermon on the Mount encourages Christians to be peacemakers (Matt 5:9) and it is important for the Christian to consider what this may look like in each difficult relationship. The Bible also encourages us to not run away from our difficult relationships but to move towards others in love and forgiveness, even our enemies (Matt 5:44). In the conversation step, wisdom is vital, and the book of Proverbs helpfully warns: "A fool's mouth lashes out with pride, but the lips of the wise protect them" (Prov 14:3).

In Step 6, I found prayer to be particularly helpful. I did not like conflict and preferred to avoid it, but to be able to commit my anxieties to a loving Father in heaven was an incredible help and tension reducer for me.

Step 7 – Review the possible conversation outcomes

In this final step, it was helpful for me to remember that we can't get very far in trying to change others. In Bowen theory the focus is always on changing self, not the other. Thus, it was helpful for me to be realistic about the possible outcomes of this conversation. As the person taking "the conflict issue" to the other person there were a few broad possibilities I was aware of:

- Possibility 1 - I may not have had all the correct information or have understood the situation correctly; and I may need to change my position
- Possibility 2 - I may have had all the correct information and have understood the situation correctly; and the other person or both of us is prepared to change positions
- Possibility 3 - I may have had all the correct information and have understood the situation correctly; but the other person is not prepared to change their position.

With respect to the third possibility there may be a mature and an immature response to dealing with the differences, and the disappointment of no change occurring. What is mature and what is immature will obviously vary depending on the context and the specific situation. For instance, in one context it might be mature to back down, while in another it might be immature to back down for the sake of, say, "comfortable harmony". What maturity and immaturity looks like in different situations can be very difficult to work out. It is always a challenge to tolerate difference and think about what an emotionally mature response might be in an emotionally charged situation. Bowen theory points a person towards working on the part that is within their responsibility to give a positive resolution a chance. Step seven for me was clearly the most difficult step. Sometimes I got it right and sometimes I got it wrong. It is all part of the lifetime growing up process, of seeking to become a more mature and Christlike person in how we respond to others.

Biblical reflection

The Bible helpfully reminds us that we can't change another. For a Christian this is a great relief to know that it is God's Spirit who causes real and lasting change. It is right for Christians to approach a fellow Christian if we think they have or are sinning against us. We firstly go on our own seeking to clarify and resolve things, then with two or three if they do not listen to us, and finally we tell it to the church if they still do not listen (Matt 18:15-20). The slow and deliberate process of dealing with difficulties here reminds us of the importance of having the humility to consider that we may not have rightly observed and interpreted the other person's actions: "Pride goes before destruction, a haughty spirit before a fall" (Prov 16:18). The Bible also reminds us of the complexity of resolving disagreements. Jesus says in the Sermon on the Mount to "turn to them the other cheek also" (Matt 5:39) but we need to consider when this response is wise and when it is unwise. As an example, Proverbs chapter 26 verse 4 says "do not answer a fool according to his folly" but the very next verse says, "answer a fool according to his folly" (Prov 26:5). Also, we know from Jesus' response to conflict situations, that sometimes he accepted the lies and insults of others, while on other occasions he stood his ground and defended himself, risking his very life. Thus, it is clear from the Bible that much wisdom, prayer, counsel, and godliness is required in resolving conflict, and there are often no simple clear-cut answers to follow.

However, the Bible does guide us very helpfully as we get into the nitty gritty of speaking with those with whom we are having difficulty: "Do nothing out of selfish ambition or vain conceit. Rather, in humility value others above yourselves, not looking to your own interests but each of you to the interests of the others. In your relationships with one another, have the same mindset as Christ Jesus" (Phil 2:3-4).

Conclusion

To conclude, relationship difficulties are never quickly fixed. My experience was that these difficult relationships did not suddenly become rosy. I had to keep working at them. Distance and tension always seemed to want to creep back in. Some helpful questions for me to continue thinking through were:

- How can I stay in good contact with this person?
- How can I resist detouring tension to a third party and thus avoid triangles?
- How can I stay responsible for representing myself with this person and not seeking to change the view of the other?

I also had to keep remembering that personal growth in the Bible is the result of God's grace and the working of the Holy Spirit. Yes, my self-discipline and effort were important according to the Bible, but the driving force behind change and growth was God's grace working through his Spirit. As growing in differentiation of self is slow and gradual, so is growing in godliness. We are being transformed into Christ's image from one degree of glory to another (2 Cor 3:18).

References

Gilbert, R. M. (2006). *Extraordinary leadership: Thinking systems, making a difference.* Falls Church, VA: Leading Systems Press.

Gilbert, R. M. (1992). *Extraordinary relationships: A new way of thinking about human interaction*. New York: John Wiley & Sons, Inc.

Kerr, M. E., & Bowen, M. (1988). *Family evaluation: An approach based on Bowen theory*. New York u.a: Norton.

Wright, J. (2009). Self-soothing: A recursive intrapsychic and relational process: The contribution of the Bowen theory to the process of self-soothing. *Australian and New Zealand Journal of Family Therapy (ANZJFT)*, *30*(1), 29-41. doi:10.1375/anft.30.1.29

Chapter 11

DENOMINATIONAL LEADERSHIP INTERVENTIONS IN LOCAL CONGREGATION CONFLICT
The Benefits of a Bowen Theory Perspective

Vivian Grice

I know of no hierarchical executive (bishop, district superintendent, placement co-ordinator) who has ever succeeded in changing a pill into a plum. While religious institutions are often seen as esoteric, they are marvellous institutions for observing family processes. They are on the border between families and workplaces, and are often family businesses.

— (E. Friedman, 2007, *A Failure of Nerve*, p. 3)

Introduction

Where anxiety abounds, triangles much more abound! Leaders are not immune to this automatic response pattern in human emotional systems. Therefore, how leaders manage *self* in the face of anxious congregational situations is important.

Focusing upon Baptist churches in New South Wales and the Australian Capital Territory, this paper explores the value of certain concepts found in Bowen theory that assist leaders to better manage self, especially in the face of anxiety and conflict. Denominational leaders often engage with the complex emotional ecologies that are church communities during times of confusion, crisis, or conflict. At such times of heightened anxiety in these systems, any "interventions" by denominational leaders run the regular gamut of reactive responses inevitably present, both within themselves and within the congregation. While the context for this paper is denominational leadership interventions in local congregation conflict situations, the concepts are valuable for any anxious, conflicted congregation situation in which a minister might be embroiled.

Drawing on Bowen theory and the work of Edwin Friedman in applying the theory to congregations, the paper will argue that Bowen theory provides a useful resource for understanding the dynamics at work in such situations, assisting appropriate leadership responses rather than the automatic reactivity to which we are all prone. It will explore how awareness of three key concepts of Bowen theory—*triangles*, *differentiation of self* and *multi-generational transmission*—can assist the leader to manage their own anxiety in the face of congregational anxiety and conflict and enable pastors to lead with increased clarity. It will illustrate these concepts through a case study of one such intervention. Throughout, the paper will engage with biblical texts, examining how these three Bowen concepts are critiqued by a biblical worldview. I will be writing from my own denominational context as a Baptist, and in my role as a denominational leader consider the issue of how we lead when we, and the congregation we are working in, are conflicted and anxious, and how this crosses denominational boundaries and leadership levels.

Ministers and leadership in anxious contexts

How can ministers and pastoral leaders manage themselves better in situations of congregational anxiety and conflict? Leadership may be very broadly defined as the capacity to influence persons. In this broad sense it is frequently conscious. Leaders *intend* to influence others. So, for instance, when the New Testament speaks about a spiritual gift of leading God's people, it says that it ought to be carried out diligently ("...ὁ προϊστάμενος ἐν σπουδῇ ..." Rom 12:8). Diligence is, for the most part, an attitude that requires conscious development. This is especially so in the dimension of leadership, if for no other reason than because of the temptation of fallen humanity to abuse the power that often comes with leadership.

However, exercised leadership invariably has an unconscious dimension. Bowen theory demonstrates that leaders influence others simply by being part of a common relationship system. We react and respond in patterns and directions of which we are not aware. We may not even intend them. In turn, others tend to respond with automatic patterns of behaviour. This is especially so in anxious times. Therefore, it is incumbent upon any leader who wishes to lead diligently to become increasingly aware of the ways that, both consciously and unconsciously, their involvement in a system and *how* they operate will inevitably influence persons. Further it argues that leaders operate more effectively when we learn to think *systems*. Bowen's understanding of human behaviour as part of relational systems, it can be argued, aligns with biblical perspectives. For instance, Scripture asserts that while we are individually accountable for our behaviour (Ezek 33:1-6; Rom 7:7-25), the influence of wrongdoing has an impact across generations (Deut 5:9)[1], and external forces can tend to squeeze us into their mould (Rom 12:1-2; 1 Pet 1:14).

---

[1] Bowen's multigenerational transmission process viewed from the perspective of God's sovereignty?

Using Bowen theory concepts, Edwin Friedman (2007) writes persuasively of how leaders may function better in the face of anxious systems. Friedman's use of Bowen theory has provided an insightful perspective on leadership, both for me as a pastor and now in my current denominational leadership role.

Specifically focusing on leadership, Friedman gives attention to churches and especially denominational leaders in their interactions with the churches they serve. After designating churches as either *plums* or *pills*, he makes this frank observation:

> The leadership lesson for a new clergy person or executive is that without well-differentiated leadership, the past dysfunctions of a "pill" can make a newly-arrived leader ineffective as well. By contrast, a modest leader in a highly differentiated "plum" congregation can appear to be an effective leader, pushed along by the effective functioning of the congregation. (Friedman, 2007, p. 251)

I concur with this general assessment. Thus, the following sentence bears a great deal of truth: "They [churches] are on the border between families and work-places, and are often family businesses" (Friedman, 2007, pp. 249-251). Many Baptist churches I know, especially family or congregational-sized rural churches, bear out the validity of this assessment.

Background

First, a little background about the ecclesiology of Baptist churches.

- Baptist churches fall into the Free Church stream of ecclesiologies, emerging in the wake of the initial sixteenth century reformation period. In large part, they arose as a reaction against the continuance of the state-church ecclesiologies in post-Luther Europe. They reacted against the principle of *"euis regio, cuius religio"*: "as with region, so religion." They declared freedom of conscience in matters of faith, and autonomy for a church freed from the trammels of control by secular rulers. Churches, they asserted, are gathered, local communities of believers, rather than religious structures imposed by state rulers or hierarchies of bishops.

- As part of this, these churches uphold what they see as a vital principle of governance: congregational government *autonomously* exercised. That is, each church is self-governing. Alongside that however, they also uphold a principle of *association*: churches gather voluntarily into associational connections to carry out mission and other functions. The Baptists are thus less of a "denomination" in the classic sense of the term, and more of an "association" or "union".

- In such an ecclesiology, what do I mean by denominational interventions? By this term in our system, I mean any effort by a denominational leader to become involved in a local congregation for reasons of pastoral discipline, congregational consultation, or conflict resolution, in such a way that the leader interacts with the emotional processes of the congregation. These interventions most frequently occur when anxiety in the system is at a heightened level, forming a basic triangle [2] of which denominational leaders need to be constantly aware: those concerned about an issue—wider congregation—denominational leader.

---

2 On the importance of the concept of triangles in Bowen theory, see Gilbert (2004), chapter 3; Marcuson, (2009), chapter 5.

- Such interventions may be *intentional*, in one of two forms: *formal* and *multilateral*; that is, at the invitation of the church, its pastor, or its wider leadership and with the agreement of the denominational leaders; or *formal* and *unilateral*, which is intervention initiated purely from the denomination's side.

- Interventions may also be *informal*, in both unilateral or multilateral forms. Denominational leaders are continually having informal and incidental interactions with ministers or church leaders, and these are interactions which in some way "intervene" in the emotional processes going on in the congregational system. As Bowen theory predicts, and experience demonstrates, the mere presence of any new person, especially a leader, in any emotional system, will have its impact, causing the system to react in some way.

- Thus, how a denominational leader manages *self* in such interventions will be a determining factor as to whether the intervention will be a blessing or a curse to the struggling congregation.

Three valuable concepts

My experience in local church leadership, confirmed by work as a denominational leader, has persuaded me of the value of Bowen theory concepts for managing my own self in the face of (inevitably interwoven) conflict and anxiety. While there are eight key concepts in Bowen theory, I will attend to just three.

Triangles

The first concept is that of *triangles*. According to Murray Bowen, triangles are an inevitable, automatic relational posture, observable in every human emotional system. They emerge because the triangle is the "smallest stable relationship system"

(Gilbert, 2006, p. 46). Two-person systems (dyads) are inherently unstable, primarily because they cannot manage for long the "anxiety" that inevitably emerges in all human interactions. That is, as people we respond to anxiety in our emotional systems by connecting with person(s) outside the dyad, forming one or more triads. Additionally, an issue may be an anxiety-binder by which the member of a triangle can distance themselves. The connecting with another person to form a triangle dissipates the anxiety from the original relational dyad, helping to return it to "balance". However, because anxiety is "catching", triangles frequently multiply and interlock.

In that it accurately reflects the human condition, Scripture provides us with instances of rebarbative triangles in situations of anxiety. For example, consider the story in Luke 12:13. A man asks Jesus to tell his brother to divide the inheritance with him. The man is in conflict with his brother. Anxiety is heightened. In order to deal with that, rather than work on it by dealing with his brother, the man brings in a third person, Jesus, producing a triangle.[3] Jesus resists being triangled or taking sides and instead tells a parable with a warning against greed that is directed to all listeners. This phenomenon of triangling is faced by all denominational associational leaders who in some way intervene in local expressions of the body of Christ.

So, whether in local church ministry or at a denominational leadership level, the skill I am learning to exercise as a leader is to be in the threesome while minimising being triangled (Friedman, 2007, pp. 242-243). By being triangled, I mean consciously or unconsciously taking responsibility to change the behaviour of persons or fix the relationships of others, apart from myself.

---

3 Jesus, of course, with divine wisdom, refuses to buy into this triangle, rejecting the invitation to intervene.

Rather, it is far more effective to take responsibility for managing my own reactivity in that potential triangle, while not trying to fix the other relationships in it. If it is true, as suggested by Friedman (2006), that triangles in anxious systems tend to transmit stress to the most responsible or motivated member, then there is a high risk that denominational leaders may be more susceptible to this than others. Why do I suggest that? I do so because I suspect that persons who tend to take on levels of overall denominational leadership are possibly those more prone to overfunction; to take on too much responsibility, a tendency commonly arising from sibling position in family of origin, among other factors (Gilbert, 2006, p. 85).[4] In such environments, a drive to overfunction is likely to be valued. Thus, it is likely that denominational leaders, as highly responsible leaders, motivated to see churches function well, are at greater risk of allowing themselves to be triangled-in when they intervene in church emotional systems, if they are not able to attain a sound level of differentiation of self. They may try to fix relationship issues that don't belong to them or take sides and try to do the work of the person or people they feel have been most hard done by.

There are a few other factors that to my mind predispose denominational leaders to being easily triangled:

- First, while all pastors carry the burden of dual responsibilities, denominational leaders frequently particularly struggle with this issue. They are there to support church *and* church leader.

---

[4] A useful introduction to the impacts of sibling position is found in Gilbert, 2006, chapter 7. Sibling position is no determinative for leadership functioning, but it is influential. Gilbert comments, for example, that "The fact that leadership most often comes easily to oldests and onlies does not mean that people in other sibling positions cannot learn to be high-functioning leaders." (Gilbert, *Eight Concepts* …, 2004/2006, p. 98)

- Second, pre-existing relationships with ministerial colleagues heighten the pressure to lose objectivity and move into more automatic responses, especially in conflicted situations, making it easy for the leader to be caught in the emotional process.

- Third, in situations of high chronic anxiety there is an increase the propensity of triangles to form (Friedman, 2006, p. 222). They tend to multiply and interlock. Denominational "interventions" tend to occur more frequently in periods of elevated anxiety: church conflict, clergy moral failure, or periods of transition. Furthermore, there is a strong pull for the leader to quickly get the system back into balance. This, of course, makes the risk of damaging triangling even greater, especially as triangles multiply and interlock.

When I am involved in an intervention, there are two fundamental arenas of triangles to which I have learnt to be alert. The first is the external arena. Examples of such potential triangles might be:

- pastor – board – denominational leader
- senior pastor – associate – denominational leader
- declining congregation – pastor – denominational consultant
- pastor – denominational leader – pastor's spouse
- theology of individual pastor – denominational vision – denominational leader.[5]

So, the list could go on.

---

[5] In Bowen theory, components of triangles are limited to persons. However, other adapters of Bowen theory include issues as part of triangles (for example, Friedman, 2006, pp. 220-221).

Yet there is what I might call an "internal" arena we must keep in view. For I myself bring to any intervention a potential set of pre-existing triangles with which I wrestle. These are drawn from my family of origin and go with me into church relationships:

- my father – self – my mother
- my sibling(s) – self – each of my parents.

From engaging with Bowen theory, I have learnt that one of the tasks of myself as a leader is, in Friedman's words, "to recognise and extricate oneself from relational binds (emotional triangles)" (Friedman, 2007, p. 171). Yet how easily, in the charged, anxious ecologies of many interventions, the sensitivities that I carry with me from my family of origin—who I align with, who I tend to avoid, who I react strongly to—trigger further interlocking triangles with the church system I enter. So, for instance, if an intervention involves dealing with a powerful, senior male leader and I have a fused or cut off relationship with my father, chances are that this will play out in the work of the intervention. My sibling position is also likely to influence my propensity to be triangled in certain situations.

Differentiation of self

A second concept integral to Bowen systems theory that I have found enormously helpful is *differentiation of self*. By differentiation of self, Bowen means the capacity of an individual to be "separate" in the emotional processes of a system, capable of taking a stand, making decisions based on well thought-through and practiced principles grounded in clear values, while staying connected to people relationally.

The Bible likewise values the capacity of a person to respond as an individual, rather than simply react in response to anxious pressures or "group-think" (Prov 1:10-16; Jer 11:18-23;[6] Rom 12:14-20; 1 Tim 4:12). Bowen theory describes the idea of someone taking a clear, differentiated position as an "I" *position*.[7] Unsurprisingly, Jesus is the outstanding exemplar of this high-level response ("You have heard that it was said ... but *I* tell you ..." [emphasis added] Matt 5:21-47).

The greater degree of differentiation of self I can develop, the more I can avoid the *togetherness forces* that tend to promote group-think (Gilbert, 2004/2006, p. 34; 2006, p. 74). The push of the togetherness force increases in power as anxiety rises within a system in which I am working. In my experience, work on myself rather than on others during interventions has meant that I can become a somewhat less anxious presence. I have learnt to work on managing my own anxieties. I try to take on less of the anxieties of others. I have found that I can be more differentiated, avoiding the togetherness push of a system by being curious about it and an analyser of it. By working on my differentiation, it enables me to be connected to people rather than cut them off because they oppose actions in the intervention. It helps me to make more observations and fewer recommendations. It supports my capacity to take a more neutral position rather than take sides.

As I reflect on my current role, an important addition to my leadership repertoire has been a (hopefully) growing capacity to apply family systems theory concepts and skills to my situation. It

---

[6] The prophets of the Old Testament consistently had to stand against anxiety in the systems around them, perhaps none more than Jeremiah. The men of Anathoth who are seeking his life in this text are the very members of his own village community, including, quite probably, members of his own family. He truly had to be differentiated within his family of origin.

[7] Taking an "I" position means being able to take a clear position, make "I" rather than "we" statements, and thus express our values, beliefs, and positions.

has assisted my wellbeing and it has also helped me to be more able to assist the pastors and congregations with whom I interact. I have had to work hard, with greater or lesser success at various times, at managing my own propensity to autonomous, anxious responses. I have sought to do this by practicing four responses:

- working on my differentiation of self: thinking for self while staying in contact with others' thinking
- becoming an *analyst* of the systems in which I find myself
- seeking to remain connected to all members of the potential triangles with which I might be in contact
- acting more as a "coach" than an all-knowing "advice-giver", or superior "superintendent".[8]

Multigenerational transmission

My third selection from the eight key Bowen concepts is the idea of *multigenerational transmission*. Broadly, this is the idea that relationship patterns and habits often repeat in subsequent generations; for example, between parents and their offspring. People move from one generation to the next with similar levels of maturity to their elders. If they are more caught in their parents' anxieties, they will transmit increased anxiety into their own functioning as adults. Similar transmission can play out in congregations across the generations, and tends to mean that patterns persist from generation to generation. Individuals in

---

[8] This is not to ignore the fact that there are some situations, especially in the areas of moral failure or abuse, where acting as a "coach" in the system is an insufficiently biblical response. While in the Gospels, more often than not, Jesus "coached" people towards the gospel and wholeness (for example in his extensive use of excellent questions), there were occasions where his interventions were far more directive, assertive, and lordly: for instance, in clearing the Temple or dealing with the Pharisees and scribes.

congregations come and go; yet patterns of health and dysfunction seem to repeat across the years, indicating that emotional patterns transcend the generational changes[9].

Awareness of this process has assisted me to be cautious of too quickly assuming a successful intervention has occurred. It alerts me to the fact that patterns can persist across generations in a congregation's history and that it is likely that one intervention is not going to resolve the problems. This awareness is developing within me, and while I am still aware of the transformative power of the Spirit, I am forming a more realistic approach to "success" and "failure", a more longitudinal evaluation of whether patterns have begun to shift, and a deeper appreciation of the energy it takes to facilitate positive, enduring change in the "family" that is a congregation.

Applying Bowen theory to ministry

Of course, it is true that knowing theory does not make one a competent workman. Bowen theory is just that: a theory, though observation-based. It is one approach to human emotional interactions. It is no cure-all for our human foibles wrought by sinfulness, nor a sure leadership approach guaranteeing denominational interventions will be successful. As Kenneth Halstead writes (1999): "Bowen Theory is a valuable tool. But all theories have blind spots and lend themselves to certain tendencies of distortion. Bowen Theory relies heavily on the ability to 'think systems' and gain a high degree of emotional objectivity" (p. 27). This could, erroneously, lead us to overly objective stances and suspicion about any level of empathy as a false means of not

---

[9] In addition to predictable patterns playing out in families as they respond to and manage anxiety, Kerr (2000) discusses how small differences in the levels of differentiation between parents and their offspring play out and present as significant differences in differentiation in family members over multigenerations.

being triangled.

Nonetheless, it has been my experience, as I have stumblingly applied many of the Bowen systems theory concepts, that there have been considerable benefits. One of the major personal benefits has been a reduction in my stress. I still constantly identify with Paul's statement at the end of his "sufferings" boast-list: "Besides everything else, I face daily the pressure of my concern for all the churches" (2 Cor 11:28). Although not made explicit by Paul, one of these pressures is the dilemma of "save the church or save the pastor", forming one of the triangulations faced by denominational leaders.

Yet by working at not assuming responsibility to "fix" a church conflict, by adopting more the stance of a coach, by endeavouring to spot the triangles (especially the ones I am in), by learning about patterns across church generations, by using appropriate humour to try to inject a more jejune atmosphere in anxious systems, by connecting rather than quitting, I discover that I am not so inappropriately burdened, am able to function more effectively, and receive more positive feedback from the interventions undertaken.

You can't always get what you want: A case example of managing self in an intervention

While thinking systems has had positive effects on my self-management in anxious congregations, it does not guarantee positive outcomes. Given the power of systems and our tendency to lose "solid self"[10] when anxious, it can be difficult to successfully apply the concepts of family systems theory "on the run" in highly anxious systems. Additionally, some systems are in such an

---

10 By solid self, Bowen theory refers to that part of "self" which can maintain a differentiated stance within an emotional system while retaining contact with that system.

anxious downward cycle that reversing this is not always possible. The example I use will be of one of the rare instances where I was involved in an intentional, unilateral "intervention".[11] The church was a small, suburban, declining congregation. The decision to unilaterally intervene in this church came at the end of over a year of more distanced efforts at helping the leadership to resolve conflict ostensibly arising from the decision of the long-term pastoral leader to cease his leadership role, move into some kind of "retirement" but stay around in the church "taking care of the nuts and bolts".

The intervention took the form of deciding to have the denominational leadership take control of the church, put a transition team in place, and seek to resolve the issues so that a healthy transition to a new pastor could occur. The result, after an eight-month intervention, was that the system ejected the denominational transition team; the nascent division in the church became a full-blown split; the exiting pastor suffered two major health issues; he then fought back to resume control of the remnant congregation, staying on to mentor a new and inexperienced pastor appointed by the much-reduced congregation. Since then, a new leadership dismissed that pastor, ceased to function, and the church closed with invited help from the Baptist Association.

Embedded in the emotional system of the church was a plethora of multiplying, interlocking triangles. The primary triangle was the pastor, a group that supported him, and a group that opposed him, but as anxiety in the system rose to fever pitch these triangles multiplied to members of the pastor's family, various others in the congregation,

---

11 Once again, by intervention, I mean any effort by a denominational leader to become involved in a local congregation for reasons of pastoral discipline, congregational consultation, or conflict resolution, in such a way that the leader interacts with the emotional processes of the congregation.

and then externally as denominational personnel intervened. Other members of triangles who interlocked in quick succession included:

- the pastor's wife
- myself
- individuals in the church supportive of the pastor
- individuals in the church opposed to the pastor
- other Baptist Association leaders
- one daughter of the pastor
- a prospective new pastor
- external members of a Transition Team appointed by the Association.

The various trigger issues behind the triangling process were:

- the sensitivity towards the long-term pastor of over thirty years
- his semi-retirement
- the elders' exhaustion
- the pastor's wife's illness and emotional reactivity
- my pre-existing friendship with the pastor
- issues connected to a coffee shop run by the church
- the financial losses of a key ministry run by the pastor's wife
- denominational processes
- previous divisions in the church's history around the pastor's leadership style
- differences in my theology of leadership and the pastor's theology of leadership.

The list could go on. Triangles multiplied and interlocked in dizzying fashion. All the accompanying symptoms of a highly anxious system (prone to chronic anxiety but now in acute anxiety) appeared: blaming, name-calling, secrecy, division into groups, sabotage, etc. And the situation was not helped because I failed to retain a level of emotional objectivity. I allowed myself to be triangled into the internal conflicts to an unhelpful degree, over-functioning by endeavouring to "rescue" the congregation. I also underestimated the power of multi-generational transmission; that is, the capacity of emotional processes to be repeated across time.

At one point, in discussing the situation with my professional supervisor I had to accept that this was not my fight. He conveyed to me something along the lines of, "They'll just have to have their fight." And they did! The church fractured. In doing so, it "spat out" the denominational intervention, so to speak, seeing it as the "identified patient". My analysis of the situation is that because of poor leadership the system did not have a sufficiently strong "immunological" response to deal with the pastor when he turned "viral"[12], caught as he was in multiple triangles between his wife, his retirement, its threat to his wife's role and standing, the elders, his declining health, and splits in the past (multi-generational transmission).

This failed intervention provided a salutary lesson to me of a few implications that flow from Bowen theory. First, I need to work hard at spotting triangles, but get triangled less. When as a leader I assume responsibility for keeping a system together it is a

---

12 For the metaphor of less differentiated people in anxious systems operating like a "virus" needing a host or a pathological response in the system, see Boers, 2002, p. 19 and Worksheet: Unhealthy Responses to Difficult Behaviours; Friedman, 2007, pp. 134-147; and Steinke, P., 2006, chapter 6.

dangerous position to take (Friedman 2007, p. 221). Second, I need to work more on my differentiation of self. Third, my experience reinforced to me the truth that we cannot change a relationship of which we are not directly a part. Fourth, it illustrated that triangles persist over time, and that the same relational patterns can re-emerge with different issues.

Bowen theory continues to offer very helpful insights about my own functioning in anxious human systems, especially when I am in a leadership role. By its very nature, pastoral or denominational leadership regularly thrusts their incumbents into anxious systems. It is part of the calling. However, in my experience, an ongoing commitment to learning Bowen theory and practicing it through working on one's own self in the midst of anxiety; seeking to increase (even if only incrementally) one's solid self; and being a curious observer of the system in which one finds oneself, and of one's self in that system, all increase the capacity to be a more differentiated self,[13] and so better serve that system rather than be subsumed into its automatic emotional processes.

References

Boers, A. (2002). *Never call them jerks: Healthy responses to difficult behaviour.* VA, USA: Alban Institute Herndon

Friedman, E. (1985). *Generation to generation. Family process in church and synagogue.* New York: The Guildford Press.

Friedman, E. (2007). *A failure of nerve: Leadership in the age of the quick fix.* New York: Seabury Books.

---

[13] "An organism tends to function best when its 'head' is well differentiated." (Friedman, 1985, p. 221)

Gilbert, R. (2006). *Extraordinary leadership: Thinking systems, making a difference.* Virginia, USA: Leading Systems Press, Falls Church and Bayse.

Gilbert, R. (2006). *The eight concepts of Bowen theory: A new way of thinking about the individual and the group.* Virginia, USA: Leading Systems Press, Lake Frederick.

Gilbert, R. (2014). *The cornerstone concept in leadership, in life.* Virginia, USA: Leading Systems Press, Lake Frederick.

Halstead, K. (1999). *From stuck to unstuck: Overcoming congregational impasse.* USA: The Alban Institute.

Kerr, M. (2000). *One family's story: A primer on Bowen theory.* Retrieved from The Bowen Center for the Study of the Family website http://www.thebowencenter.org on 26/10/2018.

Marcuson, M. (2009). *Leaders who last: Sustaining yourself and your ministry.* New York: Seabury Books.

Steinke, P. (2006). *Congregational leadership in anxious times: Being calm and courageous no matter what.* VA, USA: Alban Institute, Herndon.

Chapter 12

BOWEN IN LEADERSHIP COACHING
Walking with Leaders Through Challenging Times

Ken Morgan

This chapter examines differentiation of self in leaders of church congregations. The similarities between Bowen's concept of differentiation of self and Paul's idea of Christlike maturity are first explored. Core aspects of Bowen's concept of differentiation are reflected upon in light of the apostle Paul's injunctions to the early church. This lays the groundwork to briefly consider challenges facing contemporary churches. Three vignettes will then be presented that consider ministers' work with a leadership coach while leading systems under challenge.

Differentiation, unity, and maturity

Togetherness and separateness

Bowen described human development in terms of a struggle to manage the apparently countering impulses toward togetherness and separateness.

The balance of these two forces is embedded in all multicellular life forms: cells with different functions cooperate for the preservation and procreation of the organism. The collective success depends on cells maintaining their individual biological integrity, defined by their outer membrane and specialised function. The individual success of the cell depends on the differing functions of other cells.

A similar pattern is observed in groups of social animals where the survival and procreation of the individual depends on the survival and procreation of the group, and individuals contribute to and benefit from the collective effort.

The interdependence and interconnectedness of modern human society takes the pattern of cooperative functional specialisation to an even higher degree of complexity. At cellular, familial, societal, and global levels success for the human social mammal depends on maintaining both individuality and cooperation.

Bowen's concept of differentiation may be understood as maintaining individual integrity (adherence to personal principle and purpose) while living in cooperation with the collective.

Unity

A first glance, the apostle Paul might be accused of calling for undifferentiation: togetherness at the expense of individuality. He appeals to his hearers, "…all of you agree with one another in what you say and that there be no divisions among you, but that you be perfectly united in mind and thought" (1 Cor 1:10). However, the context of this passage sheds a different light. The Corinthian church was riven by factions, each claiming allegiance to a particular leader. The energy of the church was being diverted into conflict and away from its purpose. Paul castigated the church for their immaturity (1 Cor 3:1-2).

Later, Paul used the metaphor of the body and the diversity of its members to call the church to embrace and honour functional specialisation (1 Cor 12:4ff). He described a mature church as one where "…each part does its work" (Eph 4:16). Like a multicellular organism, an organisation, or a society, the church must have sufficient alignment of allegiance and effort in order to survive and fulfil its purpose.

Rather than calling on church members to give up thinking for themselves, Paul seems to be calling for commonality of purpose to enable the benefits of functional specialisation to be realised. Otherwise, effort is diffused by division and conflict.

Maturity

Writers in the family systems sphere use the terms *maturity* and *differentiation of self* almost interchangeably; e.g., Friedman (1999), Brown (2012), and Gilbert (2008). Undifferentiation flows from unresolved parental attachment and the extent to which the work of growing away from the parents and into an individual adult remains incomplete (Bowen, 1978, p. 382).

Paul characterises maturity as "attaining to the whole measure of the fullness of Christ", accompanied by "unity in the faith and in the knowledge of the Son of God" (Eph 4:13). Paul describes this state as being steadfast in conviction and speaking the truth in love (Eph 4:15), not "blown here and there" by divergent teaching (Eph 4:14). Maturity includes being clear and stable in what one believes, and able to articulate these convictions with the goal of collective benefit.

In Bowen's thinking and in Paul's teaching, maturity is achieved in community (Eph 4:12-13) rather than in isolation, by individuals fulfilling their responsibilities (Eph 4:12, 16) rather than experts taking responsibility to fix things, and by a multiplicity of functions (Eph 4:11) rather than a single leader "playing messiah" or "repairman".

It seems possible that Bowen and Paul might describe maturity as maintaining personal conviction and individual function in the context of cooperative effort for collective benefit.

Coaching

Bowen preferred to describe himself as *coach* rather than "therapist" to families. Coaching emphasises the agency and capacity of the client, rather than their incapacity and pathology. Whitmore (2006) describes the coach's primary function as helping the client improve their awareness of a given situation, and to clarify their responsibility to act. The coach avoids the posture of the expert charged with rectifying dysfunction, and operates more as a peer-resource, working primarily by asking questions that help the client to gain greater clarity about their current reality and to plot their course of action going forward.

Anxious times, anxious systems, anxious behaviours

Like any other organisation, Christian churches experience elevated levels of anxiety when under challenge. Declining church attendance, widespread incidences of abuse, and public indifference or even anger toward Christianity mean that today's churches face constant and multifaceted challenges. Small congregations are especially vulnerable, facing the imminent prospect of congregational closure due to decline. Church leaders feel intense pressure to respond to these challenges, which necessarily involves leaders attempting to introduce change. Pappas (2000) notes that churches deal with the sacred, and particularly in small churches, congregants tend to unconsciously conflate their ritual experience of the divine with the divinity itself. Tinkering with the worship service feels like tinkering with God and is therefore perceived as sacrilegious. More importantly, change is disruptive to the comforting familiarity the congregants have come to cherish. Ministers find themselves caught between the anxiety produced by impending demise and the anxiety produced by impending change.

Kerr and Bowen (1988) identify four behavioural patterns by which anxious systems deal with the discomfort of anxiety: conflict, distance/cutoff, projection to a third party/triangling, and impairment/under-/overfunctioning reciprocity (Bowen describes these mechanisms under his concept of nuclear family emotional process). While all of these are evident in anxious churches, conflict is universally considered particularly unacceptable in the Christian family.

So in addition to arresting decline without upsetting people's sacred sensibilities, ministers face pressure to soothe the system anxiety, resolve conflicts, create certainty, and restore calm: in Friedman's (1999) terms, to "play repairman". The role of "repairman" can create an impossible load for many ministers who move into overfunctioning in trying to manage the anxiety that belongs to members of the congregation. The perceived relational load can also lead some ministers into distancing and avoidance of the anxious fields within the congregation.

In the fourth chapter of Ephesians, Paul calls for unity of the Spirit through the bond of peace (v. 3). Paul goes on to outline the role of leadership in the church (v. 11) which is to equip the saints for service (v. 12) so that unity may be achieved through maturity, living up to the stature of Christ (v. 13). The minister is therefore further torn between the congregation's expectation to play the repairman who alleviates the congregation's discomfort, and the biblical mandate to lead the congregation into maturity in Christ.

The following coaching case examples illustrate aspects of these dilemmas for ministers and how reflecting on Bowen systems thinking is utilised to navigate particular challenges.

Leadership coaching vignettes

1: The stuck church

There was a time when this church was vibrant, growing, outward-looking, and confident. Its tiny chapel full-to-bursting, the congregation took enormous personal risk to underwrite the construction of a new, distinctive building. It was a golden era, nearly 60 years ago.

Since then the church has suffered decline, an unrealistically ambitious revitalisation plan under a charismatic but reactive minister, a season of conflict, and then an ineffectual priest who spent most of their tenure incapacitated.

Today many of those same congregational leaders from the heyday occupy the offices of the church. They have an intense sense of ownership of the church, and they fear for its future. The building, now anachronistic and deteriorating, has become somewhat "untouchable". To interfere with the smallest detail of its form and structure would somehow invalidate the faith and tradition it houses.

When the current minister commenced with the church, congregational life was marked by conflict. The church was described to the minister as "a group of groups", each mistrusting and blaming the other while quarrelling internally. The smallest changes or the most minor problems were met with over-reaction.

Letters of accusation would sometimes be exchanged between the groups, directly or via the church council, whose meetings were punctuated by name-calling and counter-accusations. Perhaps this church was reminiscent of the Corinthian church to which Paul wrote.

Unsurprisingly, there had been a steady succession of people leaving for more peaceful and purposeful churches. When the minister did not renew the contract of the clearly underperforming children's worker, the leadership were dismayed, fearing that the departure of the children's worker would lead to an exodus of children and hasten the demise of the church.

The minister was in a bind. The parish leadership expected the minister to be the church's rescuer, fixing its problems and securing its future. Yet at the same time they anticipated the worst possible outcome for the minister's decisions, and resisted even the smallest change. The minister's actions and motives were constantly scrutinised: one parish leader openly questioned the veracity of a medical certificate when the minister sought to take sick leave.

When the minister commenced coaching, she began to observe how she had become caught up in the anxious processes of the church, seeking to work harder and harder to meet the expectations of the church leadership. Her instinct was that if the leadership could be reassured of the minister's competence and commitment, they would calm down and cooperate.

As Friedman (1999) points out, drawing from Bowen theory, the results of such anxious efforts are often perverse. The harder the minister tried, the more the leaders expected and suspected. The minister was reaching the limits of her capacity.

The coaching effort

In coaching, the minister explored how her family of origin had primed her for her responses. The symptomatic second child of a distant father and temperamental mother, the minister recalled how, as a five-year-old waiting outside a specialist's office, she had patted her fretting mother's hand in reassurance.

Seeing the parallels between her efforts to calm her mother and her efforts to calm her church, the minister began seeking to pause and think before responding to congregational upset, aiming to get a clearer sense of proportion and priority.

The minister began to observe emotional process, mapping the triangles that became apparent when the congregation became upset, and recognising her own part in the web of collusions and cutoffs.

One church leader was particularly active in the triangling process, frequently coming to the minister claiming to speak for others. The minister noticed her own impulse to jump in and manage whatever particular issue was raised. In coaching, the minister sought to respond with questions, encourage the "envoy" to refer other complainants directly to the minister, and to ask the complainant about their own thoughts on the matter.

In the conflicted leadership committees such as church council, the minister took responsibility for the agenda, holding participants to account for sticking to it. When bickering arose, the minister halted discussion and declared that she would not tolerate such unbecoming behaviour. The minister sought to make clear the responsibilities of the various officers of the church, holding individuals to account for their effective discharge. After surprisingly little push-back, the committees calmed down.

Through study and coaching the minister also reflected on her responsibilities to herself, and began taking intentional "on the clock" time for spiritual disciplines and reflection. She also sought to be more disciplined in taking regular exercise and getting enough sleep, aiming to "bring her best self to work".

While the church remains vulnerable to upset, it has become markedly less conflictual and more focused on its mission and strategy. When reactivity does emerge, it tends to be short-lived and the leaders are quicker to recover their thinking.

2: The widow-maker church

This church at one stage had four clergy in succession die either in office or shortly after leaving. In more recent years, two had left with serious illness after long periods of leave. The church habitually underpaid clergy, made constant comparisons between current and previous incumbents, and employed various means to retain power in the hands of entrenched lay leaders.

The current minister knew all this when she agreed to lead the church two years ago. Having studied Bowen family systems concepts in various contexts over the previous three years, along with a couple of years of coaching, the minister was ready to test her differentiation mettle.

The church comprised two congregations meeting in adjacent suburbs. The "outlier" congregation met in a community centre, was fairly relaxed, and showed some degree of flexibility. The "main" congregation occupied the historic church building and held resolutely to a formal and historic worship structure. The church office bearers were almost entirely drawn from the main congregation. The church showed the typical anxieties about decline and future viability, coupled with the resistance to change described earlier.

The lay leaders jealously guarded their positions with their respective powers and privileges, particularly public roles such as the organist and the choir leader (although the choir was all but defunct). Various factions withheld information and at times refused to communicate altogether. Church council meetings would often descend into shouting matches, showing little regard for due process.

The regulatory framework of the denomination to which this church belongs makes it clear that the minister has final authority in most matters, her power being delegated though the denominational chain of command. However, the prevailing culture of this church was that longstanding influential laypeople dictated terms to the minister.

The coaching effort

The minister entered with a fairly lengthy ministerial career behind her, and thanks to her family systems work in the previous three years, a reasonably good understanding of her position and priming in her family of origin.

The minister was keenly aware that she had in the past shown a tendency to take too much responsibility for the wellbeing of the congregation, functioning somewhat as an "anxiety sink" for the system. In the past this had led to symptoms.

Learning from her study and coaching, the minister entered her new role eager to apply theory. Specifically, the minister sought to:

- Operate by clearly defined guiding principles
- Stay connected to the various individual players
- Be the calmest person in the room
- Focus on issues, not emotionality, no matter how intense
- Direct the leaders toward a long-range vision, choosing the strategic over the reactive.

As the minister began her work, she was shocked at the level of unregulated behaviour in the church, particularly in leadership committees. Sticking to principles, she repeatedly stopped angry exchanges and advised the group that such behaviour would not be tolerated. The minister consciously "girded [her] loins" before each meeting, determined to slow things down, stay calm, and not allow the intensity to tip her into reacting.

After some initial push-back, the committees for the most part "played nice" and the emotional process went "underground". The minister used the period of calm to bring about some significant change that had long been resisted under previous ministers. There was less reaction to the changes than the minister anticipated.

The minister began to teach Bowen theory to the leadership team, even going to the trouble of building a hanging mobile as described by Ron Richardson (2005). For several months the minister hung the mobile above the meeting table as a reminder of the interconnectedness of the congregation. Some of the leaders began to see the benefits of the minister's approach. The minister observed some long-standing hostilities soften. "Calm," observed the minister, "seems to be contagious."

The minister also sought to focus the church's attention on the central ideas of the gospel. Pointing out the gospel's central message of reconciliation, the church's history of dissension and conflict was inconsistent with their foundational ideals. A "reconciliation Sunday" offered opportunity to put old hostilities aside and begin to work together.

Some were not exactly enamoured with the new leadership style, and predictably began to form a coalition around a particular ministry, under the guise of "concern that these people are not receiving appropriate care and attention". Participants were instructed to ensure the minister had no knowledge of their meetings.

Equally predictably, the minister became aware of the meetings. Perceiving the secret meetings as betrayal, the minister's internal reactions were intense. While maintaining a calm exterior, the minister found her own anxiety climbing and symptoms beginning to emerge.

In coaching, the minister was encouraged to make regular and thoughtful individual contact with as many of the participants as possible. Since one was a staff member, the minister decided to directly discuss with them the perceived inappropriateness of their conduct.

The net effect was each participant becoming a little more reflective about their behaviour and how it affected the broader system of the church. Curiously, there were no resignations. The minister effectively sent the anxiety back where it had come from. Relative calm and cohesion were restored.

It is predicted that there will be further eruptions from time to time, gradually becoming less frequent, less intense, and of shorter duration.

3: The judicatory

Although the rate of decline had moderated by the time the new leader was installed, this denominational unit was a shadow of its former self and facing some harsh realities. While there are two small cities and several larger towns in the judicatorial region, the majority of churches are situated in small country towns where the banks and post offices are gone, and schools struggle to attract teachers. Young people leave to study or work and never return. Dwindling and mostly elderly church congregations feel an obligation to their towns to keep their doors open. The remnant of bygone prosperous days, rural churches attract the collective anxieties of the broader township. Church is where people go for nodal events, and lately most of those are funerals.

At a loss as to how to reverse the decline, many clergy simply stopped trying and merely fulfilled the minimal requirements. A common scenario saw the laypeople working themselves ragged maintaining the church and its activities, while the clergy collapsed into depression.

A new leader in any organisation will predictably surface the anxieties of its constituents. Smaller churches feared the incoming leader would shut down financially non-viable churches while others hoped some great revival would restore the church to its former glory. The denominational unit had been subject to stringent scrutiny during the Royal Commission into Institutional Responses to Child Sexual Abuse. Although the previous leader had painstakingly and courageously undertaken to "clean house", there were still some outstanding actions to take, and final responses to be made to the Commission. On top of all this, the judicatory was spending its reserves to pay the bills.

The coaching effort

None of this was news to the incoming leader. In coaching before his commencement, he wrestled with his entrance strategy. Having studied Bowen theory foundations and worked with a coach to apply theory in his previous role, the leader determined to listen well and to define himself: that is, "Help me to understand your situation", and "Here's what you can expect from me".

The leader prioritised preaching and teaching a biblically orthodox gospel and directing the resources of the church toward making disciples. He did nothing to alleviate the fears of those whose churches were marginal, or those who hoped to pursue a "progressive" agenda.

Overall the responses were predictable. Convinced of their worst fears, some distanced themselves, avoiding consultations and not returning calls. Some acted to frustrate progress through subterfuge, others were combative. Some saw the new leader's arrival as an opportunity to open up longstanding disputes, manoeuvring to recruit the leader to their side.

Knowing that these responses were both predictable and largely reflexive—or "mindless" as Friedman (1999) would describe them—the new leader declined to "take the bait", simply stating his own position. The leader saw these responses as opportunities to understand people's position, making no effort to "fix" them.

The new leader quickly determined that some painful decisions could no longer be avoided. There were simply too many non-viable churches drawing on denominational resources. Recognising that working case-by-case would result in endless lobbying, appeals, and ultimately universal dissatisfaction, the leader sought to identify a broadly applicable principle whereby each church could determine for themselves whether they were likely to be slated for closure.

Some longstanding denominational officers watched to see if the new leader meant what he said. Realising that their performance and priorities would soon come under scrutiny, they sought to retire or transition to roles outside of the judicatory. This presented the new leader with several opportunities to recruit new talent—predominantly younger, more energetic leaders aligned to the new agenda.

While the leader worked hard to be outwardly consistent, in coaching he reported wrestling with avoidance impulses, especially toward issues that had potential to upset people. In previous coaching the leader had recognised his tendency to be the broker of peace in his family of origin, with particular sensitivity to calming an easily-upset parent. This awareness helped him to be mindful of his impulses. Using coaching as an accountability structure, he was assisted in being sufficiently disciplined to tackle the "hard stuff".

So far the new leader's efforts to apply Bowen theory have largely gone according to plan, and the responses have been consistent with theory. However, the acid test will be to remain connected and on course in the face of the inevitable reactions to the tough decisions that lie ahead.

Learning reflections

Leaders set the tone

Maturity, both in Bowen's terms and in Paul's, is developed in community. The leader seems to play a disproportionately influential role in determining whether a community acts according to its ideals or out of its undifferentiation. In this regard the primary role of the leader is to work at embodying maturity, which can be understood at least in part by working to differentiate self in the community they're charged to lead.

Learn theory and get a coach

"If you know theory you can apply it, if you don't you can't" says Roberta Gilbert (2006, p. 3). Each of the leaders in the vignettes above sought to learn family systems theory and met with a coach who helped them to reflect and apply their learning.

As one outside the system, the coach is less vulnerable to the system's intensity. Thus the coach is less concerned with the content of any particular issue. With less "skin in the game" the coach can more easily be a resource by maintaining neutrality and keeping an eye on process.

Clarity is more important than empathy

A primary task for the leader is to clarify their own role and responsibilities: this enables the leader to determine where they should and should not invest their energy, and to give their communities a clear idea of what to expect. Such clarity helps to guard against being over-responsible (i.e., overfunctioning) which seems to be a common tendency for ministers.

Clarifying one's own guiding principles, and continually evaluating one's own choices and behaviour in light of these helps to prevent being "sucked into" the herd-like behaviour that characterises systems under challenge.

Clarity enabled leaders in the vignettes above to take clear and thoughtful positions, and to have a basis for holding their ground in the face of push-back reactions.

Know thyself (and thy family of origin)

A leader's vulnerabilities seem to inevitably trace back to priming in their family of origin, particularly the position they occupied in relation to both parents. Awareness of these vulnerabilities and a commitment to differentiate a self in one's family of origin seems to both subdue the leader's reactivity in other systems, and to give them clues as to their own participation in the reactivity of the systems they lead.

Watch the wheels go round and round

The anxious patterns of conflict, distancing, triangling, and over/underfunctioning are better seen as signposts to be read than pathologies to be fixed. This perspective facilitates a posture of curiosity (which is inherently more neutral), and allays the impulse to correct people. As observable indicators of emotional process, these phenomena give the leader clues as to what's going on.

The leaders in the vignettes each worked to read the emotional processes, sometimes seeing them as confirmation that the anxiety coming toward them had been sent back toward its source.

Conclusion

The examples above illustrate the complex challenges of entering church systems that are experiencing the inevitable anxieties in the face of change. Biblical principles provide a picture of the church as it is intended under Christ and the early church epistles reveal many of the same relationship ruptures that continue in the contemporary church. Having a theoretical road map for understanding the drivers and dynamics of these anxious relationship processes can be enormously beneficial for ministry leaders. While Bowen's idea of maturity as differentiation of self and Paul's idea of maturity as Christlikeness are not synonymous, they share much, both in terms of characteristics and development.

Ministers applying Bowen theory with the assistance of a coach may be more effective in helping Christian communities to conduct themselves in a manner more consistent with Christ's character and mission.

References

Bowen, M. (1978). Family therapy in clinical practice. New York: Aronson.

Brown, J. (2012). Growing yourself up: How to bring your best to all of life's relationships Sydney: Exisle.

Friedman, E. (1985). Generation to generation: Family process in church and synagogue. New York: Guildford.

Friedman, E. (1999). *A failure of nerve: Leadership in the age of the quick fix.* New York: Seabury.

Gilbert, R. (2006). The eight concepts of Bowen theory. Learning Systems, Falls Church.

Gilbert, R. (2008). *The cornerstone concept: In leadership, in life.* Learning Systems, Falls Church.

Kerr, M. & Bowen, M. (1988). *Family evaluation: The role of the family as an emotional unit that governs individual behavior and development.* New York: Norton.

Richardson, R. (2005). *Becoming a healthier pastor: Family systems theory and the pastor's own family.* Minneapolis: Fortress.

Pappas, G. (2000). *Entering the world of the small church.* Alban Bethesda.

Whitmore, J. (2009) *Coaching for Performance: Growing People, Performance and Purpose.* (4th edn.) London: Nicholas Brealey.

Chapter 13

CHURCH PLANTING AND SYSTEMS ANXIETY

Duncan Andrews

This chapter will explore the relationship between Bowen theory and the early years of new churches in the Australian reformed-evangelical context. It is a version of a paper written during my fourth year at Moore College, Sydney. As such, it was written with a deep interest in, but no personal experience of, church planting. Since then I have, by God's grace, led a church plant in regional South Australia, now approaching its fourth birthday. I have included a brief reflection from my current perspective at the end.

The paper draws primarily on the work of Edwin Friedman, a student of Bowen who went on to introduce systems thinking to a generation of clergy through his lectures and writing.[1] Friedman's approach differs at times from Bowen's, including using different terminology to express similar concepts (e.g., Friedman's use of *herding* in place of *fusion*). Some of these differences represent divergences in theory from Bowen; however most of the concepts come from Bowen theory and the core notion that anxiety belongs to a whole system and not just to an individual is consistent.[2]

Introduction

While much "how to" literature has been published concerning church planting, to my knowledge a systems approach has not yet been rigorously applied. My research involved a survey of church planters and lay leaders from a systems perspective. My hypothesis was that a critical factor for a new church to successfully navigate the anxiety of its early years is the church planter's awareness of, and differentiation within, the church's relational system.

The initial focus question for this research was:

What help might an awareness of "systems theory" bring to the leadership challenges faced in the first years of a church plant?

Upon reading the literature relevant to both systems theory in ministry and church planting, this focus question was significantly

---

[1] In particular Friedman's book *Generation to generation: Family process in church and synagogue* (1985) has been influential in taking family systems thinking to ministry contexts.

[2] A thorough review of the distinctions between Bowen and Friedman can be found in this lecture: Bowen and Friedman: Two Systems Thinkers. Carol P. Jeunnette, MDiv, PhD, Anne S. McKnight, EdD, LCSW, https://www.youtube.com/watch?v=39Vl7AXxWmk Dr McKnight's PP Slides: https://s3.amazonaws.com/bowenmultimedia/documents/Bowen+and+Friedman.pdf

modified. I will return to the modified question later. First, though, I will examine a selection of relevant literature.

Friedman's systems theory

Systems theory seeks to understand human interactions by focusing on the relational systems within which those interactions happen. In *Generation to Generation*, Edwin Friedman defines systems theory in contrast to "traditional notions of linear cause and effect" (1985, p. 15). Linear thinking isolates individual causes for particular effects. If the effect is negative, blame can be attributed to its cause/s. While this may accurately describe physical processes, systems thinking sees it as inadequate when thinking about human relationships. What happens in a relational system is not a function of the individual per se, but of the system as a whole. In terms of negative relational events, systems thinking does not look to identify "cause/s", but instead seeks to see the event in its systemic context. The "event" is a symptom of larger emotional processes and patterns, not easily accountable in terms of linear causality.

According to Friedman, understanding relational events as symptoms enables a more successful way to effect change in our relationships. However, the change we will seek is not in the input of other people: "The possibilities of change are maximised rather when we concentrate on modifying our own way of functioning, our own input" (1985, p. 18). When members of relational systems take responsibility for their own contribution, focusing not on individual symptoms but on the system itself and their place in it, they are able to bring much deeper change not only to a presenting issue but to the whole system out of which that presenting issue comes.

Friedman describes five basic concepts of family systems theory:

1. *The Identified Patient*: seeing a member with an obvious symptom not as the "sick one" but the one in whom the system's "stress or pathology has surfaced" (1985, pp. 19-20)
2. *Homeostasis*: the tendency of a system to resist systemic change
3. *Differentiation of Self*: "the capacity to be an 'I' while remaining connected" (1985, p. 27)
4. *The Extended Family Field*: seeing "the entire network of the extended family system as important" (1985, p. 31)
5. *The Emotional Triangle*: the tendency of two conflicting members "triangling in" on a third party "as a way of stabilising their own relationship" (1985, p. 35).

Friedman then applies these principles to leaders within religious institutions, arguing that what applies to families applies to church and synagogue, and that "what is vital to changing any kind of 'family' is [...] the capacity of the family leader to define his or her own goals and values while trying to maintain a non-anxious presence within the system" (1985, pp. 2-3).

Relevant for my research, Friedman in a later work identifies five predictable characteristics of a chronically anxious system:

1. Reactivity: the vicious cycle of intense reactions of each member to events and to one another
2. Herding: a process through which the forces of togetherness triumph over the forces for individuality and move everyone to adapt to the least mature members
3. Blame displacement: an emotional state in which family members focus on forces that have victimised them rather than taking responsibility for their own being and destiny

4. A quick-fix mentality: a low threshold for pain that constantly seeks symptom relief rather than fundamental change
5. Lack of well-differentiated leadership: a failure of nerve that both stems from and contributes to the first four (Friedman, Treadwell, & Beal, 2007, pp. 53-54).

A theological lens on Friedman's theory

There is much to learn from Friedman's work. However, by his own admission, he provides no theological framework. He omits quotations from Scripture, leaving it "to each reader to apply the appropriate words" (1985, p. 7). Nevertheless, there is more we can say from a theological perspective than the kind of proof-texting Friedman envisions here.

Herrington, Creech, and Taylor (2003) seek to do this by appropriating Friedman's and others' accounts of systems theory from a Christian perspective. They "use the life of Jesus and the conceptual framework of living systems" as a guide to personal transformation (Herrington et. al., 2003, p. 12), seeing Jesus as the ultimate example of a differentiated self who insisted on doing what was right in the face of extreme pressure from his relational systems to do otherwise. He kept his focus on "his Father's business", despite pressure from Satan, his family and friends, the crowds, and his enemies (Herrington et. al., 2003, pp. 18-22). Christians are those who "have apprenticed our lives to Jesus to follow him" as both our teacher and example (Herrington et. al., 2003, p. 23).

While the imitation of Christ is a biblical category,[3] more should be said in order to establish a robust theological framework for systems theory. Christian ethics has its theological basis in

---
3 E.g., 1 Cor 11:1 "Follow my example, as I follow the example of Christ."

the saving lordship of Christ enacted in the gospel; as such the claim that "imitating Jesus is the key to success as a Christian" (Herrington et. al., 2003, p. 132) is inadequate. It runs the risk of viewing Jesus primarily as an exemplar for the Christian life, rather than the church's Lord who transforms his people by his grace. When pressed, this distinction may reflect deeper theological differences. Whereas a focus on Jesus as exemplar is a position broadly promoted within the framework of liberal theology, a reformed evangelical position sees Jesus' atoning death on the cross, and his resurrection as Lord of all, at the heart of both the Christian message and the Christian life.

Ultimately it is this gracious lordship of Christ that provides both the greatest theological justification for, and qualification of, differentiation of self. It justifies the concept because the lordship of Christ frees those in Christ from the counter-claims of rival "lords". Paul describes this freedom in Colossians 2: because the Colossians had received, and were to continue in, Christ Jesus as Lord (2:6-7), no one and nothing else had any real claim over them; so 2:8-23 exhorts them to let that reality shape how they respond to the claims of rival lords, who have been triumphed over by the cross (2:15). Paul writes, "See to it that no one takes you captive" (2:8); "Do not let anyone judge you" (2:16); "Do not let anyone [...] disqualify you" (2:18). Their identity in Christ freed the Colossian Christians from all other claims on them.

With this perspective, we can modify Friedman's definition of differentiation to "the capacity to be an 'I-in-Christ' while remaining connected". This is an important qualification of differentiation of self: it is possible to be a differentiated self but pursue a wrongly directed vision. Human relationships reach their *telos* in Christ under his lordship; a Christian understanding of differentiation then becomes the God-enabled capacity to live out that *telos* in our relational systems in spite of the homeostatic resistance we will receive, neither withdrawing from nor conforming to the system.

The Leader's Journey does at times include these perspectives but gives no theological account of them. Nevertheless, it is a helpful application of systems theory to Christian leadership. Particularly helpful is the chapter on becoming a calm leader, the "leader's main job" (Richardson, as cited in Herrington et. al., 2003, p. 69). When faced with a highly anxious system, leaders need to start by "learning to see the anxiety in [themselves] and in the systems around [them]" (Herrington et. al., 2003, p. 70). This will involve exploring their own family patterns (Part 3), and developing spiritual disciplines (Part 4) that enable them to "remember that we are more interested in pleasing God than in pleasing others", helping to "minimise our anxious reactivity and choose a more constructive response instead" (Herrington et. al., 2003, p. 135).

Church planting challenges

In terms of church planting, I will focus on a recent survey of church planters in the USA conducted by researchers Ed Stetzer and Todd Wilson (2011), who presented their results in *No Church Planting Family Alone*. At time of writing, this was the most comprehensive research targeting leadership challenges, and is based on a survey of American church planters connected with *Exponential*, a US-based movement aiming to accelerate multiplication of faith communities.

The report identifies seven top challenges facing the planters surveyed:

1. Leadership development and reproducing culture
2. Financial self-sufficiency and viability

3. Team development and volunteer mobilisation
4. Systems, processes, and cultures
5. Vision casting and avoiding mission drift
6. Evangelism and discipleship
7. Spiritual, physical, and mental health of planter and family (Stetzer & Wilson, 2011).

The report focuses its recommendations on creating wider support systems for planters, including thorough assessment, coaching and training, ongoing support networks, and practical training in e.g., project management. While these strategies provide vital means of support, little attention is given to the planter's awareness of their relational system and their role within it.

The focus of my research was initially an investigation of the main challenges facing church planters in Australia, using these seven challenges listed as a point comparison, and being curious about what systems theory might contribute to understanding and potentially helping the presenting dilemmas. However, it became apparent that this could easily become an exercise in what systems theory is working against—that is, focusing on symptoms rather than deeper processes. Without addressing these core issues, even the best responses targeted at the identified challenges will not be as effective. Targeted responses to individual issues run the risk of linear thinking. They may have some effect; but without addressing the underlying relational systems the problem will likely resurface in a different way.

This concern led to a modification of the original focus to include the wider systemic context in which leaders were operating. From a systems perspective, what is more urgent than addressing specific challenges is the need to identify underlying levels of anxiety when confronted with possible symptoms. The advantage of this approach is that it is relatively easy to measure. As mentioned above, indicators of anxiety in a system are predictable: reactivity, herding, blame displacement, the quick fix, and undifferentiated leadership. The survey asked questions seeking to expose these indicators.

The following questions were surveyed:

With reference to the first year of your church plant, rate each of these statements (from 1 being *never* to 5 *very often*).

Testing reactivity:
1. Conflict emerged over issues I felt were inconsequential or secondary.
2. The launch team had regular times of laughter and playfulness.

Testing the herding instinct:
3. New ideas put forward by team members were welcomed and thoughtfully discussed.
4. Disagreements were welcomed and thoughtfully discussed.

Testing blame displacement:
5. During conflict, those involved blamed each other for what they had done wrong.
6. Members recognised when they had said/done something wrong and quickly apologised to the people involved.

Testing the quick fix:
7. The launch team relied heavily on church planting manuals and "how-to" literature.

Testing undifferentiated leadership:
8. When faced with significant challenges, either external or internal, the plant leader became anxious and indecisive.
9. The team leader's reaction to conflict was to withdraw and not directly address the issues being raised.

10. The team leader's reaction to conflict was to take more control in the situation.
11. The vision of the church plant was clearly communicated and referred to when making important decisions and responding to challenges.

Analysis and results

The high levels of change in the first years of a church plant create fertile conditions for anxiety to become entrenched. According to the literature, a critical factor for successfully navigating this anxiety is the church planter's own awareness of and differentiation of self within the anxious system. I sought to test this through surveying a selection of both planters and lay leaders of new churches, asking the questions above as a way of testing key indicators of chronic anxiety. It is important to recognise that these are indicators of *chronic* anxiety as distinct from acute, or time-limited, anxiety. Anxiety, as a basic response to threat, "can be lifesaving" (Herrington et. al., 2003, p. 35). However, when anxious modes of relating become endemic, or chronic, it "creates a terribly ineffective state for a person to live in for any length of time" (Herrington et. al., 2003, p. 36). Therefore, while every "emotional system sustains some level of chronic anxiety", the higher the level, the "more difficult it is for [a] system to function in a healthy way" (Herrington et. al., 2003, pp. 36-37).

Limitations

The research had a number of limitations. Firstly, the small sample size limits the extent to which these results can be generalised. The anonymous nature of the survey also limits its usefulness. While both lay leaders and planters were surveyed, it was not possible to track which lay leader matched which planter. This would have yielded insights into how a specific planter and lay leader both viewed their particular planting experience. As it is, the observations here relate to the group as a whole and to anonymous individuals. "Named" surveys, or even focus groups, would enable both more accurate data and more direct application of the results to individual churches, although respondents may have felt less free to answer frankly.

Also, a final evaluative question testing the overall "success" of the plant would have aided the research. If this had been done, particularly for longer-established plants, firmer links between early indicators of chronic anxiety and the longer-term health of the plant may have been drawn. As it is, our research only focused on these early indicators. The best we can say is that, according to the literature, those church-plants exhibiting chronic stress in their first year are likely to have these patterns continue and become embedded, with the system being placed under long-term stress. Again, according to the literature, a critical factor is the differentiation of the leader within the anxious system. The higher the levels of chronic anxiety, the more "homeostatic force" the leader will feel to continue these patterns; and the harder, and more important, it will be to maintain differentiation of self in order to influence the system into more mature, less anxious ways of relating.

Results

Fifteen respondents—nine planters and six lay leaders—rated a series of statements, from *virtually never* to *very often*. Each question was assigned a weighting from 1-5. For "negative" statements the weighting aligned with the rating; that is, *virtually never* was weighted 1, and *very often* weighted 5. For "positive" statements the weighting was inverted. In this way, the higher the weighting, the higher the levels of chronic anxiety indicated.

With this in mind, Figure 4 indicates the average weighting for each indicator, given as a score out of 100. On average, chronic anxiety levels are moderate in the sample group as a whole, with each indicator falling within the range of 45-52. The fifth indicator—undifferentiated leadership—is consistent with the others, aligning with a systems perspective in which the presence or absence of a well-differentiated leader is a critical factor in addressing other indicators of anxiety (Friedman et. al., 2007, p. 88).

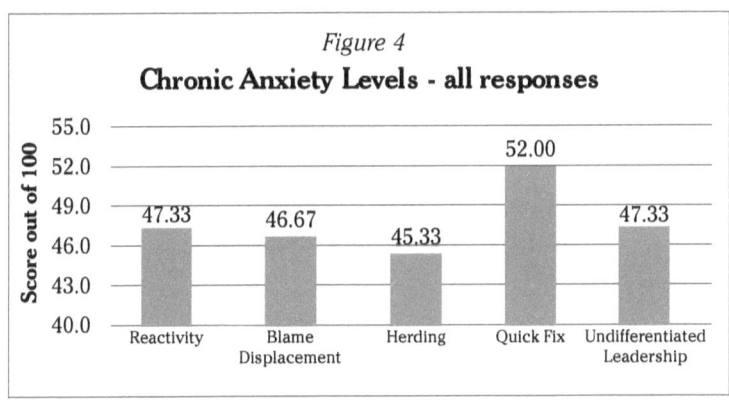

For individual responses, however, the range increases significantly. Figures 5 and 6 show the overall levels of chronic anxiety, averaging their responses for all questions. The score out of 100 is proportionate to the overall levels of chronic anxiety indicated by each person. The scores are presented in random order, and there is no correlation between planters and lay leaders—that is, Lay Leader 1 is not (necessarily) in the same church as Planter 1 and so on.

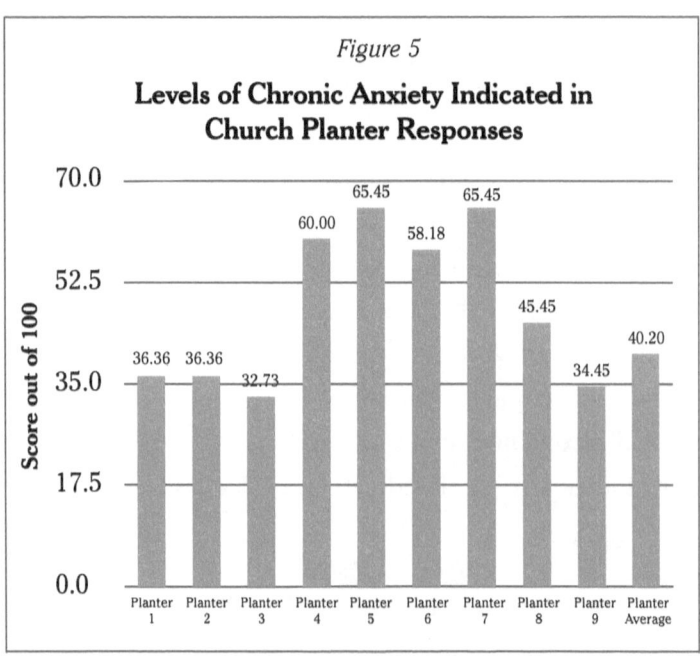

Figure 5
Levels of Chronic Anxiety Indicated in Church Planter Responses

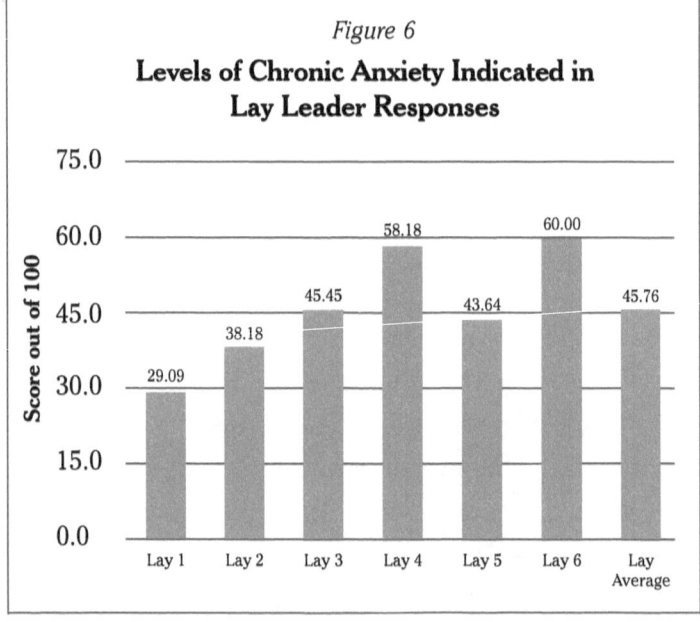

Figure 6
Levels of Chronic Anxiety Indicated in Lay Leader Responses

Given these data, a few observations are of note. First, lay leaders on the whole indicated slightly lower levels of chronic anxiety than planters, with an average score of 45.76 compared to 48.28. This may be accounted for by planters being overly self-critical, or lay leaders being overly generous. In either case, the difference is not vast, indicating that planters and lay leaders were in general agreement.

The second observation is that respondents were generally consistent across their answers. That is, those who indicated low levels of anxiety in one question generally indicated low levels across the board, and vice versa. In one exception, "Lay 1" indicated very low levels across the board, except in one question testing "blame-displacement", or the "tendency to look outward for explanations rather than inward" (Herrington et. al., 2003, p. 64). The question read: "Members recognised when they had said/done something wrong and quickly apologised to the people involved". The respondent answered with *virtually never*, and so received a "5" weighting for this answer, indicating high anxiety in this regard. However, they left a comment explaining their rating with reference to the harmonious, long-term relationships in the plant team which meant that members did not apologise, not because of "blame-displacement" but simply because there was so little conflict. While a "congregation free of conflict might simply be dealing with its anxiety in other ways" (Herrington et. al., 2003, p. 58), the consistently low anxiety levels indicated in this respondent's other answers suggest that their system is functioning well in terms of chronic anxiety. If we re-allocate their score to a 1 instead of 5 for this question, their overall score is even lower at 21.82/100.

On the other hand, respondents who indicated high levels of anxiety in one area were likely to indicate this across the board. The two respondents with the highest overall levels—Planters 5 and 7—gave answers consistently weighted between 3-5, each with only one answer scoring below 3. This general consistency in answers concords with the basic assumption of systems theory that individual events are "symptoms" of underlying system processes rather than the result of a linear chain of cause-and-effect (Friedman, 1985, pp. 14-17). As such, a less-anxious system would be expected to "score" less across all indicators of chronic anxiety, and vice versa. The higher average levels of chronic anxiety indicated by Planters 5 and 7 were not due to occasional "spikes", but to consistently medium-high weighted responses, as one would expect in a system that is stressed.

Focusing on the planters, five out of the nine indicated lower levels of chronic anxiety (weighted below 50/100), and four indicated higher levels (above 50/100). The five indicating lower levels of chronic anxiety fell within a weighting range of 32 to 45; and the four indicating higher levels between 58 and 65. This clustering again aligns with what would be expected from a systems perspective—that a well-functioning system will be less anxious across the board, and vice versa.

Turning to the specific questions, a few observations are salient. Most striking is the difference in average response between two of the questions, both testing the fifth "indicator", undifferentiated leadership. The statement "The team leader's reaction to conflict was to take more control in the situation" was given the highest weighting across the board (62.67/100), with 11 out of 15 respondents scoring between 3-5. In contrast, the statement "The team leader's reaction to conflict was to withdraw and not directly address the issues being raised" scored the lowest average weighting (36/100). Both these questions were designed to test for undifferentiated leadership, each from a different perspective. Well-differentiated leaders "are able to stay in relationship with those they lead, without having to control them or without being done in by them" (Herrington et. al., 2003, p. 65). Undifferentiated leadership, then, can react to relational conflict either by an over-assertion of control or the opposite extreme of becoming "indecisive, not wanting to offend any of the parties" (Herrington et. al., 2003, p. 65). The group indicated low levels of the second reaction (an indecisive avoidance of conflict); however, the high levels of the first reaction (a confrontational assertion of control) suggest that undifferentiated leadership may be manifesting itself in this particular way.

There are indications that the leader's assertion of control in contexts of conflict is viewed by some respondents as a positive trait. One lay leader, stating that the planter became more assertive and controlling under stress, qualified this as a function of his personality—and therefore not necessarily a negative feature. However, while qualities such as assertiveness may be seen as beneficial in those undertaking a task as uncertain and intense as planting a church, when that assertiveness manifests itself in controlling others so as to limit conflict it can be just as much a sign of an insecure and undifferentiated leadership as the leader who avoids conflict through indecision. Especially when the conflict involves two other members of the plant team, a leader's taking control becomes an instance of "emotional triangling", in which an individual tries to change the relationship of two others by taking on their stress as his/her own. However, according to systems theory, "the way to bring change to the relationship of two others [...] is to try to maintain a well-defined relationship with each, and to avoid the responsibility for their relationship with one another" (Friedman, 1985, p. 39). In other words, well-differentiated leadership allows space for conflict between other parties, seeking neither to control or abdicate from it, but remaining in direct and non-anxious contact with both parties.

More positively, several encouraging results are apparent. For the statement "The launch team had regular times of laughter and playfulness", no one responded *virtually never*, with 10 of 15 respondents rating between *sometimes* and *very often*. Given that "[p]erhaps the most easily discerned characteristic of an anxious system is the loss of playfulness and humour" (Herrington et. al., 2003, p. 63), this result suggests systems that, while undergoing the inevitable "acute" stress of planting a church, nevertheless have moments of non-anxious "stress-relief".

The statement "New ideas put forward by team members were welcomed and thoughtfully discussed" tested for the "herding instinct" in which the force for togetherness smothers the force for individuality (Friedman et. al., 2007, p. 67). All respondents answered with *sometimes* or above, with nine of the 15 answering either *often* or *very often*. While one lay leader commented that it often felt that meetings only functioned to "get us all to the point of agreeing with the leader's already decided way", the overall results are nonetheless encouraging. The welcoming of diverse opinion encourages experimentation, adventure, and the team's investment in the decision-making process.

The statement "The vision of the church plant was clearly communicated and referred to when making important decisions" was also in general answered positively, with only two responses in the *seldom* category. Clarity of vision—and the capacity to hold to that vision "despite the resistance and pressure of their relationships in the system"—is a sign of well-differentiated leadership and thus an important factor mitigating against anxious patterns becoming chronic.

Synthesis

The research yielded varied results across the church plants surveyed, with some exhibiting lower, and some higher, levels of chronic systemic anxiety. In each case, the levels of anxiety exhibited in the first four indicators—reactivity, blame, herding, and the quick fix—coincide with the levels given in the fifth and, according to the literature, the decisive factor—the leader's differentiation of self. This suggests that our hypothesis—that the first year of a church plant provides fertile ground for anxiety, and that the leader's role is critical in successfully navigating this anxiety—is valid.

Evaluation

The value of seeking to identify chronic stress indicators is, firstly, that it aids clarity in assessing the health of our relational systems, and, connected to that, enables leaders to analyse and critique their own contribution to those systems. Effective leadership involves having "enough emotional maturity [...] to remain connected with those who differ with the leader or the majority, and to remain a calm presence when anxiety arises" (Herrington et. al., 2003, p. 46). As I indicated earlier in the chapter, more work needs to be done in establishing a coherent, theologically grounded framework for systems theory; nevertheless, it provides helpful insights into the dynamics of human interaction and the important place of non-anxious leadership in forming and sustaining healthy communities.

Reflection

As mentioned in the introduction, since writing this paper I have led a church plant in regional South Australia. I am in no doubt that whatever good has come as a result has been entirely the gracious gift of God. Much good has come, more than I could have hoped for, for which I am deeply thankful.

I am also in no doubt that, under God's hand, a significant factor that has helped me navigate the early years of a church plant has been the awareness of my relational systems that systems theory has given me. My experience has not been free from anxiety; there have been many moments of intense strain as I have responded to my own and others' sins and weaknesses. Nevertheless, a commitment to focus on my own contribution rather than others', a desire to express and pursue a clear gospel vision for our church, and an appreciation of others' contributions alongside a commitment to make decisions driven by the gospel and not external expectations, are all areas in which whatever progress I have made has by God's grace been enhanced by systems theory.

I remain convinced that few things are more urgent for the cause of Christ than the ongoing and widespread planting of biblically faithful, evangelistically focused churches. My prayer is that as church planters learn to see the inevitable anxiety of a new church within its relational system, and attend to their own contribution within that system, God may grow in them a relaxed confidence in his sovereign grace that enables the kind of calm, focused leadership that will foster mature and fruitful churches, for the progress of the gospel and the glory of his name.

References

Friedman, E. (1985). *Generation to generation: Family process in church and synagogue.* New York: Guilford.

Friedman, E., Treadwell, M., & Beal, E. (2007). *A Failure of nerve: Leadership in the age of the quick fix.* New York: Seabury Books.

Herrington, J., Creech, R., & Taylor, T. (2003). *The leader's journey: Accepting the call to personal and congregational transformation.* 1st ed. San Francisco: Jossey-Bass.

Stetzer, E., & Wilson, T. (2011). *No church planting family alone: Leading voices weigh in on top challenges facing today's church planters.* Retrieved from Stetzer's website: www.christianitytoday.com/assets/10182.pdf

Section 4

PERSONAL ACCOUNTS OF APPLYING
BOWEN THEORY AS A CHRISTIAN

Chapter 14

"ANGELS AND DEVILS" IN THE FAMILY
An Exploration of Reciprocal Functioning in the Moral Domain

Margaret Wesley

Murray Bowen wrote that there are no angels or devils in a family (Bowen, 1994, p. 492). Was he right? Are there angels and devils in your family? What about your congregation? Are there people who seem to lead faultless lives while others never seem to get anything right? What about you? Are you an "angelic" Christian leader? Do you like to be seen as a good Christian? If so, then examining your ministry under the lens of moral reciprocal functioning may be disconcerting, but it also may be liberating.

Bowen observed that people who overfunction in emotional systems, such as families and churches, support processes that allow others to underfunction. This chapter will invite you to consider the impact your moral functioning may be having on the people around you. It will look at moral extremes in the Bible and in my family and will seek a path out of moral overfunctioning into humble discipleship to Jesus who was not afraid to break the rules in order to bring healing and hope.

Reciprocal functioning

A few words about reciprocal functioning will be necessary as we begin. All emotional systems include some people who overfunction and some who underfunction; some who take on responsibility that belongs to others and some who give away their responsibility to others (Brown, 2012). It is like a seesaw whose angle increases as anxiety in the emotional system increases. When there is more stress on the relationship system, overfunctioners will often take on even more responsibility and underfunctioners will function even more poorly, sometimes developing physical, emotional, or social symptoms.

When we begin to see our congregations and other communities through the lens of reciprocal functioning, we will think again about that member of our ministry team who we had seen as lazy, and we will ask, "How am I contributing to a system that invites that person to underfunction?" When we notice we haven't taken a day off in weeks, and hear ourselves saying, "There is just too much work", we will learn to ask, "What tasks am I really responsible for here? What responsibilities have I taken from others?"

Reciprocal functioning is an automatic process. Nobody chooses to overfunction or to underfunction. We are not even aware of these processes unless we stand back and observe the system through a Bowen family systems theory lens, and even then we rarely catch more than a glimpse of our own contribution to the process.

Reciprocal functioning in the moral domain

The longer and harder we look at life through the lens of Bowen theory, the more clearly we see these dances[1] of reciprocal functioning. As I was looking long and hard at my life and ministry

---

[1] I was introduced to Bowen Family Systems Theory by Harriet Lerner's *Dance of...* series of books. (See for example Lerner, 1985.)

in 2013 a scary thought occurred to me. What if reciprocal function takes place in the moral domain as well as in the domains of workload and decision-making? What if my good moral behaviour, as a Christian minister, is actually fuelled by overfunctioning? What if my moral overfunctioning is contributing to a system that allows others to underfunction morally?

Are you seeing why this was a scary question? Christian leaders seek to set a good example for others through our kind, patient, self-controlled behaviour. What if this exemplary behaviour is potentially producing the opposite result to that which is intended? What if the members of our congregations are not increasing in their moral functioning but rather forfeiting their moral responsibility to us?

What if, by working so hard at being an "angel", I am inadvertently contributing to a system that is producing "devils"? By asking the question in this way I am making reference to Bowen (1994) who wrote that, "More knowledge of one's distant families of origin can help one become aware that there are no angels or devils in a family" (p. 492). There are no angels or devils in our churches either but, let's face it, we are sometimes tempted to think of our fellow congregation members in just such terms.

Moral extremes in the Bible

One of the reasons we are tempted to think of people in stark angel/devil categories is that we do see real examples of moral extremes in society, in our families, and in the Bible.

The first siblings mentioned in the Bible, Abel and Cain (Gen 4:1-16), both born after the fall, set the scene for the family conflict we find punctuating the biblical narrative. However, this story is not just about conflict; it is also about moral contrast. In Genesis 4:7 God says, "If you do what is right, will you not be accepted?"

Cain does not do what is right. Instead, he murders his brother. We know nothing about Cain's behaviour before the sacrifice, but God's rejection of him implies that he had not been doing what is right, and his subsequent actions bear this out. We are told almost nothing about Abel except that God had regard for him and his sacrifice (Gen 4:4), implying that he did "do what is right." It would be reading too much into the narrative to find moral overfunctioning in Abel's behaviour but we do find a stark moral contrast between two siblings who were raised by parents experiencing huge levels of anxiety.

This foundational story introduces the good son/bad son dynamic that is so common in the Bible. The most detailed discussion of this is in Genesis 37-50. Joseph was his father's favourite son (Gen 37:3) and we can observe a clear triangle in which Jacob's preference for Joseph led to enmity between Joseph and his brothers (Gen 37:4). Joseph's sense of his own superiority is seen when he reveals his dreams of family dominance to his brothers in the presence of their father. We know from the end of the story that these dreams were genuine predictions of future events (Gen 42:9) but his choice to talk about them shows him revelling in his favoured status. The fact that he brought a negative report to his father about his brothers (Gen 37:2) also suggests that his sense of superiority had a moral dimension. These family processes appear to contribute to lowered moral functioning in the brothers, especially Judah, whose idea it was to sell Joseph into slavery (Gen 37:26-27).

Joseph's journey to maturity required him to leave behind the privileges of being the favoured son and destined leader and become a slave (Gen 39:1) and then a prisoner (Gen 39:20). This path of humiliation appears to help him mature. Through this period we see him choosing to be the leader God had gifted him to be rather than revelling in superiority that he had not earned.

By the end of the story we find him using the superior position he has gained to serve his family, rather than to shine a spotlight on himself (Gen 50:21). He has learned, as all moral overfunctioners need to learn, the right answer to the question, "Am I in the place of God?" (Gen 50:19). God had given him all he had: his leadership gifts and his moral strength. They were given for the good of others, not for him to boast about or use as tools for holding on to power and privilege.

He was able to say to his brothers, "You intended to harm me, but God intended it for good" (Gen 50:20). As he recognised the activity of God in all their lives, he was able to let go of his sense of moral superiority. He was not an angel. His brothers were not devils. They were all in God's hands. If we had more space we could also look at the complexity of the brothers Jacob and Esau, or at the relational processes behind good men such as Eli (1 Sam 2:11-17) and Samuel (1 Sam 8:1-5) raising bad sons. Instead, I will simply encourage you to keep your eye out for these ideas when you are reading the Bible, especially the historical books of the Old Testament.

Jesus and his brothers are an intriguing example of family process. If we assume that Jesus was fully differentiated[2] as an adult then we cannot describe him as morally overfunctioning. However, his brothers do appear to underfunction in relation to him (John 7:1-9). Perhaps they were reacting to their parents' preference of their older brother, even though in their case the favoured brother was humble and gracious.

---

[2] By suggesting that Jesus was fully differentiated I am not claiming that he found relationships any easier than we do. He was fully human. (See my analysis of Jesus as a son in a family in Wesley, 2015.) However can we observe him holding to his identity and autonomy while maintaining emotional connection with others, even when anxiety levels became extreme? This warrants further discussion about the concept of differentiation of self, which other papers in this book deal with in greater detail than this paper allows.

Considering family of origin

Having observed moral reciprocal functioning in the Bible, you might be tempted to turn immediately to analysing similar processes in your church. I urge you instead to study your family of origin first. You will gain essential insights there that you will then be able to apply to your ministry. Your family of origin is where you learnt the patterns of behaviour you typically contribute to emotional systems. Your family is also the best place (though also the hardest place) to make slow but permanent changes to your functioning.

Murray Bowen (1994, p. 545), with his typical scientific restraint, wrote:

> My experience is going in the direction of saying that the most productive route for change, for families who are motivated, is to work at defining self in the family of origin, and to specifically avoid focus on the emotional issues in the nuclear family.

The emotional issues in your church or ministry may, perhaps, need to be faced eventually, but the most productive work you can do initially, especially if you are a leader, is in your family of origin.

As an example, I will now outline my own efforts to observe the moral reciprocal functioning that gave me the illusion of "angels" and "devils" in my family of origin. Out of respect for my family members, I will not include the level of detail that I might share in a group where confidentiality agreements have been made, but hopefully my outline will be sufficient. My parents had both died before I began this work. I therefore offer the following as an example of family of origin research where interaction with living parents is not possible.

I would like to begin with a verse from a poem I wrote as I was emerging from adolescence. At the time, my father had been dead for about five years and I was struggling to sort out the implications of his life and death. My mother was still living, and I was seeking to separate myself from her and work out who I might be as an autonomous adult. In this poem I describe my childhood self as:

> A helpless onlooker
> In the eternal struggle
>   of good and evil,
>   of love and hate,
>   of Mum and Dad.

I share these few lines, not because they give an accurate description of myself or my parents, but because they capture how I thought at the time about my parents as representatives of good and evil, as an "angel" and a "devil", along with my feeling that I had no room to move in response to that stark contrast of powerful moral forces. I will now introduce my parents in the language of my stark thinking at that time.

When I was a child my father was an alcoholic who was violent at times. Though very intelligent, he found it difficult to maintain employment. As a result, we were very poor, especially during the years in which Mum was unable to work because she was at home taking care of the six children she produced because he refused to allow her to use contraception[3].

My mother not only raised a large family of her own but also attracted to her hearth all the troubled children and teens of

---

[3] It is one of my life's little paradoxes that I disapproved of my father preventing contraception yet, as the youngest of my siblings, I would almost certainly not have been born if he hadn't.

the neighbourhood, with many of them calling her "Mum". She founded an emergency housekeeping organisation to help local families with childcare, cooking, and cleaning in times of crisis. When the Housing Commission began building homes in our town, ours was the first family to be given a house.

That is the black and white snapshot of my parents that I held in my head as I moved into adult life. My parents both died before I began to seriously investigate family systems theory, so I have relied on the recollections of other family members to fill in some shades and contours I will now present to make this picture more true to their complex reality.

My father appears to have been raised by two Irish Australian "angels". At least, I have found that their children have not been willing to admit to any fault in them. I remember his mother as a gracefully ageing woman. She was a devout Roman Catholic with a gentle but robust presence. She visited us once when she was in her eighties and the lounge chair she was sitting on somehow overturned and landed on top of her. We were all horrified that an elderly person in our home should be so mistreated by our furniture, but we found her under the lounge giggling about the funny predicament she found herself in!

I never knew my paternal grandfather because he died from cancer when my father was just 18, but the stories I have heard suggest a sweet, gentle man. I am told that he would play the fiddle at bedtime to help his children sleep. His wife's only complaint about him was that she could never get him into an argument because he was always too ready to agree with whatever she said.

This agreeableness and my grandfather's early death from cancer suggest that this couple dealt with anxiety through the development of physical symptoms, not through conflict. I am also very aware that today my father's family members tend to be highly child-focused; I might even say child-obsessed. That may well have also been true for this couple. I can easily imagine their mounting anxiety, in the middle of World War II, as their four boys headed towards their eighteenth birthdays.

My grandfather's cancer and death was part of the storm of trauma that tossed my father into adult life. When his father became ill, my father had been required to leave the prestigious school he was attending on a scholarship in order to find work to support his family. A little later he turned 18 and joined the war in New Guinea.

A number of years ago I was given a pile of letters that he had written to his mother during the war. In one of them he mentioned that his girlfriend had died in a car accident in Melbourne. I hesitate to imagine the impact of such news on a young man who believed he was fighting to protect the people he loved.

When the war ended, my father was part of the occupation forces in Japan. By all accounts this was a huge party. One of my uncles suggested that it was during that time that Dad's alcoholism developed.

One of my father's younger brothers, Terry, could be described as our family's most evident "angel". He also went to New Guinea but was not there for as long as my father. He was part of the medical corps as an ambulance driver and remained an ambulance officer for the rest of his working life. He was a man without a single apparent vice, except overeating. He didn't drink, smoke, swear, or gamble. He was the father, grandfather, and great-grandfather of an enormous family clan, yet he treated each member, including his nieces and nephews, as though they were the most important people in the world.

These two brothers show how similar experiences of adversity can contribute to very different life functioning in siblings. I cannot be certain about the processes that contributed to this difference, but I wonder if reciprocal functioning had begun to develop between these brothers even before the war? Perhaps my father had been labelled as the intelligent son and Terry as the good son? Perhaps a slight reciprocity was exacerbated by the enormous anxiety surrounding their entry into adulthood.

As I have considered the trauma surrounding my father's entry into adult life, I have gained compassion for the boy who was so overwhelmed by that trauma. As I watched my nephews, and then my son, turn 18 I have imagined them in his place and I cannot see them coping any better than he did. I thank God that none of them have faced such challenges.

When Bowen (1994, p. 492) wrote that "there are no angels or devils in a family" he added that even the most devilish family members are "human beings, each with his own strengths and weaknesses, each reacting predictably to the emotional issue of the moment, and each doing the best he could with his life course." By doing my own family of origin work I have come to see my father in a very different light. And in that gentler light I can have compassion for his weakness and honour whatever efforts he made to improve his functioning and to do "the best he could."

Through family research I had come to see that my father was not a devil after all. This was an important first step, but the next step, of accepting that my mother was also not an angel, was more challenging. However, the evidence that she was a mere human was there for me to see as soon as I was willing to look. Just one example of her tarnished halo was the way that she and a close friend had disagreed sharply about how their emergency housekeeping organisation should be managed, and they had never reconciled.

My mother was not as robustly angelic as I had thought, but she was certainly a good person, so I wonder why she would marry my father? What did she bring from her family of origin that led her to him?

My mother was the eldest of her siblings and was given (and accepted) responsibility for the safety and upbringing of the younger ones long before she was of an appropriate age. Her tendency to overfunction seems to have developed early in life and was firmly fixed by the time she met my father. Perhaps his lack of responsibility felt like a good match for her over-responsibility, in the moral domain as well as in others.

As I look at my mother I see that it is possible to give every appearance of being a good person without necessarily being a mature person. How many of her generous actions flowed from a kind heart and how many from an anxious heart that needed to be liked and depended upon in order to feel comfortable? I can't answer that but I can be sure it was not 100 percent either way. Emotional processes in our families may give us a predisposition toward good behaviour, but are unlikely to lead to better moral functioning in the system as a whole.

My role in the primary triangle of my family of origin was to cling to my mother and cut myself off from my father. So, you can guess how I might behave in other relationship systems. I tend to become attached to good people and distance myself from people I perceive as abusive. When a "good" person acts in an abusive manner I can become disoriented. I feel more comfortable when good and evil are clearly delineated.

My moral overfunctioning sits alongside a theology of radical grace that I have embraced since I was a teenager. Our beliefs about God are powerfully transformative, through the indwelling Holy Spirit, but the patterns of behaviour from our family of origin resists transformation. On the side of the Holy Spirit, we need to exert our conscious efforts to observe, challenge, and uncover the roots of our usual patterns of behaviour.

Jesus and moral over-/underfunctioners

Jesus did not align himself with the moral overfunctioners of his day. In the deeply anxious times they lived in, Pharisees hoped that strict observance of the law would help maintain Jewish identity and God's favour. I see them standing at this critical turning point in history, believing that they held the future of their people in their hands. These were ideal conditions for moral overfunctioners. The Pharisees were balanced by moral underfunctioners. The temple hierarchy and high-priesthood were corrupt, the Roman authorities were inclined towards military provocation, and numbers of people were easily encouraged to seek God's kingdom through violence. Jesus criticised all these approaches, but his most strident words hammered against the Pharisees (Matt 23). Those of us inclined toward moral overfunctioning need to pay attention. It might make us feel comfortable and superior, but it does not bring us closer to Jesus.

One of the most fascinating things about the Gospels, when viewed through a Bowen family systems theory lens, is the way Jesus stays out of the intense moral reciprocal function of his community. We see this most clearly in his refusal to meticulously comply with the Sabbath and purity regulations that were practiced by his contemporaries. This morally perfect person was not at all scrupulous about mere law keeping. Instead he responded lovingly to each situation and each human need that he encountered. He healed people on the Sabbath (e.g., John 5:1-9), he touched lepers (e.g., Matt 8:1-3), and allowed a haemorrhaging woman (Mark 5:25-34) and a sinful woman (Luke 7:36-50) to touch him.

When moral overfunctioning drives our behaviour we may be so distracted by a need to do the "right thing" that we forget to do the loving thing. We may be concerned about setting a good example and about enhancing our church's reputation, or even God's reputation. These are good things, but when our eyes are on the rulebook they are often not on the person or situation in front of us.

I noted earlier that a theme of good son/bad son reciprocity is introduced toward the beginning of the Bible and expanded upon several times as the story unfolds. Jesus takes up that theme in Luke 15:11-32. What if the bad (prodigal) son repents and returns home? What happens to the reciprocity of the relationship? The good son's familiar patterns of behaviour had always been a reaction to the bad behaviour of his brother. What will he do now that the pattern has changed? The good son is stiff with fear and anger, but his father knows what to do. He throws a party.

Coming to the party would require the good son to step out of his moral reciprocity and celebrate with his family: celebrate his good father and his "bad brother". He is invited to stop reciprocating and start celebrating! How does he respond? We are not told, perhaps because many of us are that good son. The question then becomes how will I respond to Jesus' invitation to celebrate my relationships with the angels and devils in my family and my church?

Living on autopilot is easy in every domain, including the moral domain. Following the rules, embodying the role of the "family angel" or the "church angel", is easy. It is harder to make thoughtful choices based on realistic assessments of what is needed; and to act on those choices even when we might be accused of acting wrongly, and when we know we might be mistaken. But this is the example Jesus gave us.

Concluding reflections

I would like to return to my family for a moment. My father eventually stopped drinking when my mother found the strength to do what was necessary rather than what was morally and socially sanctioned. She asked the police to place him in rehab and prevent him from ever coming back. She chose to face the world as a single mother (in the 1970s) rather than going on being a morally upright abused wife. I'm not sure how this was resolved, but I know he did come back, and that from this time on he took his recovery seriously.

The way out of overfunctioning in the moral, or any other, domain begins with observing the patterns of behaviour we learnt in our family of origin and carried into adult life. Once we are familiar with our own patterns, we can observe the impact of those patterns on our church or other emotional system. With these observations we can give ourselves some freedom to think more clearly about the real needs of each situation. We might then choose a behaviour that is outside our usual pattern. It feels much more natural to continue our familiar patterns or else to flip over to the opposite extreme and become underfunctioners. Exhausted Christian leaders who flip from moral overfunctioning to moral underfunctioning have done great harm to God's people. That is not our calling. We are called to do what we thoughtfully conclude to be in accord with God's character in each situation, rather than relying on socially sanctioned behaviours that make us look like good people.

References

Bowen, M. (1994). *Family therapy in clinical practice.* Northvale: Jason Aronson.

Brown, J. (2012). *Growing yourself up: How to bring your best to all of life's relationships.* Wollombi: Exisle.

Lerner, H. G. (1985). *The dance of anger.* New York: Harper & Row.

Wesley, M. (2015). *Son of Mary.* Eugene: Wipf & Stock.

Chapter 15

THREE PSYCHOLOGISTS AND A FUNERAL?
A Personal Reflection on a Bowen Theory Approach to a Family Crisis

Michael Crichton

Why would anyone seek to apply Bowen family systems theory rather than adopt more conventional forms of psychological assistance when faced with emotional or psychological challenges in the family? This paper is a personal reflection on my journey in Bowen theory as a full-time minister when one of my own children became ill with a significant mental disorder. I will share my learnings along the way and also consider if Bowen theory is consistent with an evangelical biblical theology.

Introduction

As a minister in the Anglican church for over 30 years I have had the privilege of listening to many people as they shared the challenges or crises they have faced. When it came to medical or mental issues all I could do was pray with them and encourage them to see a professional in that field. However, it is surprising that when my own family faced a crisis my wife and I did not ultimately take the conventional course of action when our daughter became symptomatic and showed signs of a mental illness. We chose to adopt a Bowen family systems approach based on our understanding of the theory. In a nutshell this meant taking steps to avoid having her institutionalised and continuing to try and help her take responsibility for her life and actions. We sought to avoid labelling her condition as this has been shown to retard rehabilitation (Friedman, 1985). This paper is a description of that journey and the application of Bowen theory and the observations we were able to make. The main events I will be describing occurred between 2012-2015. It should be noted that this paper is a collaborative work that involved consultation with all members of the family.

The family at a glance

My wife and I had been married for 25 years and in full-time Anglican ministry when our family started to unravel. We were married in 1988 and had children in 1992, 1993 and 1996, a boy followed by two girls. Both our girls were gifted dancers (Jazz Ballet, Contemporary Dance and Classical Ballet) but the eldest had a particular determination. She excelled, winning numerous awards in both the local and interstate/national competitions in all fields of dance. When she reached the age of 16 it was decided she would leave school and attend the local ballet school full-time. During that year she was encouraged to pursue a full-time career in dance and she attended a summer school for ballet in New York City. My wife accompanied her on this trip and she acted as a "house mother" in the dormitory accommodation for a period of 8 weeks. This was a positive experience and it was decided our daughter should apply to different ballet schools throughout the United States. She was accepted into a ballet school in Washington DC and began there in September 2010.

A crisis develops

Once again, my daughter excelled and she was considered one of the best in the school. Despite her obvious talent, the pressure to be "skinny" started to take effect. As she was living at a distance it was difficult for us as parents to know how well she was looking after herself. She was living in ballet school accommodation with a house mother giving oversight and we believed she was in good care. We were thankful that she had been 'adopted' by some Christian families at the local Baptist church. My wife had established these connections when she first took our daughter over to Washington DC. This was important in giving us a sense that others were looking out for her as we were unable to be there. We also had several phone calls and Skype conversations per week with her which initially was always very exciting. During January 2011, however, it became apparent that our daughter was struggling with various issues, some social, others to do with eating habits, and still others associated with the pressure she was under to perform at such a high level. At the end of each year the ballet school puts on a performance as a way for students to have that experience and "show" their families how they had progressed. Our daughter was chosen for a lead role.

To cut a long story short, her anxiety and dysfunction had reached such a level that she did not believe she could perform. We were surprised because she had always performed extremely well under pressure. We felt she only had to get through the next month and she would be on her way home to Australia for the summer break. Little did we realise the situation was far more complicated.

She had a breakdown of sorts and was admitted to hospital. My wife flew immediately to Washington DC and brought her home. The ballet school were very concerned because she had mentioned to another student that she wanted to kill herself.

My wife and I were naively thinking she would get through this unusual "episode" and she would be back for the start of the new year in September 2011. My wife convinced the ballet school our daughter would seek medical help and that, all being well, she would return in September.

Our daughter never returned and has never danced again.

When she arrived home in Sydney it quickly became apparent that she was sicker than we had anticipated. She was refusing to eat, and her social behaviour was self-destructive. My wife had heard of a way of treating eating disorders called the Maudsley approach, so as a family we attended these sessions for six months.[1] I took three months of carer's leave in an effort to keep our daughter safe. Despite our best efforts this method of treatment proved counter-productive as our daughter was at the older end of the age spectrum for when this approach is best applied. Some of the advice she was given was also in direct opposition to our Christian beliefs. For example, she was told that she could sleep around if she felt like it and that getting drunk was not an issue.

We took her to a variety of psychiatrists and psychologists over an extended period of time hoping to find someone who could make a "connection" with her and convince her to co-operate and at least "try". To be perfectly honest our daughter felt most of these doctors were unhelpful and that they did not understand her unique complexities, and we were beginning to agree with her. They prescribed various medications for depression and anxiety on a trial and error basis. Nothing seemed to make any difference

---

[1] This is a type of treatment that involves the whole family rather than just the individual in overcoming anorexia nervosa. See http://www.maudsleyparents.org/whatismaudsley.html for further details.

and her symptoms continued. Unfortunately, one size doesn't fit all—as we were beginning to find out.[2]

By this stage she was self-harming, drinking heavily, and continuing with self-destructive sexual relationships. Within an 18-month period she had tried to overdose at least three times. On each occasion God was gracious and she was found before the overdose could reach its full effect. We spent many days beside her bed in intensive care units. This would be followed by a few days in the mental health section of the hospital for observation and to stabilise her condition. Each time created high levels of anxiety within our marriage and family, especially as we had tried to do everything we could to assure her of our love and keep her safe. It felt like we were fighting a losing battle.

It was becoming clear that there was a pattern developing and we needed to find a way to break the cycle if at all possible.[3] Our daughter had little sense of self or self-love which we all need if we are to function well. Her *differentiation of self* was extremely low[4] (Bowen, 1978). It did not matter how much we told her we loved her or that life was worth living—she did not believe it. To top it off our daughter had decided to go "cold turkey" off all medication.

---

[2] Through our experience we felt that while there are common features around diagnosis of eating disorders their treatment is very complex as each individual sufferer has a unique combination of emotional, physical, and relational factors which brought the illness about in the first place. We were not convinced this was always taken into consideration.

[3] In fact, there were many patterns, too many to list here but one standout pattern was that as soon as it appeared that her mental state was improving, and she was taking more responsibility for herself, we felt it might be a good time to take a short break—we were exhausted. Her condition would deteriorate as soon as she realised we were going to leave her.

[4] Bowen uses the term *differentiation of self* as a way of describing the core emotional maturity of a person.

My wife and I were desperate for help as nothing conventional seemed to be working. We were faced with two main options:

1. Have her institutionalised which would have been for at least a six-week period initially. This would also mean she would not be able to complete her TAFE course which only had a few months left, but at least she would be safe.
2. Try and keep her out of the hospital system, keep her at TAFE, keep her safe at home as best we could and try and apply Bowen theory to our precarious situation.

The turning point

We chose option two after her first suicide attempt. We had been to more than three psychologists and came close to attending our daughter's funeral. We were desperate. We turned to Bowen family systems coaching for help.[5] I had done some introductory courses at the Family Systems Institute in Sydney and suggested my wife and I get some marriage and family coaching. She was willing to try anything!

That may seem a rather odd course of action to take when the "problem" was with our daughter. Yet one of the foundational teachings of Bowen theory is that the marriage is the key relationship within the family unit. If there are problems with the children, the first place to start is to consider the marriage and to work on it (Bowen, 1978). The degree to which the parents can manage their own anxiety will have a huge impact on the anxiety within the family unit, as leadership can either elevate anxiety or reduce it within a family system, depending on how they respond.

Most of the clinical advice we had received was based on a cause and effect approach focusing on fixing the individual with the symptoms, whereas systems thinking was a radical new way

---

5 We attended the Family Systems Institute at Neutral Bay, having 1-hour sessions on a monthly basis. The FSI offers a variety of training courses for those interested in exploring Bowen systems thinking. See www.thefsi.com.au

for us to consider our situation. Systems thinking broadened our horizons to consider that a wide range of interconnecting relationships all had a part to play in any family, both in contributing to and maintaining symptoms in members of the family, but in also bringing relief and healing to the family.[6] Our family was a unified emotional system in which our struggling daughter was a part. Each of us were affecting the other and if any person could change their part, the experience of every individual will change.

Through our coaching and its application, we started to recognise the following:

- We needed to focus on the emotional process in the family rather than the symptomatic content. Family systems thinking also locates a family's problems in the nature of the system rather than in the nature of its parts (Friedman, 1985).
- The effects or dysfunctions in our family are outworkings of our *family relationship patterns* rather than an end point in a linear chain of cause and effect.
- The way to eliminate symptoms was best achieved by modifying the reactive patterns rather than by trying to change the dysfunctional part or person directly (Friedman, 1985).

Shifting the focus from the "problem child" to the family system

Family anxiety

According to Bowen theory, anxiety is part of all our relationships and flows throughout the family system, seeking to find a point of dynamic equilibrium (Kerr & Bowen, 1988). With our daughter's

---

[6] There are eight concepts in Bowen theory. The simplest explanation of the theory we have found is in *The Eight Concepts of Bowen Theory* by Roberta M. Gilbert, M.D Leading Systems Press. See www.hsystems.org

mental illness and the instability it generated, our family system was operating with a very high degree of anxiety. This was layered on top of our previous ways of managing the anxieties of family life. The family dynamic was changing dramatically. The dynamic equilibrium of our family's emotional processes was changing on a daily basis as the anxiety moved around our system[7] (Gilbert, 2004). My wife was yelling a lot as she vented her frustrations/anxiety at a child intent on destroying herself. The role I played was one of trying to be a resource to my wife but also being as calming an influence as possible. The other two children became angry as they saw their sister destroying their parents and their family. They withdrew and dealt with their own challenges, not wanting to further burden Mum and Dad. It was interesting that some years later both these children confessed to having personal challenges at this time but decided not to burden their parents and faced them on their own.

Through our marriage coaching my wife and I discovered that we had been unknowingly projecting our anxiety onto the children in unhealthy ways.[8] One of the significant lessons we learnt revolved around "child focus".

Child focus

Bowen identified that in most families, child focus is a reality. Child focus usually involves one if not both parents giving undue focus to a child. This would normally mean taking too much responsibility for the child and thus overfunctioning on behalf of the child.

---

[7] I have always enjoyed the illustration of how anxiety passes through a herd of cows. If one cow stands too close to the electric fence and gets a shock, it is not long before their reaction is passed through the whole herd. The rest of the herd "catch" the anxiety.

[8] It is worth noting that this is nearly always unintentional but present in all families in varying degrees.

> The child focused family is one in which sufficient family anxiety is focused on one or more children to result in serious impairment in a child. The higher the anxiety in the parents, the more intense the process. (Bowen, 1978, p. 297)

Child focus often seems loving, but it does not allow the child in question to grow in emotional maturity; in fact it tends to lead to immaturity because the child does not have the space to grow independently or take responsibility for their own actions.

When there is a seriously ill child in the family it is difficult not to focus on the child especially if their situation is life threatening, so we had to learn a new way of dealing with our children.

If we were to help our "sick" or symptomatic daughter to get emotionally healthy then we had to find ways to help her take responsibility for her life and choices—as risky as that may sound. We had to change our thinking in the way we responded to her and dealt with our own anxiety surrounding her behaviour. We had to treat her based on her potential best and not treat her as a patient, where we expected the worst[9] (Brown, 2017).

With our daughter being a 19-year-old woman, we had to change our relationship "dance" if she was to have any chance of growing a healthy self[10] (Lerner, 1998). We had to come to a fresh awareness

---

[9] A person's potential best is what they are optimally capable of in their given situation and circumstances. This will vary from person to person and the situation they face. It involves not taking on another person's functioning or responsibility. You need the wisdom of Solomon to sometimes work out what that involves because we so desperately want to step in and rescue people and not give them the chance to "rescue" themselves.

[10] The metaphor of a dance in our relationships is helpful and commonly used in applications of Bowen theory (See Brown, 2017, p. 231 and Lerner, 2005). Every dance has dance steps and patterns; so it is in our relationships. If the relational dance is going to change, someone has to alter the steps and over time the pattern can change also.

that it was not our job to fix our daughter or rescue our daughter but to treat her as a responsible adult. She was not a project!

For this to happen my wife and I had to change the way we (as a couple) related and the way we processed our anxiety. For starters we had to be more honest with each other in expressing our *I position* in a calm and open way[11] (Kerr & Bowen, 1988). We needed to focus on our relationship more than our children's "issues". One of the practical implications of this was that we planned short trips away to focus on our marriage and enjoy time together, which had been a rarity in our busy ministry life. The response of our symptomatic daughter was interesting because she thought it was irresponsible to leave her while she was still unwell. The "push back" we got from our daughter was substantial.[12] She did not like the fact that we were taking the focus off her, and she was being "forced" to take responsibility for her life. Invariably she would threaten to kill herself or start harming herself. We stood our ground and still went on our trips. The challenge for us was to manage our own anxiety when such a threat was hanging over us.

My wife came to realise that verbally projecting her anxiety at our daughter was counter-productive and damaging to the relationship. The challenge for me was to speak up even when my wife was in such a stressed state and encourage her to speak less. Without a doubt this was a difficult time for our marriage, but we had to change the dance in our system. It was a painful but worthwhile

---

11 Stating one's I position is at the heart of Bowen's concept of differentiation of self. To state one's I position is not about being selfish but rather an attempt to openly express one's core beliefs and principles.

12 The term *push back* is used to describe the reactivity of someone who wants the "system" to go back to the way it once was, prior to the changes.

part of the journey[13] (Gilbert, 2004). My own challenge was that I had to find ways to not act as the overfunctioning absorber in the family and encourage members to deal with their own anxiety rather than me being the dumping ground.

This was actually an uncomfortable part of the journey for me as it meant speaking up and telling people I had heard enough and did not want to hear any more. Once again this felt unloving, but it was a small step in the process of helping others be responsible for their own anxiety and not projecting it onto a third party.

Togetherness forces

Whilst our symptomatic daughter was trying to destroy herself and push us away through physical and emotional distancing, it was interesting to see how the rest of the family formed even stronger bonds at the height of the crisis. Our two other children grew closer together and put aside their own challenges in order to support their parents.

Bowen theory talks about the reciprocity between togetherness and separateness forces. The more our daughter pushed us away, the tighter we clung to each other. The new closeness was very comforting at one level as the degree of care and support for one another felt almost cathartic.

However, it also made it difficult to be an individual, which led to high levels of disagreement when it came to discuss the best way to deal with the ongoing situation. One of the continuing personal challenges the situation brought to each of us was

---

[13] In Bowen theory the issue revolves around the reciprocity in the marriage relationship. What that means is that there is always an overfunctioner and an underfunctioner in every marriage which sets the pattern for the "dance" in that marriage. See Gilbert (2004) pp. 17-20.

how to be a mature thinking person rather than an emotionally reactive one. When a new crisis point was reached, my wife would often become emotionally reactive rather than bringing her best thinking to the situation.

My wife readily admits that the turning point for her was recognising how unhelpful her reactivity was to our situation. As she worked on being less reactive with our symptomatic daughter and instead responding more calmly and thoughtfully, it had a significant impact on the whole family structure.

Through our coaching sessions my wife came to realise that she had a strongly fused relationship with our daughter, which was damaging to both of them. We also came to realise that physical distance did not solve the emotional issues; it just appeared that way.

As parents the reality was that we needed to take small steps to back away from our daughter so that she could take responsibility for herself. Doing this was counterintuitive as it felt like the most unloving thing to do—yet it was the most powerful demonstration of our love for her that we could make. We loved her enough to allow her to take responsibility for her own life no matter what the consequences.[14] We came to recognise that healthy relationships require both togetherness and separateness for emotional maturity to blossom. However, getting the balance right is an ongoing challenge in all our relationships.

Triangles

These togetherness forces created some interesting triangles within our family. A number of interesting triangles formed between family members at times of heightened crisis. With any

---

14 Jenny Brown (2017) in her book *Growing Yourself Up* (Revised Ed.) offers some helpful suggestions. See pp. 237-239.

triangle two people are on the inside and one person is on the outside. On reflection the triangles did not stay the same but changed as circumstances did. Some notable triangles were:

- Brother and sister – symptomatic sister on outside
- Sister and sister – brother on outside
- Father and mother – symptomatic daughter on outside
- Mother with second daughter – husband on outside
- Father and son – mother on outside
- Mother and symptomatic daughter – father on outside
- Father and symptomatic daughter – mother on outside

We came to recognise that triangles in relationships were unavoidable and that they could be destructive and limit our growth to emotional maturity.

In responding to this new awareness, my wife and I made a commitment to spend individual time with each of our children. The impact was significant. Instead of speaking *about* each other we spoke *to* each other. It strengthened individual relationships and led to a deeper appreciation for how each individual was feeling in the situation. Surprisingly, this did not lead to greater fusion or togetherness but rather to a stronger sense of individuality while remaining closely connected.

When one of us started to talk about another member of the family we were quick to recognise the triangle and encourage each other to speak directly with that member of the family.

How does Bowen theory sit with a biblical worldview?

In the midst of this period of heightened family crisis when we were learning to apply aspects of Bowen theory to our lives, we were also constantly wrestling with whether this theory contradicted our Christian faith or undermined our biblical understanding of the human condition.

Faced with the complexity of our family system, and a symptomatic child, many would have suggested (and did) that we should just pray and trust conventional methods of mental health treatment. We certainly prayed (a lot) and had many others praying for us.

We also did initially explore conventional methods of dealing with mental health issues but the more we explored Bowen systems thinking the more we felt it was common grace wisdom that we would be foolish not to investigate.[15]

Based on years of clinical observations, Bowen theory seeks to describe patterns of human behaviour that keep repeating across the generations. The patterns that Bowen describes (some of which have been highlighted in this paper) rang true in our experience. We also found that rather than contradict or undermine a biblical view of humanity, they reinforced them.

In an attempt to be brief, I would suggest that a biblical anthropology sees people as made in the image of God (Gen 1:27-28) and therefore the pinnacle of God's creation. Yet, through wilful disobedience, humanity is now less than was Adam and Eve were created to be (Gen 3). We still bear the image of God, but that image is fractured and broken (Rom 1:18-3:20).

We are now to the very core of our being fragile and broken—in every way; emotionally, physically and intellectually. This is the

---

[15] By "common grace" I mean a number of things. It contrasts with saving grace which we experience through faith in Jesus Christ, his life, death and resurrection. However, common grace refers to God's good gifts available to everyone no matter who you are or what you believe. Common grace comes in many forms including rain and food but also the wisdom that comes through other people and their learning.

result of what the Bible calls "sin". Our brokenness is evident in our selfish and self-centred behaviour patterns. Bowen theory actually helps me better understand the way our sinfulness works itself out in our relationships and behavioural patterns.

For example, the Bible speaks of "the sin of the parents to the third and fourth generation" (Deut 5:9; Num 14:18), which carries the idea that the impact of sin within a family can be felt down through multiple generations. Bowen's observations of the way patterns of relating can influence the following generations resonates with this biblical idea when it speaks of multigenerational processes (Kerr & Bowen, 1988).

It is because of our fallen nature that our behaviour patterns are unstable. It is because of our frailty that we resort to mechanisms such as triangles, overfunctioning and underfunctioning, which Bowen theory helpfully identifies as part of every family unit. Bowen observed that these patterns are passed down through the generations.

Rather than undermine our biblical view of the human condition, Bowen theory helped us come to a deeper understanding of the complexities of human behaviour that result because we are sinful. This recognition also confirmed our need of God's redeeming grace if we are to ever break the patterns that are so deeply entrenched in all our relationships. So rather than threaten our biblical worldview, we found Bowen theory actually strengthened, reaffirmed, and deepened our understanding of ourselves and others, as people made in the image of God but sadly damaged by the sin that invades us all. Having identified the patterns within ourselves and our own family system we were in a much stronger position to prayerfully take steps that might lead to healthier relationships and emotional maturity.

And they all lived happily ever after?

The application of Bowen theory is not a magical formula that guarantees you will end up with the perfect family. The work of applying Bowen theory to our situation was painful, difficult and often felt unrewarding. Nonetheless, we stuck to it because it made sense of our family relationships and we believed that over the long term we would see some small changes and growth in emotional maturity for us all. Even after we had begun applying Bowen theory our daughter still attempted suicide a few more times. Yet, we stayed the course and kept on working on managing our own anxiety and not making a project out of her.[16] It seemed like madness but slowly and surely patterns began to change. We do not think our approach should be prescriptive for anyone as every situation and family is unique, but we hope what has been shared will give a helpful insight for others. Our daughter started to take small steps in owning responsibility for her life. Her self-destructive behaviours did not disappear but slowly began to reduce. She completed her course of study, then she held down a full-time job. She subsequently re-trained and became a successful personal trainer and body builder. We wanted to save our daughter's life but the only way we could do that was by working on our own anxiety and marriage and entrusting her to God.

Our marriage has grown and changed through this time, more than we could have imagined. My wife has learned to be less

---

[16] Our coaching appointments were usually about a month apart over a three-year period—it was certainly no quick fix! To be clear, the coaching we received was not about giving us support through a crisis but rather helping us to learn a process of relating that would over time grow our marriage in emotional maturity and ultimately be a blessing to our children. Whilst the crisis may have passed, we continue to receive marriage coaching from time to time.

reactive to anxiety that may be directed at her; she acknowledges that she now speaks less and thinks more; she is less focused on rescuing the children; I am learning to express honest opinions that previously I would not share with my wife; we have both learned to take more responsibility for our own anxiety and not look to each other to fix it.

Our family continues to be complex and have its struggles, but it is now three years since our daughter's last major symptomatic episode. She still has her challenges, as do we all, but we consider her life a gift of God's grace. He spared her life but in a very real way we are convinced that the application of Bowen theory to our family system was instrumental in the hands of God in halting dysfunctional behaviour and putting our family on the road to recovery. To him be the glory!

References

Bowen, M. (1978) *Family therapy in clinical practice.* Maryland, USA. Rowan & Littlefield Publishers, Inc.

Brown, J. (2017). *Growing yourself up: How to bring your best to all of life's relationships* (Revised Ed.) Chatswood, Australia. Exisle Publishing Pty Ltd.

Friedman, E. (1985). *Generation to generation: Family process in church and synagogue.* New York, NY. The Guilford Press.

Gilbert, R. (2004). *The eight concepts of Bowen theory: A new way of thinking about the individual and the group.* Pompano Beach, Florida. Leading Systems Press

Kerr, M. & Bowen, M. (1988) *Family evaluation: The role of the family as an emotional unit that governs individual behaviour and development.* New York, NY. W.W. Norton & Company.

Lerner, H. (1998) *The mother dance: How children change your life.* New York, NY. Harper Collins Publishers

Lerner, H. (2005). *The dance of anger: A woman's guide to changing the patterns of intimate relationships.* New York, NY, US: Perennial Library/Harper & Row Publishers.

Chapter 16

GRAPPLING WITH BOWEN THEORY IN MINISTRY
An Interview with
Simon Flinders and Paul Grimmond

Lauren Errington

I had the privilege of meeting with two seasoned ministers to reflect on how they have found grappling with Bowen theory and its application to their ministries a challenging and enriching endeavour over the years. This conversation gives a flavour of their careful scriptural critique, personal reflections and the usefulness of their continued meeting together to understand and apply Bowen theory in their relationships and ministries. I am grateful for the generosity of Simon Flinders, Senior Minister at Northbridge Anglican Church in Sydney, and Paul Grimmond, Dean of Students at Moore College in Sydney, for their participation in this interview.

Lauren Errington (Interviewer): Thanks for being willing to participate in this conversation today. To begin with, I was wondering how you both first encountered Bowen theory?

Paul Grimmond: I have spent most of the last 16 years in university ministry with students, and I was two years out of [Moore] College when I took over as the senior person in charge of a large university ministry at the University of New South Wales. I did this for the next five and a half years until I got completely burnt out. As I got to this point, one of the things that became apparent was that I needed to do some work on my marriage. At the time, Jenny Brown introduced me to Bowen theory as a conceptual framework to think about my personal engagement with burnout. In particular, it was a framework for thinking through relationships and pastoral work. I then started to use it in the team I was responsible for, and I helped trainees think about it in their university ministry. It has also been extremely useful in thinking about my new role at Moore College which is a different organisation and system to where I have been before.

Simon Flinders: I came to Bowen theory in the reverse order to Paul. I first encountered Bowen theory in the context of ministry, then personally. I have spent 17 years as a minister in different parishes, the last eight at Northbridge, and now as the Senior Minister. I first came across Bowen theory when I was working at a church where Jenny Brown and Peter Frith were congregation members. I learnt some of the vocabulary, and from there did some further reading on the theory. Three years ago I joined a reading group for people thinking about Bowen theory in ministry, which has continued to meet after the formal group finished up. It's been very stimulating to chat to others about the theory and application in a ministry context. More reading on Bowen theory sparked interest in my own family of origin, which I have since started to explore and found helpful in personal application for my life, and family, and health.

Lauren: It sounds like one of the things you have both found helpful is thinking about systems and its application to workplaces too—do you think this has helped you transition in different roles?

Paul: That's hard to answer, because I understood my previous work system better and had a long history of relationships there. I have a shorter history of relationships in my new role at Moore College and am still finding my feet in the system. What I am aware of, though, is that my personal inclinations carry across to new systems, and Bowen theory has helped me to be aware of this.

Simon: I have done most of my thinking about Bowen theory as a senior minister, but what I have found helpful is having a colleague familiar with the theory too. The women's pastor at my church has also found Bowen theory to be useful, and it is helpful to be able to share the same language as we reflect on what we are observing and encountering at church.

Lauren: Both of you have mentioned the family of origin work you have done in your thinking over the years. I wonder if you could say more about this and how it might have helped you tune in to your own patterns of functioning in ministry relationships?

Paul: My process of experiencing burnout was a massive moment for me. It was public, visible, and high profile. At the time I would have said it was due to external circumstances being overwhelming for me, but I have since realised that I had anxiety and depression. Understanding Bowen theory has helped me to see that the system was big and complicated. What was helpful, and awful, was recognising personal things about myself and realising I functioned in a way that was unhelpful for me and the organisation.

Lauren: Can you give an example of this?

Paul: Yes, so for example I avoid conflict, and part of this is that I have a somatic response to pre-empting conflict and so avoid it. I began to understand that I have had this sort of response since I was young, particularly with my mum. When mum was upset, I felt responsible. In ministry, the effect of this meant I got more tired and had strong reactions to particular people in ministry and would avoid tackling those. This helped me avoid conflict, but didn't help the organisation as a whole. At another level, understanding my own family of origin and my functioning in relationships, such as not wanting to express frustrations in my marriage and how this contributed to our patterns of communication, helped me understand how I contributed to situations. So in particular, I was challenged to speak up even if it brought anxiety to the system I was a part of, in family or work relationships.

Lauren: It's interesting that you've observed the same patterns, what Bowen would call distancing I think, in your own growing up and in your ministry relationships. I'm curious about what you notice now about your anxiety?

Paul: I used to react to my somatic response; now I use it as a sign that I am uncomfortable in a relationship. Then I ask—what can I do to react better? This includes trying to think, and to get enough distance to think. I am thankful to God that I can say that my experience of anxiety has changed over time, and that I can function better in situations that used to overwhelm me. As I look back over the past ten years, I think I experience anxiety less deeply but I still can't overcome the initial reaction to conflict. I am also aware of the sinfulness attached to some of those drives in me—particularly in wanting to please people. I have had to let the gospel challenge me in that my job is not to keep people happy, and part of that is learning to give people space to come to their own conclusions.

Simon: What Paul has been saying has really resonated with me, the idea that we need to work on self and recognise what we contribute to the system and relationships. It is a big mental shift to be content to work on that, just to work on myself rather than try and change others. The application of that to ministry is that it is helpful to remember that problems aren't all "out there."

Lauren: Simon, what is it about your own reflections on your family of origin that have helped you in your ministry relationships?

Simon: I am a self-confessed overfunctioner. In my family, I think my sibling position contributes to this as I am the eldest of two, and both my parents were also the functional eldest in their families. When I was a teenager my parents divorced. I stayed with my mum and found myself being thought of by others as the "man of the house." I think all of these things have led to patterns of overfunctioning and feeling responsible for things that were not my own. But it's been quite confronting for me to realise that I function differently in my family than in my ministry. I observed that in my family I was good at offering practical support, but was a bit allergic to offering emotional support. In ministry it is the opposite, I am very emotionally connected to people in the congregation.

Lauren: It is really interesting that your experience is not that relationship patterns translate directly from your family of origin into the church relationship system, but in fact they can appear to be the opposite forms of overfunctioning.

Simon: This has been the most helpful part of family of origin coaching for me—working out my principles and where I am, or am not, living them out. I find I'm more able to do this in ministry, but in my family of origin I often don't operate in line with my principles. I'm now teasing out more about what gets in the way of that, what causes me to be reactive in family rather than acting on my principles.

Lauren: Something you've both talked about in your experiences with Bowen theory is the process of understanding yourselves more and, in particular, the way you function in relationships. Something I often come across when talking with people about Bowen theory is the concern that self-awareness is a navel gazing exercise, and inherently selfish. I wonder what your thoughts are on the attention to self in Bowen theory?

Simon: I think that sort of response has a shallow understanding of the theory. In my experience, a higher level of self-awareness allows for more capacity to love the others that God has entrusted to my care. Five years ago I thought I had a good grasp on how my family shaped me as a person, but a Roberta

Gilbert book helped me to see that more self-understanding from my family of origin actually means I am more able to help others. This has underlined for me the principle that more awareness of self is important in ministry. For me, it has shifted work on the self from "psychological curiosity" to an "act of love." I was a sceptic at first about Bowen's focus on family of origin work, but I now have impetus to do more work, even on previous generations in my family.

Paul: At Bible college [as a student] I was anxious about the concept of self-awareness, but I think understanding the concept has been a revolution to me. I am more and more persuaded that self-awareness is fundamental, because if you don't understand yourself, you are just shifted around and reactive to the system around you. This is now so important that I've been part of a team at [Moore] College seeking to embed self-awareness in the Ministry and Mission course to help students grow in their skills for self-awareness, wanting people to act from conviction rather than coercion.

Simon: That's so important because the fruit of poor self-awareness can be very damaging. A lack of self-awareness can be disastrous to senior ministers and the systems they are involved in.

Lauren: The idea that developing a sense of self is about being clear about one's own convictions, rather than being coerced by the system, is a helpful way to describe that value. I'm curious to ask both of you what helps you to stick to your own relational principles along the way?

Simon: Primarily being immersed in the word of God. Secondarily, and I'm intentional about it being second, is having conversations with people who understand the language and concepts of Bowen theory, such as with Paul, or my colleague, or our reading group.

Paul: For me, reading the Scriptures and working hard at them has helped establish core principles. What Bowen theory showed me over time, was that there was a gap between my core principles, and how I enacted my self and my relationships. Now, I realise this might sound a bit dangerous to some people, but what it's given me is a language and a way of engaging with Scripture at a deeper level, if I can put it like that. What Bowen theory showed me was that in reading the Bible there are some principles I have held more tightly and more unconsciously than others, which has affected the way I relate to people. It's the awareness of systems thinking that has helped me realise that I have been privileging certain aspects of biblical reality over other biblical principles. In other words, I have come to see how my anxious sensitivities have reduced my capacity to wisely apply my Bible-based life principles.

Lauren: Can you give us an example of what you mean by that?

Paul: One of the values I held very deeply as a pastor was compassion. I think this was a significant contributing factor to my burnout. Because I held that as a core value, the way I cared for people meant I would immediately overcommit to try and look after them, no matter how senior in a ministry position I was in. This conviction was held firmly in place by what I believed about the gospel, and what it meant to be a Christian, but I realised over time that it had an effect on the system. I had 800-1000 people in the student ministry, and I was overcommitting to a few people. I had to ask, what biblical principles did I need to pay attention to as a leader?

And how should this affect how I committed my time? I realised that I had privileged certain biblical truths over others, and needed to work out how to re-align my actions according to my actual role, in ways that were healthier for me, for the system, and ultimately, for everyone who was involved in this ministry. So it has been a process of working out what biblical principles I hold, and how they fit together, not just in isolation.

Simon: I think one of the things that makes Paul such an attractive conversation partner about Bowen theory is that we have a mutual respect for each other and similar theological rigour. Over the years I have seen people with theories, including Bowen theory, run away with them and become less biblically grounded. I think we share a commitment to finding ways in which Bowen theory can provoke us to think about the Scriptures more deeply, not less.

Lauren: That's very helpful, and leads me to ask, as you keep the word of God central, how have you found systems theory fits best? Or on the other hand, where do tensions arise?

Simon: It's a huge question isn't it? I think a core observation about the theory is the emphasis on personal responsibility, and I think that's a snug fit with the biblical view, as the Scriptures ask me to take responsibility for myself before God. Bowen theory offers a lot of tools to help us do that. So that's quite significant for me. I find a lot of resonances with Bowen's focus on anxiety and the Scriptures. Not that I think that anxiety itself is a massive category in the Scriptures, but that I think it is related to lots of other theological ideas—fear, fear of other people, fear of God, and the dynamic of that and trusting God. So I think Bowen's idea of anxiety, where it comes from and what it produces in us, shows a connection between the Bible and Bowen theory.

Lauren: And tensions?

Simon: We've talked lots over the years about points of tension. I think there are gaps in Bowen theory, but you would expect that because it doesn't have a theological agenda. So I don't think it is right to hold the theory up to a standard to which it never sought to attain. We have thought a lot about where sin comes in, and that notion of personal responsibility. The theory itself doesn't have a vocabulary of sin, and I think there are dangers in Bowen theory in thinking about yourself in the system, and what you contribute to it, in less "moral" terms as we would with the Scriptures.

Paul: Yes, it kind of articulates the problem as an accident of history or dysfunctionality, but it doesn't situate that in a relational context, particularly in relation to a God who has created us. I remember when I was teaching some of the concepts to some students, and one of them reflected that you can become mature emotionally either away from God, or close to God. And it's true—you could follow the concepts and become healthier and better at doing that, but you could do that in a way that is entirely opposed to God and the truths of the gospel. Bowen theory by itself without the Scriptures could lead you in any one of many different areas, whereas the Scriptures give you a revelation of a shape that comes from outside you and that adds some flesh to what maturity actually looks like. We have a conviction that there is something external to us that provides some framework for establishing the principles we want to hold on to and what the heart of some of those things actually look like in relationship with each other.

Simon: Bowen theory believes in your I position and your principles; it doesn't really care about what your principles are as long as you have some that you have come to thoughtfully, not reactively. I guess what we are saying is that we think those principles themselves should be shaped by a higher authority. Probably one of the other tensions we have thought a bit about is that lots of Bowen theorists are quite pessimistic about change. That's something I hear a lot, about the limited capacity of the system or another person to change.

Lauren: Do you mean such as the limited, incremental change a person is able to make in a system?

Simon: Yes, and there is something about that that I like, that is realistic, and I think takes a good account of the doctrine of sin and its consequences. But again, the theory doesn't account for God's great power to radically transform people's lives. Again, I wouldn't expect the theory to do that, but it is one of the areas where I think there is tension, because I think Christians can afford to be more optimistic about God's power to transform people even though there is wisdom in having low expectations and patience that accounts for sin.

Lauren: You've both obviously thought a lot about the tensions over the years; are there other ones you have grappled with?

Simon: Probably the biggest area of tension for me is what I might call "interdependence". I think the Scriptures talk a lot about positive interdependence with one another in a Christian family and the ways in which we can serve each other where some emotional enmeshment, such as weeping with those who weep, is actually healthy Christian engagement. Sometimes when I read Bowen theorists I wonder if the emphasis on autonomy and emotional independence might lead Christians to be too wary of sharing each other's emotional burdens. It is a tension for me because I can see the worth of what Bowen is saying about the need for a person to consider how they can best serve the other from a strong position of differentiation, but I also want to be someone who is not hesitant to engage with—and even enter into—another's emotional distress/joy when needed.

Paul: Yes, and I think some of the vocabulary of Bowen rings alarm bells for Christians very easily. Attention to self, for example, compared to the Bible's language around selflessness and self-sacrifice. And it seems initially that you can't hold those things together, so I think it requires some deep theological thinking about what's going on, rather than just the surface differences that exist between those things. What Bowen theory has helped me to see is that often in our system, things like fear, or a response to power, or wanting to please people, mean that people hear things and want to do them not because they have formed an understanding of why those things matter to God, and why they are true of what has been revealed in the gospel, but just out of the pressure of relationship, or the system they are a part of. I think the tensions I have felt with Bowen theory can be eased significantly by appreciating, if you're thinking about it Christianly, that I want to persuade people to have real convictions that they believe, and then to have enough space to enact those and to learn not just to react to the system or to people or anxiety or their fears.

Simon: And that's the great helpfulness of the theory, right, because everyone thinks they are acting in line with their convictions...

Lauren: And we can all find examples where we are deceiving ourselves!

Simon: Yes, get 50 pastors in a room and we all think we are doing exactly what we planned to do! But what the theory might do is to help you learn about your own reactivity and that you are operating out of that. And it's certainly been the case for me, that in certain situations I've realised I'm actually reacting here, I'm not acting on my principles, and Bowen theory has given me some tools to help me to see that about myself, to grow in that self-awareness. So then we can do what we thought we were doing in the first place!

Paul: I think in ministry contexts we need to be really thoughtful about the vocabulary we use, or how we help people appropriate the vocabulary and see its significance. I have used the term triangling a lot with people in talking about pastoral ministry. But triangling is at least significantly correlated with things like gossip, for example, in the Scriptures. And so to just talk about triangling independent of biblical truths that represent what is going on in relationships, I think heightens people's anxiety and fear around those things. Whereas I see the triangle as a helpful objective way of seeing the relationship dynamics that are going on, in which things like gossip takes place. So the theory is describing some of the observable fundamental dynamics about what is going on in the world, and those dynamics then need to be explained and understood in light of biblical truth. They are not an addition to it, or an alternative to it, but a different description of the same reality.

Lauren: So there is wisdom in those things that goes with the gospel conviction. And you can't make someone have a gospel conviction, but you can urge them toward the gospel and you can help bring these things as wisdom that can be paired with that.

Simon: And what Paul is saying, is that it deepens both, in a dialogue between them. As Bowen theory becomes more useful to you, the more theologically reflective you are with it. My theological framework has enriched my experience of the theory.

Lauren: One thing I do want to ask you both before we finish, is how has an understanding of Bowen theory, and an awareness of your self—Simon, you said you were an overfunctioner, and Paul, more of a distancer—how has it changed the way you relate to people in your communities, especially when there are strong emotions?

Paul: Again I think this is where the idea of conviction has been helpful for me. Before, when I encountered people who were struggling with sin, I just desperately wanted them to stop. Which is right, and exactly what we should want to happen. But I think that desire ended up with me laying down ultimatums, which I think in the end was making them respond, or not respond, in reactivity to me rather than thinking deeply about the situation.

Simon: Yes, I think for me in situations probably similar to Paul, where people were stuck in situations or in sin, I would often overfunction for them. I can remember a time when I pursued someone too much, but now realise that this sort of thing might lead to people changing because of a felt need to please the pastor rather than them coming to their own convictions in their relationship with God.

Paul: My other observation is that most people would come to me with decisions and issues about Christian liberty, and trying to choose between options. And honestly, under God, they are free. 1 Corinthians 8 and Romans 12-14 help us to think about using our freedom in truth and in love for one another. And I want people to grow not by being forced, but by being personally persuaded about what is right. So now, in my ministry, I work to reflect with people on what is happening, and to reflect with them about what significant things the Bible might have to say, and then to leave them with as much freedom as possible to make their own decision. Which actually really annoys some people—

Lauren: Do you mean they are actually saying: "Tell me what to do!"

Paul: Yes, and it's hard and frustrating for both parties as I have to fight myself at that stage, because I think I know what might be the best thing for them to do, but to fight my urge to want to direct the outcome, and to really let people think it through and come to their own convictions.

Lauren: It sounds like a dilemma in parenting.

Simon: It's helpful you say that Lauren, and it's probably one of the things we could have said before about the resonances between Bowen theory and the Scriptures—that there is obvious connection between families and the church of God which is so often described as a family, and there ought to be some obvious points of connection there. So a parenting framework as a way to think about pastoral relationships can be very helpful.

Lauren: What about for you Simon in your ministry?

Simon: I have learnt along the way that in conflict, my anxious response is to find a quick fix. On reflection I have learnt how self-interested this is to calm my own anxieties, and I've realised that a slower process of resolution will sometimes be better and so I am learning to sit with my anxieties in this. One area I notice my reactive instincts kick in is with highly anxious people, who can be a great drain on leaders' time, and I go straight to setting boundaries up and distancing. One of the gems from Bowen theory that I have found really helpful along the way is that staying relationally connected doesn't mean staying connected on an anxious issue, but just staying connected. So just being able to have a different conversation, which means I'm less likely to get drawn into stuff I don't want to get drawn into, but not creating distance that might heighten the other person's anxiety. Bowen talks about this as having one on one contact, which I think is really helpful pastorally.

Paul: It's just sparked another thought for me, that pastorally I've made a change to inviting others to reflect and ask questions themselves, rather than me telling them what I see and explaining. So I used to say, "This is what I see, and this is why this is happening", whereas now I am slower in my response, and might say, "This is what I hear is going on for you; how are you feeling and thinking in that space?" So working harder to not offer my own interpretation or solution in a situation, but describing the facts of a situation and then trying to invite responses to encourage self-awareness and for them to take responsibility for themselves.

Simon: One of the things I have learnt to love is that Bowen theory dignifies small steps when managing a system. The leader or pastor often carries cultural or big picture anxieties, but Bowen theory values small steps, like in personally becoming more Christlike and taking small steps for things to happen.

Lauren: We need to finish, but what I am noticing from both of you is a deep desire for God to be the one working in people's lives, rather than people responding in reaction to you as leaders. Part of this seems to be about creating space for people to come to their own convictions as they search out the Scriptures. And I have heard how this has meant tolerating the discomfort as a leader that accompanies that! Thank you both for your time, it has been a really stimulating conversation.

INDEX

A
Acts 32, 130
anxiety
   acute *4,* 76, 205, 235, 242
   in Bowen theory 69, 140, 284
   clinical 265, 283
   chronic 4–6, 76, 197, 229, 235–243
   in churches *see* church – systems anxiety
   in biblical texts 69, 71, 75–6, 288–9
   managing own 111, 124–7, 145, 191
   physiology 4, 140, 146
   in relationships *see* relationships; triangles
   in workplaces 171–2
   see also differentiation of self; fusion; triangles
approval
   desire for 115, 118, 154
   people-pleasing 104, 112, 118, 284, 291
   see also togetherness

B
Bavinck, Herman 31
beliefs
   Bowen theory 45
   developing own 7, 12, 29, 39, 112, 293
   'borrowing' 7, *78,* 113

Bible
   biblical truth 1–2, 9, 58
   genealogies 24, 66
   worldview 1–2, 26, 52, 59–63, 274–6
blame
   in the Bible 26–27, 177
   cause-and-effect thinking 53, 228
   displacement 229, 234–9, *237*
   in relationships 5, 61, 83, 109
   see also sin
Boers, Arthur 83, 205
Bowen Family Systems Theory
   see Bowen theory
Bowen theory
   and the Bible 1–2, 274–6, 287–300
   key concepts 3–6, 268
   origins 2–3, 38
   summary of 2–8, 111, 268f
   see also change; humanity
Bowen, Dr Murray 2–3, 38, 53–8, 252
Bridges, Jerry 12
Brown, Jenny 10–12, 128, 210, 270, 281
burnout 123, 135, 150–166, 281, 287–8
   see also sustainable ministry

C
Calvin, John 25, 45, 88–9
care *see* pastoral care
cause-and-effect thinking 9, 22, 53, 65, 126–7, 267–8

Index   297

change
- Bowen theory 6–9, 28–9, 56–8, 112
- biblical view 10–12, 30, 45, 63–4, 129, 290, 299
- *see also* emotional maturity; goals; sanctification

child focus 5, 56, 255, 269–271
- *see also* family projection process

church
- anxious togetherness *see* fusion; togetherness
- body of Christ 9, 32–4, 59, 152–4
- community 32–3, 155–6, 222
- as an emotional system 8–9, 32–3, 69–70, 153, 196, 260
- Ephesian church 71–76
- leadership *see* leadership
- planting 226–44
- relationships 140–1, 160
- systems anxiety 15, 75–6, 163, 211, 233–243
- unity 105–8, 209–210

coaching
- case studies 120, 127, 213–222
- goals 124
- therapy as 7, 53, 124, 211
- rescuing versus *125–6*, 129–132
- *see also* rescuing

Colossians 88, 99, 129, 131, 231

connection
- balanced 3, 31
- mature 105, 108
- *see also* fusion; separateness; togetherness

conflict
- avoidance 106, 184, 283
- biblical examples 74, 186, 210
- church 189–190, 202–6, 212–16, 234
- family 56, 113
- management 159–162, 177–9
- triangles 135–8, 147, 197, 229
- workplace 171–3
- *see also* self management; triangles

Corinthians
- First letter of 8, 33, 99, 129, 131, 147, 152, 210
- Second letter of 30, 129, 131, 187, 202

creation
- of humankind 11, 22, 26, 40, 275
- doctrine of 90–6, 99
- relationships 63, 176

cutoff
- broken relationships 45, 178
- fusion 107
- relationship patterns 45, 173, 177, 215
- response to anxiety 5, 29, 212
- *see also* distancing

D

Darwinism 3, 11, 40, 43, 60–1
- *see also* evolution; natural selection

depression 120, 135, 220, 265, 283

detriangling *see* triangles

Deuteronomy 191, 276

Dever, Mark 105–106

differentiation of self
- basic level 29
- biblical examples 31, 45, 70, 199, 224
- Bowen theory 97–8
- efforts on own 11, 182, 145–6, 199, 206, 273
- lack of 106, 230
- responsibility for self 54, 108
- scale 28–9, 39, 77–8, *78*
- and spiritual maturity 146, 154–5, 187
- *see also* emotional maturity; emotional immaturity

distancing
- anxiety response 5, 23, 46, 111, 177
- conflict avoidance 80, 118, 187,

293
family of origin 55, 107, 258
see also emotional cutoff

E

eating disorders 264–278
emotional
  discomfort 106, 111, 124, 136, 155, 165
  process *see* multigenerational transmission process; relationships
  reactivity 6–8, 29, 156, 224, 229, 292–293
emotional immaturity 65, 98, 117, 179, 185, 237, 270
  see also cutoff; distancing; triangles
emotional maturity 5, 28, 105, 154, 210, 215–16, 289
  see also differentiation of self; triangles
empathy 42, 201, 223, 287
Ephesians 28, 31, 62, 68–84, 105, 129, 131, 132, 152–4, 210–11, 213
evolution
  adaptation 11, 21, 39
  human evolution 65, 94, 97
  natural systems theory 10, 40–1
  see also Darwinism
Ezekiel 191

F

family
  in biblical texts 63, 84, 249–251, 276
  diagram *see* genogram
  as emotional unit 4, 38, 56–7
  togetherness *see* fusion; togetherness
family of origin
  coaching 156, 215–224
  examples 112–16, 179, 252–8
  influence on styles of relating 116–18, 128, 157, 198, 282–6

multigenerational patterns 7, 23
research 41, 57–65
see also genogram; triangles; relationships – patterns
family projection process 5–6, 269–271
Family Systems Institute 267
feeling
  awareness of 174–8
  and thinking processes 28, 77, *78*, 95, 112
forgiveness 26–7, 47, 62, 151, 181, 184
Freudian theory 2, 22, 53
Friedman, Edwin
  church and family 32, 189
  genograms 57
  differentiation of self 210
  leadership 160, 192, 205, 212, 240–2
  systems theory 228–230, 61–2, 268
  triangles 147, 195–198
fusion
  anxious togetherness 23, 29, 103, 106–9, 159
  between thinking and feeling *78*
  cutoff 29, 159
  in relationships 5, 115–16
  see also herding

G

Galatians 118, 131, 132, 143
genealogies *see* Bible – genealogies
Genesis 11, 24–5, 44, 46, 130, 174, 176–7, 249–251, 275
genogram 23, 52–8, 65
Gilbert, Roberta 123, 172–3, 181–3, 196, 199, 223, 286
goals
  defining own 38, 160–2, 181, 229
  see also coaching; leadership
gospel 23, 34–5, 60, 74, 86, 166, 219
  see also beliefs; Bible
gossip 115–16, 118, 137–8, 148, 292
grace
  characteristic of God 31, 35, 66, 129–130, 187, 231

common 59–60, 275, 275f
salvation by 12, 26–7, 62–3, 276
see also humility
guilt *see* blame
group mentality *see* herding instinct; fusion

H
Halstead, Kenneth 201
Hebrews 131
herding instinct 40, 229, 234, 242
see also fusion; Friedman
hermeneutics 69–70
Holy Spirit
change 10–12, 126, 165, 181, 186–187
dependence on 34, 165
indwelling 72, 131, 152, 258
unity 104, 106, 213
humanism 21, 28, 37, 42, 62
humanity
biblical view of 30, 43–5, 95, 276
Bowen theory view of 21–2, 60–2, 98, 214, 275
broken relationships 177, 191
God's image 11, 13, 24–30, 44, 130, 174
individual responsibility 11–12, 27, 47, 62, 108
natural systems theory 39–40, 209
see also sin
humility 42–3, 144, 156, 161, 186–7

I
image of God *see* humanity
individuality
and togetherness 33, 38, 44–5, 109, 209
as separateness 3, 107–110, 161, 214, 272–3
loss of 29, 103, 229, 242
see also fusion; togetherness
interlocking triangles 5, 116, 137, 144, 198, 203

'I' position 106, 183–4, 199, 271, 290
Isaiah 65

J
James 129, 131, 143, 180
Jeremiah 25, 90, 199
Jesus Christ
differentiation of self 199, 230, 251
head of the church 105
humanity's redemption in 26, 63–4, 166
ministry of 98, 129
relationships 33, 251, 258
teaching 60, 86, 104, 157, 181, 184
triangles 195
see also Bible; church; gospel; sin
John 104, 129, 152, 251, 259
John, First letter of 30, 131, 174

K
Kerr, Michael
differentiation of self 109, 178, 183
view of humanity 42, 97, 176
multigenerational patterns 23, 26, 201
natural systems theory 40–1, 94
Kings
First book of 93
Second book of 24

L
leadership
biblical examples 75, 129–130, 213, 250–1
see also Ephesians
coaching 211, 213–23
conflict 138, 161, 180, 200, 234–5, 240
differentiation of self 77–83, 198–200, 223
family of origin 157, 224, 252
goal-directed 153, 232, 287
interventions 192–4, 202–6
managing self 156, 191–2

patterns of relating 173
togetherness 114, 160
see also sustainable ministry; workplace
linear thinking *see* cause-and-effect thinking
Luke 33, 104, 130, 148, 195, 259

M

Mark 27, 60, 86, 98, 259
marriage *see* spouse
Matthew 157, 178, 181, 184, 186, 199, 258, 259
maturity *see* emotional maturity/immaturity; spiritual maturity
McGoldrick, Monica 56, 61–2
ministry *see* church; leadership; sustainable ministry
Moore College 226, 280–2, 286
morality 27, 60–1, 74–5, 247–8, 258–260, 289
multigenerational transmission process 6, 22–4, 65, 190–1, 200, 205

N

narcissism 59–60, 98, 109
National Institute of Mental Health 3, 53
natural systems theory 3, 10–11, 22, 39–43
see also Darwinism; evolution; Kerr
non-anxious presence 34, 82–3, 145, 241–3
nuclear family emotional process 5, 33, 212, 252
Numbers 276

O

objectivity
in family of origin 7, 55
limitations in 42, 59, 176
in patterns of relating 41, 45, 146, 292
in thinking 39, 42, 95, 174, 184
see also self awareness; thinking
observation
in leadership 160, 175, 206, 248
of relationship patterns 41, 47, 76, 156, 173, 179
of self in relationships 6, 121–7, 131, 146, 214–18
of triangles 137–8, 194
see also self awareness
overfunctioning
in family of origin 116, 258, 272, 284
pastorally 122–5, 162–5, 205, 223
reciprocity with underfunctioning 212, 249
in relationships 108
in the workplace 177–8
see also rescuing, underfunctioning

P

Papero, Dan 29, 107
parenting 6, 56, 95, 106, 262, 294
see also child focus; family
pastoral care
awareness of self 121–4, 161, 294–5
purpose of 129, 132, 155, 164
systems awareness 21, 33–4, 70
see also coaching; empathy; rescuing; sustainable ministry
Paul, the Apostle
and anxiety 71–3
on church 8, 28, 33, 202, 209–210
ministry 81–3, 130, 213
maturity 31, 222, 231
see also Ephesians
people-pleasing *see* approval; togetherness
Peter
First letter of 35, 129–132, 148, 152, 191
Second letter of 143
Philippians 34, 104, 130, 187

Piper, John 148
Powlison, David 9–10, 58, 60–1, 65–6
principles *see* beliefs
problem solving 122, 127, 142–3
Proverbs 87, 90–6, 115, 142–3, 146, 176, 184, 186, 199
Psalms 45, 58, 90, 95, 131, 146
psychology
    and the Bible 70–1
    and Bowen theory 57, 63
    and a Christian worldview 8–9, 12, 61, 66, 187

Q

questions for reflection
    anxious togetherness 121
    beliefs 12
    church 9
    family of origin 121
    gossip 115
    leadership 170
    objective thinking 180
    pastoral coaching 131, 305
    patterns of relating 167, 183–4, 191, 257
    psychology 10
    sustainable ministry 164–5
quick-fix mentality 140, 146, 237, 241, 286, 304

R

reactivity *see* emotional reactivity
reciprocal functioning 9, 29, 55, 125, 167, 255–7
relationships
    balance 3, 56, 110, 159, 273
    perceived threats 4, 69, 103, 109, 140
    restoration 30, 34–5, 47
    seeing patterns 5–6, 23, 55–9, 63–66, 116–17, 127
    sensitivities 6, 117, 159, 160, 163, 198
    tension 3, 23–4, 104–6, 136, 162
    see also approval; observation; togetherness; triangles
repentance 57, 61–2, 147, 181, 259
rescuing
    biblical lens 129–133
    coaching versus 120–8
    fixer mentality 111, 121–2, 205, 214
    others from discomfort 155, 159, 165, 270
    triangles 5
    see also coaching; overfunctioning; problem solving
Revelation 24, 129, 152
Richardson, Ronald 9, 33, 47, 74, 79–82, 157, 218, 232
Romans 25, 26, 30, 47, 63, 65, 129, 152, 180, 191, 199, 275, 294

S

salvation 12, 25, 86, 99, 135
Samuel, First book of 251
sanctification 30, 62–3, 66, 117
    see also change; Holy Spirit
secular theories 8–11, 60–1, 87–95
    see also Bowen theory; natural systems theory; psychology
self
    awareness of relationship patterns 7, 41, 56, 121, 155, 243, 284
    awareness of vulnerabilities 224, 285–6
    differentiation *see* differentiation of self
    pseudo self 78, 80
    regulation 37, 111, 156
    solid self 31, 50, 84, 157–9
    taking responsibility for 7, 50, 112, 161, 190, 295
    see also emotional maturity; objective thinking; relationship patterns
selfishness 36–41, 60, 180–3, 276, 285
selflessness 36–7, 49–50, 291
    see also care; pastoral care

separateness *see* distancing; individuality
sibling position 6, 53, 173, 198, 256, 284
side-taking 5, 7, 59, 141, 144f
   see also approval; triangles
sin
   biblical view of 24–7, 45–7, 153, 177–181, 276
   Bowen theory 10, 43, 45–7, 57, 60–3, 289
   pastoral care 130, 155, 293
   see also humanity; Jesus; salvation; self awareness
societal emotional process 6, 33–4, 209–210
spiritual maturity 146–7, 154–5
   see also sanctification
spouse 5, 56, 113, 134–140
stress *see* anxiety; sustainable ministry
sustainable ministry 36, 150–66, 243
   see also burnout; overfunctioning
systems thinking *see* thinking

T

Thessalonians
   First letter of 130, 132
   Second letter of 130
thinking
   group-think 40, 106, 108–9, 199
   linear 66, 121, 228, 233, 240, 268
   systems 8, 42, 202, 228, 267–8, 287
   see also cause-and-effect thinking; feeling; herding instinct; objective thinking; togetherness
Timothy
   First letter of 68–84, 130, 199
   leadership 77–83
   Second letter of 68–84, 131
togetherness
   anxiety driven 3, 40, 45, 106–9, 199
   Christian community 33, *80*, 103–6, 209
   desire for *see* approval

   examples 109–111, 112–17, 272–3
   see also fusion; herding instinct; individuality
triangles
   and the Bible 95, 142, 250, 292
   definition 5, 134–7, *137*, 229
   detriangling 7, 82, 144–9
   interlocking 5, 116, 137, 144, 198, 203–6
   observing 34, 137–8, 194–8, 215
   primary 113–16, 198, 257, 273–4
   in the workplace 173, 177, 180
   see also family of origin; gossip; side-taking
Trinity 38, 44, 48–9, 70

U

underfunctioning 4, 122–5, 162, 178–181, 224, 247–261
   see also overfunctioning; rescuing
undifferentiation 5, 209–210, 223, 234, 240–1
   see also differentiation of self; emotional maturity/immaturity
unity 28, 103–7, 118–19, 152, 209–210
   see also fusion; togetherness

V

validation *see* approval
values *see* beliefs
vision *see* goals; leadership
Volf, Miroslav 47, 49, 152

W

wife *see* spouse
wisdom 86–99, 143, 180, 184, 275, 293
work
   Bowen's workplace 8
   conflict at 171–2
   managing relationships at 173, 179, 182
   gossip 115
   value of 89
   see also conflict; triangles

www.ingramcontent.com/pod-product-compliance
Lightning Source LLC
Chambersburg PA
CBHW032028290426
44110CB00012B/710